Claude Debussy

The Piano Works of

CLAUDE
DEBUSSY

By E. Robert Schmitz

Foreword by Virgil Thomson

DOVER PUBLICATIONS, INC.
NEW YORK

Published in Canada by General Publishing Company, Ltd., 30 Lesmill Road, Don Mills, Toronto, Ontario.
Published in the United Kingdom by Constable and Company, Ltd., 10 Orange Street, London, W.C. 2.

This Dover edition, first published in 1966, is an unabridged and corrected republication of the work originally published by Duell, Sloan & Pearce, Inc., in 1950.
This edition is published by special arrangement with Appleton-Century-Crofts, Inc., an affiliate of Meredith Publishing Company.

Library of Congress Catalog Card Number: 66-20423

Manufactured in the United States of America
Dover Publications, Inc.
180 Varick Street
New York, N.Y. 10014

1521315

To those of my family, assistants, students, and friends who shared with me the exalting task of fighting for ultimate sincerity in the interpretation of this alchemy of sounds . . . this book is dedicated

Cathedral of Bourges
(12th Century)

Examples of arches:
Notre Dame de Paris

Author's Note

This book is not intended to subtract from those which have been written about Claude A. Debussy. Nor will it attempt to dispose of the private life and inner thoughts of the man whom I profoundly admired. This book is solely concerned with a part of the musical heritage he left us—that part written for the piano.

As time goes on, Debussy's recommendations, his criticisms during the many hours spent in his studio accompanying singers or reading piano works—these recommendations seem to crystallize with an ever-growing and firm command as does his music, the witness of his intent.

It is true that literary commentaries on music are dangerous procedures to the extent that they detract from the very essence of that music which lies outside of conceptual notions; the intrinsic value of music is in its own perfection, which long survives both the primum mobile of its composition and its specifics of technique. Yet, before a music can be liberated to assume its status of a pure art form, a correct appraisal of its source and ways and means must have been made, understood, and then discarded as having served its purpose in orientating the listener and performer to the quality of beauty, of perfection, which this music will thereafter spell for them.

The whole being of the listener must participate in the reception of the beauty contained in music, but it is often necessary to stimulate the imagination by commentaries to obtain a state of receptivity. Little by little the commentary will pale, only the musical substance "per se" remaining in the memory.

The insistence of this book upon intellectual commentary on the works it considers is motivated by the repeated experience of imperfect or erroneous conceptions and perceptions of the piano works of Debussy, by both performers and listeners.

The causes of these imperfections are multiple. Wrong, preconceived notions of this music, built on hazy, not to say lazy, commentaries, have done untold harm. Early criticisms, baffled by the original and daring innovations contained in this music, either glibly pass it off with few knowing terms of little service to the student, or belittle it in a reactionary mood of distrust, or outright envy.

Sometimes the insufficient learning, or imperfect discriminative reaction, may establish a wrong perception which scientific and true education may help to correct. Erroneous perception also may consist in attributing to one object the reaction appropriate to a somewhat different object; or different objects may stimulate the receptors in ways so nearly alike that different reactions can never be built for them.

It can also happen that failure to integrate the complete content of a work may result in substituting illusion for actual sensory content.

So the disturbing factors range from emotional states, biased and biasing ideas, lack of education, or lack of discrimination. It seems then, in the face of these elements, that commentary about Debussy, if conscientious and based on many years of performance and study of his piano works, may not be amiss. Literary connotations, pictures reproducing views of objects that might have been, or actually were, sensorial stimuli to composition, can serve an end, most particularly when coupled by melodic, rhythmic, harmonic, contrapuntal, structural analysis.

It is my hope that these will rectify certain notions and complement the intrinsic musical audition and perception of those who, through limited experience of the world of travel or of peaceful contact with nature, through biased and narrow musical study, or through insufficient classical schooling, have been deprived of the multiple imaginative resources to recreate with truth in their interpretations the colorful and genial piano literature of Debussy.

Foreword

VIRGIL THOMSON

Historically viewed, Debussy is the summit toward which, during the two centuries since Rameau's death, French music has risen and from which, at least for the present, it seems to decline. Internationally viewed, as Fred Boldbeck lately pointed out, he is to the musicians of our century everywhere what Beethoven was to those of the nineteenth, our blinding light, our sun, our central luminary.

So high a content of expression, of communicable meaning, in structures at once vast, monumental, and bold, is not to be found in any other music than that of these two composers. Neither is so masterful a workmanship in all the musical elements—rhythm, melody, harmony, and their offspring, orchestration—in music that, for all its technical sophistication, speaks so directly to the heart. For musicians and for laymen, both are in their epoch peerless. And for culture they are classical, which is to say, basic both to pedagogy and to the repertory of public execution. Without them music is Europe without Napoleon, *Hamlet* without the Prince.

Just as Beethoven, not Bach nor Mozart, really summed up the German temper—all emphasis and ordered planning, jollity and private meditation—so Debussy, not Berlioz nor Bizet, encompassed most fully the French, with its dramatic contrasts of reason and sensuality, of irony and tenderness, stiffness and grace. From France, the home of liberty, too, came the firm freedom of Debussy's style and structure. Among all our musical masters, I should say, Claude Debussy was the least weighed upon by the dead hand of formula. Yet neither was he an improviser. This latter art, indeed, among all the compositional techniques, is the one most servile to rules of thumb. Debussy's operation was more thorough. Like any Frenchman building a bridge or cooking a meal, painting a picture or laying out a garden, he felt, he imagined, he reasoned, he constructed—and in that order.

It is in that sound French order, too, that E. Robert Schmitz built up his book about Debussy. Love is in it, and a spontaneous enlightenment, studied penetration, logic, and the completeness of a vast experience with the material. He knew Debussy and Debussy's music; he knew classical esthetics and contemporary; he knew the pianoforte. He early created from all these a method of piano playing at once radical and comprehensive. He made that method, I insist, both *out of* and *for* the music of Debussy. That is the source of its value and the test of its strength.

The techniques of that method are laid out in *The Capture of Inspiration*. Their application to Debussy's piano music is the subject of the present book. Debussy's thought is here correctly analyzed, each keyboard work exposed in full detail. Schmitz knew what every one of these is about, what it should say, how to make it speak. He also knew, from long experience as a teacher, all the pitfalls. He knew how faulty fingering or pedaling, erroneous rhythmic or harmonic analysis, can make any work by Debussy lose precision, turn subjective, sound like a sketch.

Schmitz has left us in his two books contributions to pedagogy and to the understanding of great music. It is regrettable that he did not also complete his third project, undertaken with the RCA-Victor company several years before his death, for the complete recording at his hands of Debussy's solo piano works. His astounding executional and interpretative powers, save as recorded on a few discs, must remain now merely a memory in the minds of those living. That which will survive our memories and which will be E. Robert Schmitz's monument is the one here raised to a master who is not only the chief musical eminence of our century, but a keyboard composer whose work will not fail, I believe, to be esteemed of posterity beside that of Chopin and Sebastian Bach.

Contents

THREE: PIANO WORKS 1905–1910

FOUR: PIANO WORKS 1910–1915

FIVE: PIANO WORKS 1915

Illustrations

Manuscript of a letter from Claude Debussy to E. Robert Schmitz (1913)

The Piano Works of

CLAUDE DEBUSSY

CLAUDE DEBUSSY by Marcel Baschet

1.

General Commentary

Achille-Claude Debussy was born on August 22, 1862, at Saint-Germain-en-Laye. His ancestry being solely made up of shopkeepers, peasants, and employees of the Paris suburbs and the Côte-d'Or, he received but a slight and general early education with a few piano lessons by Cerutti. Madame Mauté, Verlaine's mother-in-law and a pupil of Chopin, took him in hand and in 1873 he was admitted to Lavignac's *solfège* class at the Conservatory, there to win the medal for *solfège* and to follow up in Marmontel's piano class. In the year 1874, he received his second "accessit" (honorable mention), then the second prize in piano (1877), and first prize for accompaniment in 1880. Nothing was awarded him in Durand's harmony class because of his persistent unwillingness to accept the established rules!

Thanks to Marmontel, and having become the pianist for Madame Nadiejda von Meck, Tchaïkovsky's famous Egeria, he is able to visit Switzerland, Italy, and Russia. Following his studies in composition with Ernest Guiraud, he obtains a second grand prize at Rome in 1883 and the first grand prize for his cantata "L'Enfant prodigue" in 1884.

From the Villa Medici, where he remains for two dull years (1885 to 1887) he sends his "Damoiselle élue," which is accepted with reserve, and, upon his return to Paris, composes the "Suite Bergamasque" for piano in 1888. Two pilgrimages to Bayreuth in 1889 and 1890 take him from delirious enthusiasm to the most hopeless disappointment. It is then that he chances upon the authentic score of Moussorgsky's "Boris Godounov" and befriends, as his natural allies, a small group of writers and artists who are in some way or another connected with symbolism.

A memorable date in the musician's evolution is the year 1892 when he finishes his first symphonic work which is no less than his "Prélude à l'après-midi d'un faune" and when, having discovered Maeterlinck's theater, he decides to put "Pelléas and Mélisande" to music. This composition will take him ten years to accomplish.

Meanwhile, in 1893, he offers the "Quatuor à cordes," and his "Nocturnes" for orchestra are favorably received at the Concerts Lamoureux on December 9, 1900. "Suite pour le piano" follows in 1901.

As a result of the controversial feud over his "Pelléas and Mélisande," Debussy who had kept away from the conflicts which he had occasioned, retires into a haughty solitude and, from then on, his life and works become as one. The year 1903 is that of the "Estampes" for the piano.

After six years of marriage, he separates from Mademoiselle Texier in 1905 to marry Madame Emma Moyse, publishes the second book of "Fêtes galantes"; a real symphony, "La Mer", wrongly named "symphonic sketches"; and two selections of "Images" for the piano, closely followed by "Images" for orchestra.

In 1910, the year of the first book of the "Préludes," he conducts his works in Vienna and Budapest. Ida Rubinstein then requests a rapid writing of an important score for a "mystère" by d'Annunzio, "Le Martyre de Saint-Sébastien," which had its premiere on May 22, 1911. Immediately after this, the Ballet Russe asks for the music of "Jeux" of which the theme and choreography are by Nijinsky. By 1913 the second book of "Préludes" is completed.

A triumphal tour of Russia in 1914 precedes the advent of the war, by which Debussy is so affected as to be unable to write, but, despite the appearance of the first symptoms of an incurable illness, he reacts and composes the twelve monumental "Études" for the piano and plans to write "six sonatas for various instruments, by Claude Debussy, French musician." He composes three of these before entering into a long and painful agony which ends on March 26, 1918.

CHARACTERISTICS OF DEBUSSY'S PERSONALITY

To those who enjoy an infinite number of choicely and beautifully expressed details, I suggest reading the works of Maurice Boucher,

Charles Koechlin, Leon Oleggini, and Oscar Thompson on the subject of Debussy.

This is only a résumé of personal recollections, and the quotations of a few paragraphs that we found particularly adequate to outline briefly the most salient characteristics of Debussy. Of course, more details will be brought out in the chapters that follow.

Independence is the dominant factor in his character. "The joy of being free" induces him, from his Conservatory days, to liberate himself as much as possible from all laws and restraint, if so compelled by his musical instinct.

"At first, one must disobey," said Maeterlinck ("Ariane et Barbe-Bleue"). "It is the primary duty when order is menacing and cannot be explained." This phrase sums up Debussy's view that logic is first and pre-established order last.

His tastes were those of a refined artist, sophisticated and exacting. They were multiple, too. He hated vulgarity in any form, and his epicurean or sybaritic impulses often deprived him of the sheer material necessities, yet they were essential to his heart and soul. An esthete with a taste for the rare, the exotic, and the perfect, for order in fantasy, he was also inquisitive, yet discreet.

Habitually silent, and what might have seemed distracted, he needed peace to better hear his soul's song; solitary, taciturn, and tormented, a sudden and compelling need to see or hear a friend would incite him to leave his work in order to share a joy or the emotion of a propitious creation; then his verve, colorful but always in good taste, as was his music, would relieve him of the almost constant worries that were generally his habitual climate.

For truly he was often anxious and possessed by a curious sense of guilt, probably due to the lack of balance between the material necessities of his daily life and his refusal or inability to create speedily, or publish works he did not find satisfying; he would write to J. Durand, his publisher, as in 1907:

"It is nice of you to think of the nervousness of your poor friend who now imagines the worst catastrophes with regard to a mere forgotten flat; think of what can come of it when it concerns things which affect one directly. Excuse me if my nerves are in 'triplets' today. Excuse this outburst of spleen. Unfortunately, they are so frequent in my life. . . ."

Or in another letter of the same year: "Please forgive me for the delay; I work like a factory and I am progressing in spite of terrible and tiresome jumps backwards."

Debussy, as we see, worked slowly and was rarely completely contented with his creation. No one knows as yet how much music he wrote which he destroyed. He often announced the completion of a work, then, after playing it over, he would suppress it and say: "I have started all over."

It took him from 1893 to 1902 to conceive and finish "Pelléas and Mélisande"; and many of the acknowledged stimuli of his piano works were perceived years before the moment when the work was actually finished and ready for the publishers. In contrast to these rather serious aspects of his character was his great "*à-propos*" in humor.

When music expresses a feeling of joy, it is important to come out of the mist and let the sun burst forth, to be incisive without being brutal, to dance, play, laugh. As a person Debussy could be witty and he adored paradoxes. "His humor was not exactly irony or fantasy, nor sensitiveness, nor bitterness; it was all fashioned in a peculiar tone which added new elements and affected the subjects as a sharp or a flat affects the tone." (Maurice Castelain in the *Revue Anglo-Américaine*, 1927.)

His mocking sensitivity, his ironic languor, the unusual twist of his humor, were elegies that pirouetted into epigrams, all blended into a subtle alchemy.

"What is humor? It is a password, a sign of complicity, a complicity which involves all the players of the game, invites the witness to partake of the jeering. The victim is mocked and the mocker himself becomes linked to the trial, both as judge and defendant. Humor appears thus as an ironical confession of the blunders and bunglings in a universe, of which one is not too confident of being the least offender. With a secret delight, the humorist is apt at turning the derisive mirror toward himself, at the cost of its blurring as it discloses the reflection of his own grimace." This is an extract from Thérèse Lavauden's "Humor in Debussy," an excellent article which should be quoted in its entirety.

"Humor is the arrow that man uses to bluff God!" In his music, Debussy reaches humor through the irony of *entrechats*, the recall of an old melody, colored by our astonishment, hustling seconds, unexpected stops, jostling of rhythms, and splashes of arpeggi.

Thus, in "Hommage à S. Pickwick," the grandiloquence of the phrase completes the buffoonery of the sudden intrusion of the English national anthem.

In "General Lavine-eccentric," "Minstrels," or "Golliwog's cakewalk," the stubborn hammering of an out-of-tune and badly played cornet, drum tattoos, or a dirty joke followed by a burst of laughter; these are the simple suggestions of Debussy's fun. Likewise, in "La sérénade interrompue," we witness the lilliputian drama of the lover interrupted by everything, including the night-watchman with the crippled rhythm of his wooden leg. The instillation of the smothered sound of rockets and of fragments of a sleepy "Marseillaise" in among the firecrackers of "Feux d'Artifice" is another example.

It is humor tinted with tenderness which makes "semi-quavers sprout as bristles" on the mean "Gradus" of "Children's Corner." It is humor again in the amusing takeoffs on "Tristan," embodying that impertinence which children cherish so much.

But also, this humor is an expression of Debussy's all-embracing love and pity, of his understanding of children and adults alike, and of his putting himself so often in others' "shoes." A sympathy which is full of grace and of deep tenderness, gives him a perception which is childlike, and at the same time paternal, and initiates him to the juvenile universe of his beloved little Chouchou. Is it the memories of his own childhood which permit this spontaneous transposition which he shares with the adored child, of reality into the world of fantasy?

Love, tenderness, and pity are at the depth of Debussy's soul. Pity, which can be of a pagan nature when Debussy contemplates the sea or the reflection of the water, or dreams of the motion of clouds. Human pity, with which he imbues the mysterious figures of Mélisande and La Damoiselle élue. Human pity, when, with a few poignant notes, he

7

transmutes into sounds the words of old Arkel: "If I were God, I would take pity on the hearts of men."

Debussy's synthesis of love was double-edged. In one aspect it was deliberately accepted as sinless, as almost divine, as an ultimate fusion into ambient poetry, a dream inviting the heart's tenderness and exaltations in the beholding of the charm of things and of beings.

It was also that all-embracing love of which Charles Koechlin speaks: "Debussy does not spiritualize matter; he does not deny its existence nor does he suppress it; but he endows it with the adoration of the heart, like the love of life . . . the gratitude of him who has known voluptuousness."

Through the widely differentiated sensualities of Debussy's perception, voluptuousness had an unlimited scope—voluptuousness of a look, of hair, of perfume, or of music.

PERCEPTIVISM

What are the mysterious component elements that transform a human being into a creative genius?

Further in the book we will deal with Debussy's characteristics, and the analysis of the form, structure, melody, harmony, rhythm, counterpoint, and modality that he used. But now, with the help given us by the science of psychology, we would like to examine what the resources of the human mind are and how they may function:

"The activities of the total range which make up the life of an individual, whether normal or abnormal, may conveniently be divided into six groups each represented by a typical sort of activity; these activities have conventionally been termed: sensing, perceiving, thinking, feeling, willing and doing. . . .

"*Sensing* is exemplified in the acts of seeing the color of a rose, tasting the flavor of a fruit, or smelling the odor of a perfume; there are other sensings for which we have no specific verbs; for example, the sensing of cold, heat, tickle, and pain; we sense also contraction and relaxation of muscles and sense many other conditions and occurrences within our bodies.

"*Perceiving* may be initially described as sensing and something more. . . . Under *Thinking* we include imagining, remembering and anticipating; you imagine, for example, the sound of a violin or of a bell; the blaze of a fire—at moments in which none of these are actually sensed or perceived. You remember the meeting with a friend yesterday . . . the cold wind of last week, etc. . . .

Under *Feeling* we have no subordinate terms. At various times you feel pleasure, depression, hunger, anger, elation, pain. *Willing* occurs when you hesitate as to whether you will do a certain thing or not. *Doing* or dynamic acting includes all cases in which action on your part modifies or changes your environment or changes your relation to it." *

From the quotation above, we may deduct that the creation of art presupposes: to sense, to perceive, to think, to feel, to will or to do, and/or any combination of such. . . . Plus. . . .

At the time of perception, the mind takes possession of a concrete matter as perceived by the senses (some form of vibration) and reforms a mental synthesis of it, an idea which then becomes its own. Sensory perception, as an impression made on us by that which is outside of us, then disappears as such, along with its cause, and the resulting feeling in the mind remains in the memory. The depth (or value) of the intuition of things in space and the intensity of the perception of concrete things are the result of the quality of each personal and particular sensitivity, also of the individual knowledge acquired through studies, and most probably of the many hereditary factors.

Looking back on some of the ideas of Mr. Dunlap, whose admirable book could be quoted at length, one can conclude that . . . if sight governs space and perceptions, touch helps in measuring the forms, resistances, and densities, and the body as it approaches the object can appraise what the eye has seen, what the nose has smelled, and what the ear has heard, thus grasping the three dimensions: breadth, height, and depth.

Through *special training*, the eye will perceive the color gradations, the dispersions of light; the *educated* ear will discern noise from those sounds which are music. Thus accumulated in the memory, these recollections will be the mines from which the stimulated mind will draw its creative material. These very memories will be infinitely varied, as illuminated by the colors of the days, seasons, years, the revolutions of the outside world, and the evolutions or revolutions of the inner life of the individual. In brief, the senses manifest through the mind the synthesis of objects, forms, savors, perfumes, light, and vibrations of all kinds in time and space.

* *Elements of Psychology* by Knight Dunlap, p. 23.

"When the several direct sensory reactions have become amalgamated into a single perception, the details of this perception will be determined, not by the characteristic sense stimulation of the object alone, but by it in conjunction with the various other stimulations playing upon the receptors of other senses and by the reactions (whether perceptual or ideational) which have preceded." *

As an illustration of this quotation one can take any very ordinary object, in its visual perception (for example); confronted by this sensory stimulus, each person will have a different reaction, depending on association and past experience toward the set object. (A clock may suggest . . . schooldays, waiting in hospital corridors, first date, zero hour, childbirth, mechanical precision, abstract design, the approaching of old age, tension of deadlines, taking a train, mathematical division, duty, a Harold Lloyd film, tick-tock music, late for the concert, etc.)

The acuteness with which the senses perceive, the acquired education, and the various comparisons that foster the grasping of relations of things to one another, allow for a sublimation of the sensations which, in a true process of alchemy, induces the sum total of the thus accumulated experiences into creative principles. From the historical point of view, we find in the development of mankind, an interesting parallel evolution between the sense of sight and the sense of musical hearing.

The German Hugo Magnus tells us of the historic evolution of the sense of color: "At first the rainbow was thought to be all one color; Homer saw it purple; later Xenophon saw it as a purple cloud, red and yellow-green; two centuries later Aristotle sees three colors, red, green, blue; three hundred years later . . . and Ovid sees a thousand dazzling colors which he cannot distinguish separately; red, being the lowest of color vibrations, was perceived first."

So has it been in music as its overtones were perceived: the unison was first; then the organum with consecutive fifths; then gradually we perceived the triad; then the seventh; and, at the apex of contemporary experience, Debussy perceived the complete harmony of the ninth, eleventh, thirteenth, as the true expression of nature which they are.

Now comes the very question that was one of the many incentives which led to the writing of this book:

* *Elements of Psychology* by Knight Dunlap, p. 199.

"Is the subject-matter of music to be accounted for solely in terms of the tonal structure itself or is it necessary, for a complete account of music to recognize the existence of a subject which although symbolized by the music is itself beyond the limits of tonal form and material?" *

By what precedes and what will follow, I feel that our answer is: Music should not be accounted for solely in terms of the tonal structure.

In this book one will find note of a number of points of interest relating to the extraordinary innovations used by Debussy in his compositions and relating to musical technique per se, but paralleling these will be considerations of the stimuli of creation as they bear and clarify the intents. For we have realized how the content of a certain object creates a chain of thought-reactions both in the creator and in the auditor or interpreter, and we have admitted that they soon separate the direct from the indirect content and set the symbol over the meaning.

It is then of importance to try to decipher, however hard the task, how this transmutation occurs in the creative process of Debussy, in order to duplicate it, as nearly as possible, in the approach to his works— the end products of this procedure—either as listeners or performers.

It was earlier brought out that education and heredity may be strong factors in this process, but when we consider the type of school experience that Debussy received in his youth, we are bewildered by the acuity of his perception and the universal scope of his cultural acquisitions in *later years*. His classical studies were of short duration, busy as he was with his music. Heredity and surroundings were unpretentious, his ancestry denoting storekeepers, small merchants, and the like. But, come the adolescent and matured years, Debussy, a student at heart, and an ardent seeker of knowledge born from beauty, adds to his amazingly acute sense of perception the understanding of all arts: literature, painting, sculpture, architecture, mythology, Greek and medieval chants, primitive scales of the Orient which number in the thousands. To these artistic endeavors, Debussy adds the cult of all that vibrates in Nature: clouds, moonlight, passing breezes—either carrying the upper partials of bells of nearby or faraway churches, or the fading notes of military bugles, the wind at sea or in the plains, sun-

* *The Meaning of Music* by Carroll Pratt, p. 204.

11

rays on a golden roof, or the shimmering lacquer of a Japanese panel.

In Nature, music is revealed to him by the perfumes of warm evenings, trees stretching their branches, the silvery leaves trembling in the emotion from the dirge of All Soul's Day, or by a laughing sun glancing ironically through the rainbow, and the everlasting beauty of sunsets, the sea, angry or frolicking. To Debussy, Nature was a Cathedral in which his mystic intensity paid homage to God in the infinite beauty of its creation, possessed as he was by what I shall call a "religion of the beauties of Nature."

From all these perceptions, and in striking musical progressions Debussy synthesizes the essence of landscapes ("Bruyères," "Collines d'Anacapri"); personal moods of the moment ("Brouillards," "Les sons et les parfums . . ." "Mouvement," "Feuilles mortes," "Cloches à travers les feuilles"); Nature's angriness ("La Mer," "Ce qu'a vu le vent d'ouest"); loneliness ("Reflets dans l'eau," "Des pas sur la neige," "Canope," "Hommage à Rameau"); manly, robust, or fierce qualities ("Danse," "L'Isle joyeuse," the twelve "Études.")

It is incredible how close a contact with the vibrant expression of beauty Debussy sought; it is incredible to realize how impressions made by beauty were stored (in some cases for a long time, and often subconsciously) and integrated into the intimate fabric of his being, to be gradually transformed into sounds as the urge arose.

His is indeed that balanced interaction of senses and mind toward creation which embodies the theory of perceptivism. From a multitude of passing and heterogeneous stimuli, Debussy, in the crucible of his imagination and by a genial transmutation, fashions an alloy richer than the purest metal and attains by his modern alchemy one of the most fascinating apexes in the historic evolution of the Art of Sounds.

IMPRESSIONISM

It is perhaps well to turn our attention now to "impressionism," and to investigate once and (we hope) for all what this term can infer toward Debussy, what are its drawbacks, its limitations, its possible interest or reality, and its incapacities.

In a letter of March, 1908, to his publishers, Debussy mentions this term ruefully: "I am trying to do 'something different'—in a way, realities—what the imbeciles call 'impressionism,' a term which is as poorly used as possible, particularly by art critics."

As a matter of fact, from its very first usage, it had a rather insulting connotation; used for the first time by Louis Leroy in the French paper *Charivari*, April 25, 1874, it applied to the painter Monet and his followers with an undertone of derision. It has never since lost its sense of disdain and its subconscious association with inconsistency and degeneracy, with vagueness of intent and of expression, despite the illustrious creative artists it is applied to.

True, impressionism has been from time to time reassessed and redefined, for instance by Oscar Thompson in 1937, as follows: "In literature, in painting, in music, the aim of these kindred artists was to suggest rather than to depict; to mirror not the object but the emotional reaction to the object; to interpret a fugitive impression rather than to seize upon and fix the permanent reality." *

Other sources even include in their description the techniques employed by Debussy (such as modality, pedal-points, pentatonism, wholetoned series, bitonality, etc.) as part of the description of the term 'impressionism.' But is that not begging the point? Or, rather, trying too late to amend terminology to make it fit in foolproof fashion the entire work of Debussy.

It is a similar evolution to that of the rash of political terms in "isms," which were perhaps genial in their first usage, but which in the mouths of thousands of people have come to convey so many sins, to mean so many heterogeneous concepts, to represent such varying political techniques as to have lost any vestige of meaning, any resemblance to scientific terminology.

We feel toward impressionism in music as many students and researchers in political science must feel about other "isms." We rue the day the term was invented, and wish for the day when it will disappear, so that it may not continue to befog the study, the assimilation of the style of Debussy to his normal position in the history of music. We have had time enough since he created, and should have perspective enough to have the historian's long view of his output, and to no

* O. Thompson, *Debussy, Man and Artist*, p. 21.

longer cite it as a temporary "curiosity" with a special and unfit terminology—but rather to view it as a genial but normal result of what came before, and what, in the unremitting evolution of the art, was to come after.

In this light we will consider that for a time Debussy, whose close friends included a number of so-called "impressionist" painters and a number of so-called "symbolist" poets, may have been passingly influenced by their aesthetics, by their contrast of unmixed colors, by their uses of equivalences rather than realities, by their stippling technique, by their synthesis of the emotion of the stimulus rather than the onomatopoetic reality in description. In a very limited number of works, for instance, "Nuages," "Brouillards," Debussy gave a most diaphanous and evanescent form to his music, through the choice of subject and the necessary technique to do justice to that subject.

The public, imbued with Wagnerian aesthetics, quickly exchanged study of these works for a rapid and easy label, which, if thoughtfully applied to a limited one percent of Debussy's works, might have been ingenious, but which, poured on indiscriminately, has resulted for decades in blurred, vague, sloppy, wrongly pedaled, innocuous performances of Debussy's works.

For the rest, the major portion of his works, Debussy adapted and fashioned his own technique and aesthetics to many varied sources of inspiration, to stamp them indelibly with Debussyism, with that power of sensorial transmutation discussed under perceptivism.

Because he set to music the Dante Rossetti poem "The Blessed Damozel" do we call Debussy a Pre-Raphaelite? Because he was a pupil of Massenet, a good friend of Satie, and an admirer of Moussorgsky, do we call him a Massenetist, a Satist, or a Moussorgskist? No, because in doing so we would only be indicating an infinitesimal aspect of a whole which is so completely stamped by the individuality of the Debussy genius. The same applies to "impressionism," with the added drawback of its insulting and inaccurate connotations. One can only resolve to substitute for the laziness of this terminology the far more gratifying knowledge derived from the deep study of Debussy's harmonies, forms, tonalities and modalities, rhythms, melodies, and the interpretations needed to do them justice. One will then find that Debussy stands at a midpoint betwen romanticism and neo-classicism, effecting in his works the transition in the cycle between these two aesthetics, and adding his own embodiment of perceptivism in manifold techniques as a further heritage.

ROMANTICISM

It is a well-known adage that "one must always be the son of someone," and that however original one may become in one's full blossoming, the early shoots are the product of a seed which is not truly ours.

It is therefore not idle to inspect the long and powerful movement, mostly German, which had preceded Debussy and his relation to it. In so doing we must first establish the fact that the Romantic movement, by the time of Debussy's adulthood, had passed its culmination, exhausted its powers temporarily at least, and was branching afield to try to renew its tarnished glory and exasperated energies.

In accepting this immediate heritage, Debussy was quick to realize this situation and to grasp both its dangers and challenges. Economic of means, as all truly French artists are, he began by rejecting from romanticism all aspects of form and expression which were large, colossal, pompous, in favor of conciseness, compactness, and a close adherence to the precept that "brevity is the soul of wit." This brevity very automatically banned the romantic fascination—I would almost say, hypnosis—of repetition.

A second national trait, that demanding clarity and logic, as a basic aesthetic consideration, makes him discard from the romantic tradition all disorderliness, chaos in structure, chaos in the logical sequence of cause and effect in music, and the amount of subjectivity which in its morbid exploration of individual psychoses loses sight of universally shared emotions. One could say that if Debussy's emotions are refined and sometimes specious in their cultural implications, they yet belong to normal psychology rather than to psychopathic research.

Noting these specific ways by which Debussy made his departure from the romantic movement let us consider the many details, some of them fairly large, by which he accepted this heritage, even in metamorphosing it.

One of the prime traits of the romantic, in literature and in music, is his attempt to evade reality and live in a dream. This escape assumes varied forms in the romantic movement, some of which are found again in the choice of subject matters, as stimuli in Debussy's piano works. In rapid survey, there is escape in space (travel, exoticism), escape in time (the past, antiquity, medievalism), escape in literature and legends (the fictitious or supernatural), escape into imaginative suggestions of the new world to be created by science.

A next romantic trait derives from the first and that is the interest shown by Debussy in contemporary poets, their influence, and his very rich and remarkable song cycles. His own literary achievements in "Proses lyriques" and as critic for the *Revue Blanche* and numerous other publications (later collected in the book called *Monsieur Croche: Dilettante Hater*) bring a parallel to the diversified cultural palettes of the romantic musicians, who, far from limiting their interest to music, gave free rein to their curiosity in other fields. His interest in graphic arts is given substance by his borrowing of the terms "estampes," "esquisses," and "images" from their vocabulary, as well as by his intense interest in colors, musically and otherwise.

Love and sublimation of nature have been, since the German literary inception of the romantic movement, potent factors: brooks, meadows, forests, moon, and sun each in turn provoked thousands of words investing them with various degrees of charm, magic, evil, or joy as backgrounds for the subjective drama of moods to be projected. Debussy's love of nature greatly extends this realm in two directions. First, the diversity of the aspects of nature that beckoned to his artist's soul, or rather to his perceptivism, had a tremendous range, encompassing clouds and fog, the sea and wind in all their aspects, water, snow, trees, as well as the more usual pastoral scenes and moonlit luminosity. And second, but much more important, is the fact that, unlike the romantic, Debussy does not intrude upon nature; he lets nature intrude upon him. He gives nature a soul, a will and personality, which he observes with the keen insight of those who really love. His depiction of nature is the result of a fond objectivity, in which the object through Debussy's abstraction is given freedom of any heavy-handed molding of nature's expression to his ends!

16

It naturally derives that in the musical language used in response to the highly diversified aspects of nature and to the various exotic, literary, legendary sources of stimulus Debussy would have adapted to his technique of composition—with tremendous transmutations—certain traits of the classic and romantic heritages. The first will soon be discussed; in the latter one may cite the use of folk materials or their spirit, the attention to color and therefore to orchestration and its transference to the piano, resulting in orchestral as well as piano virtuosity (but not as a means unto themselves), extremes of compass and extremes of dynamics, pictorial effects, and the association of certain motifs, harmonies, or rhythms to certain objects, emotions, or situations. This last item alone could furnish material for a research thesis.

Thus, Debussy's relation to the period preceding him is that of a refining of some of its still usable traits, a complete discarding of those points which had been overindulged, a clarifying, a tensing of its techniques, the giving of an orientation through sensitive logic, plus, and that is the capital point, the numerous genial innovations, the stamp of the personality of Debussy, which, from his own resources, bridged the gap between this partially usable inheritance and the multi-faceted renaissance of the early twentieth century.

CLASSICISM

Before undertaking the examination of detailed aspects of the musical language as used by Debussy, one must examine a heritage which we feel is more potent than romanticism in applying to his method and the resultant works, i.e., classicism of aesthetics and neo-classicism in certain aspects of technique, though again, one must warn the reader that this is only another fragment of the Debussy aesthetics, the whole not having yet received an adequate name.

Classicism of aesthetics. . . . In looking up the terminology, we find that it presupposes a lasting quality born of the very beauty, of first-class rank, of that which is dubbed "classical"; quality which may be the result of subordinating the forms of expressing human emotion to the perfect balance of logic and keen sensitivity. Classicism is the art of expressing oneself with sovereign mastery, but without restraint, with-

17

out fear; translating inner emotion, whether intellectual or sensual, by the simplest means and avoiding useless chatter. In other words: genial imagination and knowledge—controlled by spiritual intelligence and logic.

We postulate that: had we invented it, we still could not have found a description which better fits in every respect the general aesthetics of Debussy, except in that it does not go far enough, does not encompass all that he means to the history of music.

As to neo-classicism, that is, the return to forms of classicism earlier employed, it is one of the weapons Debussy used to emancipate himself from that which in the romantic movement was incompatible with his tastes and development. In so doing, he revivified the creative air, fertilized the musical soil, fructified the vocations of countless disciples, and paved the way for a widespread and felicitous neo-classical movement.

His contrapuntal conception of voice leading, and of independently evolved and developed horizontal levels, is probably the most important single item of his neo-classicism. It presupposes—and in Debussy this is confirmed—a terracing of dynamic levels, great individuality of phrasing of the superimposed voices, a non-metric (i.e., non-accentual) conception of the bar-line, sensitive attention to appoggiaturas and their resolutions, polyrhythmic stresses resulting from the non-conforming rhythms of each voice, and, as by-products, a tremendous diversity of pedal-points and of motivic patterns which are in direct descendance of the "divine arabesque" of Bach.

Sharp contrasts of dynamics, of scoring, of texture, remind us of the art of chiaroscuro of the baroque period, and the minute attention given to ornaments in symbol—or written out in the melodic line—gives more than a passing bow to the "style gallant."

The classical dance suite is brought to light again in the "Suite Bergamasque," "Hommage à Rameau" (a slow saraband), and in "Pour le piano," the last having many traits in common with the organ style of Bach and his precursors. The ricercar, with augmentation, diminution, inversion, etc., comes back in "Hommage à Haydn," "Reflets dans l'eau."

In thinking of the dance suite, we naturally think of the clavecinistes; Debussy's texture is greatly imbued by the clarity of pattern and by the keyboard style of these masters, from whom he also borrows little tricks such as the crossing of hands, arpeggi and scale passages, ornaments.

The symmetry, compactness, proportions, and balance of Debussy's form are classic, as are the structures which served as inspirations for the evolving of his own, very specific, molds. They clearly adhere to the classic principles of dramatic unity and literary and musical construction: the statement of a situation, the unfolding of action, the climax, the denouement, the end.

The return, after so many centuries, to the medieval modes was an immensely important move in its melodic, rhythmic, and harmonic inferences, in the richness they brought and in the problems they required to be solved in their modern use, and in the opening of a veritable mine of musical materials; true, Debussy was not the only one to advocate and practice the return to modes, but he was, among its earliest champions, one of the best-equipped to deal with its harmonic subtleties and to popularize its uses by his own example. Though it is likely that his efforts in this direction may have caused him troubles, as we see in the following which he wrote:

"It is admittedly less dangerous to preach Palestrina to the crowds than the Gospel to savages; yet one may meet with the same hostility—the difference is only in the penalty: in the one case scalping, in the other yawning." *

One could also mention that, if Debussy had subject matters, so did the clavecinistes, and that, when couched with logic, discretion, refinement, and universality of expressed emotion, they become as classical as are the compositions on abstractions—to which Debussy also gave generous attention in the suites, the études, and the instrumental sonatas.

FORM

One must not be led by the descriptive titles Debussy gives to some of his works to conclude that the form, in following a program, will be incompatible with classical premises of structure. Nor must one be

* *Monsieur Croche*, p. 97. (Dover edition, p. 35)

blinded by the use of Chopin terminology in the designation of pieces; ballade, valse romantique, mazurka, nocturne, prélude, étude, these terms are passing acknowledgment of his deep respect for the great romantic, whose pupil, Madame Mauté de Fleurville, was Debussy's early teacher; they in no way infer the use of Chopin's architecture.

Debussy's forms are strictly classical, but they are evolutions of former forms, adaptations, revaluations, not copies. On this subject, Debussy is quite rabid; he felt with justice that forms must not stagnate and that, in the post-Beethovenian symphony, for instance, the medium had lost aesthetic significance through a childish tracing of the form:

"A symphony is usually built up on a chant heard by the composer as a child. The first section is the customary presentation of a theme on which the composer proposes to work; then begins the necessary dismemberment; the second section seems to take place in an experimental laboratory; the third section cheers up a little in a quite childish way interspersed with deeply sentimental phrases during which the chant withdraws as is more seemly; but it reappears and the dismemberment goes on; the professional gentlemen, obviously interested, mop their brows and the audience calls for the composer. But the composer does not appear. He is engaged in listening modestly to the voice of tradition which prevents him, it seems to me, from hearing the voice that speaks within him." *

From this scathing report, one may deduce Debussy's impatience with lengthy developments, and his even greater impatience with unimaginative subservience to traditional form. Bach, in writing a fugue, never wrote a letter-perfect textbook fugue! Haydn, Mozart, Beethoven, in writing sonatas, never twice used the same form in its identical details! Theirs was a constant experimentation, a live sense of organic rapport and proportion, and not the feathered beds of complacently accepted molds. Debussy not only preached, but also practiced this art of a logical linking of cause and effect of the materials used, arriving at a classical form through the dictates of this discipline of conciseness, nonrepetition, and proportion of phrases, rather than by a preconceived selection of a mold.

What is the resultant form? To what may we compare it from our experience or our vocabulary of known quantities?

A number of isolated cases have the alternation of sections which are

* *Monsieur Croche*, p. 37. (Dover edition, pp. 18-19)

the property of rondo form, that is, the basic arrangement of A-B-A-C-A, etc., such as is found in "Poissons d'or," for instance; or the alternation of only two materials, A-B-A-B and coda (based on both materials), for instance, in the "Second Arabesque." Still another resultant repartition is found to be ternary A-B-A, as in the "First Arabesque."

But, in most of the works, the resultant form is more complex and partakes of elements of rondo form and of first-movement sonata form, with that constant logic of growth of the materials and contrapuntal independence belonging to the fugue or the ricercar.

The problem of terminology now places itself before us. You may ask, why not call this form, in Debussy's wide but varied usage of it, a rondo-sonata form? The answer is in the descriptions of sonata and rondo forms prevalent in nearly every textbook we turn to, in which a mass of details, "ifs and buts," so clutter the general principles of these forms as indeed to make their academic application to the works of Debussy unthinkable. It may not be amiss here to take a little time to view this strange situation of terminology, for if the sonata form (or the rondo form) is to mean a rigid set of rules as to keys, number of themes, repartitions of materials, types of cadences, relative lengths of sections, *und so weiter,* it will only apply to a very short period of musical history, and even in that period one notes the exceptions made to it by its "fathers," Haydn, Mozart, and Beethoven. It will never continue or be enriched; its literature will have stopped before it began. Yet we realize that this strict conception of the sonata, like the strict conception of the nonexistent textbook fugue, was never that of its pioneers, and is only prevalent in textbooks through the rigid postmortem assessment of the past, a result of the oversimplification and the over-detailed German statistical methods therein glorified.

From that standpoint then, it is impossible to call Debussy's most prevalent forms "sonata" or "rondo," with the general principles of which he, however, did discipline, invigorate, and create his medium.

If some day analysis becomes reasonable and logical, and, acknowledging the existence of certain basic molds, or structural tendencies, or aesthetic principles of architecture, keeps from the temptation of setting down in minute details their non-universal aspects, too—befuddling the poor student into thinking that composers of genius write thus according to law, instead of creating anew in each work—then, and only then, could one see the marvelous evolution of these basic principles through infinite ages of development, and apply them freely to composers of very different schoolings, aesthetics, harmonic and melodic techniques. To these forms, their plurality of use would indeed be their glory.

In our opinion, then, the basic and only assumption of a rondo form would be its frequent return of a principal material (be it a motif, a theme; be it varied, identical, shorter; in this or that key, or no key) between sections which contrast to this principal refrain in any way desired by the composers (another material, a development of the first material, a free cadenza, a series of harmonic progressions), anything which shows a break of texture if not of content from the refrain.

For the sonata, the basic and only valid assumption would be its tripartite arrangement of exposition, development, recapitulation. That the exposition should contain long themes or mere motifs, one or twenty such, in tonic, dominant, supertonic, or raised fifth, is of no consequence to the form at large, only to the specific piece at hand. That the development should be long, short, on one or ten materials, or should even elect a new material to strengthen its argument, is also of no import to the form, does not destroy its fundamentals; nor is the condensed recapitulation, or the restatement of two materials juxtaposed instead of succeeding each other, or the recapitulation of materials in an order different from that of the exposition.

These are all individual treatments of a basic assumption, enriching its scope, its variety, its development, its plasticity—and, therefore, its usefulness and reason for being. The sonata then assumes in its exposition-development-recapitulation sequence the basic aesthetics of logic, as found in Debating (statement of problem, argument, summary), in novels and drama (the characters and situation, the action, the climax and denouement).

But until such a general conception is prevalent, one cannot use current terminology in Debussy (or in the analysis of the majority of late nineteenth- and twentieth-century composers), for, although his form is strict (disciplined) and classical (proportioned), it is *evolved from*

22

but not *identical to* the classical forms it most resembles—as they are now described, i.e., with a set content.

We could invent a series of terms then to describe the Debussy form: micro-sonata, symmetro-nuclear form, epitomic form, polaroid-contra-tilophony, prisma-sonata. But in doing so, would we not be adding our piece of straw to the tendency we have just decried, and to the even worse twentieth-century tendency of dividing heritages by parcels, of failing to see logical continuity in history, of brilliantly making a crazy quilt out of a long curve of events. No, it is the wiser course to describe the form (as is done later on in the consideration of the piano works of Debussy), to show the sections, their contents, their functions, their relations, their proportions, and to await a future in which perspective will have allowed a philosophy of formal analysis in which Debussy's vital contributions will mark another step in the long and rich evolution of the rondo-sonata and sonata forms.

HARMONY, MODALITY, TONALITY

In the coming of age of an intimate relationship and cooperation between acoustics and musicology, it has been pointed out more and more strongly that the evolution of harmony is a constant growth, embodying humanity's slow but steady perception of the partials of any fundamental tone. As a partial is perceived and assimilated into usage it finds its way eventually into harmonic theory, and its acceptance may considerably change the relationship of harmonies previously recognized.

So it was that the perception of the perfect fifth, the perfect fourth, and the octave brought music from homophony to polyphony, that the perception of the third and sixth (long contested as dissonances) formed the supplemental factor to form the triad and its inversions, that the perception of the next partial, the minor seventh, paved the way for the dominant seventh chords, and so forth. Since each tone contains an infinitely subdividing range of partials, it in fact contains the history of harmonic evolution from earliest times, to the present, and to the future, at the rate of growth governed by the perception of acutely sensitive prophet-composers, their uses of these additional partials, and their eventual acceptance by theorists and the public ear.

"The Debussyist harmony created a scandal in its day. Its richness and novelty were not at first understood, because of a failure first to integrate it in the system in which it fit. People saw only an arbitrary nihilism there, where in truth a logical growth of value was prevalent." *

Dissonance, which is a relative quantity, can be defined as the unusual, the shocking, the highly colored, the non-conforming element of a progression. It is obvious then that, in a texture concerned mainly with triads, a seventh is a dissonance, but that in a texture mainly made of sevenths or ninths, the dissonance will have to be an eleventh, thirteenth, or a bitonal aggregate, and one could even conceive of a texture in which widely superimposed chords used in abundance could, by contrast, make a triad sound as a dissonance, i.e., a non-conforming element.

Our understanding, then, of consonance and dissonance in Debussy, as in any composer, will be based on what the harmonic 'norm' of the particular passage under observation is, and not on a preconceived notion, which already in the romantic movement would not have held true. For the seventh and ninth chords, already in powerful effect in Schumann, invade the Wagnerian harmony, with the capital difference that these "dissonant" chords are now treated as consonances, as resolutions, as conclusions and cadences.

Further, the staticity of the tonic chord is avoided, delayed, dodged, and replaced by a dynamic tendency toward its coloring, an urge which sometimes is granted, sometimes frustrated throughout. Further, tonalities and modalities combine, and, in the tense friction of major and minor superimposed seconds, it is possible frequently to consider both components of the tension as sovereign tones, rather than, in the classical tradition, to attribute tonal rights to one, and subserviency, with the duty of resolving, to the other. Yet this mode of treatment is not *parti-pris* in its sensitive usage in Debussy, for frequently too, the retards, appoggiaturas, acciaccaturas are resolved in classical manner.

Having considered the two important points of the normal expansion of harmony through perception of its overtones, and the very relative

* André Coeuroy, *La Revue Musicale*, p. 117, Paris, May, 1921.

24

quantity of dissonance and consonance, we may look briefly into the amazingly diversified harmonic language of Debussy, that wide vocabulary which he developed to the service of the vertiginous effects he demanded and obtained from music. First, let us examine the systems, i.e., the modalities and tonalities before considering specifics of progressions and chords.

DIATONICISM. It would be an error, and a grave one, to overlook in the early enthusiasm over more exotic colorings, the infinitely sensitive and widespread treatment of the diatonic system by Debussy. In its use, the range is from classically sober adherence to the scale degrees, through the Faurean dexterity of supple modulation to the enrichment of altered chords, to bi-modality (superimposition of major and minor, or their intimately linked successive use), to bitonality and polytonality.

BITONALITY and polytonality find their systematic use in Debussy, and for that reason and in view of succeeding historical developments are of particular importance in those works and passages in which they occur. This simultaneous use of two or more diatonic scales assumes three distinctive forms in Debussy.

(1) It is sometimes the result of chordal superimposition (several independent triads juxtaposed), or of the harmonization of a conjunct melodic passage with consecutive major thirds, giving the effect of a series of major tonics and of consecutive polytonality.

(2) It is more frequently the result of the superimposition of completely independent contrapuntal levels, each evolving quite completely in its own key.

(3) It is also found in the rapid mirroring of short motifs, of which the intervals are retained integrally, but which start a major or minor second below or above each time, an effect which for want of a better expression we have called 'successive polytonality,' for the rapidity of the succession precludes the formalities of modulation, while bringing characteristic changes of tonal center incommensurate with a single tonality. Under this general heading one can see further the analysis of "La danse de Puck," "Brouillards," "La Puerta del Vino," "Les tierces alternées" "Feux d'Artifice," "Hommage à Haydn," "L'Isle joyeuse," and the interesting cadenza of "Poissons d'or," which in 1907

superimposes C major and F♯ major, much in the manner in which Stravinsky, though probably arriving at it independently, superimposes the same two tonalities in "Petrouchka," completed in 1911.

ANCIENT MODES. In his use of medieval modes Debussy shows the same ease and fluidity as he does in the use of diatonicism; his is not a turn toward the rigidity of archaism, yet it is a very complete revaluation of their uses, not just a passing coloring. A marked preference is shown for Aeolian, Dorian, and Phrygian, with less frequent usage of the Lydian and Mixolydian modes. A note of warning: in the works of Debussy, these modes are nearly always transposed, and do not confine their compass to an octave. Further, the differentiation of the position of the dominant in plagal and authentic modes is not necessarily maintained. For instance, the Aeolian mode sometimes functions as the plagal form of Dorian, and sometimes as an authentic mode with its dominant at the fifth. Debussy also frequently uses a mode pentatonically or hexatonically, i.e., with some of its tones missing, which, however, a later phrase of the melody may supply.

The use of the modes in his works is a horizontal process, which is "harmonized" by a counterpoint freed from its earlier limitations of dissonance. Further, modality has a definite influence on the cadential uses in Debussy. His fresh attention to the subdominant and submediant chords, both in modal and diatonic passages, is worth noting here as a heritage of plagality, as is his use of the Phrygian cadence. Typical passages of modality will be found in "Suite pour le piano," "Hommage à Rameau," "Et la lune descend . . . ," "Suite Bergamasque," and a number of others.

CHROMATICISM. The use of chromaticism in Debussy, as compared with that of his romantic predecessors, is restrained. It is frequently limited to transitional passages, to pictorial tensing of the texture either as a humorous twist ("Minstrels," "General Lavine-eccentric," etc.) or in the mounting fury of elements, and the wind particularly. We find in his letter to J. Durand, February 29, 1908, the interesting remark: ". . . by this weather, when the wind abuses its chromatic privileges."

A further use of chromaticism is made by Debussy in "slide" modulations, in which a rapid chromatic succession on a uniform pattern can effect a wide change of level nearly without a break in texture. Enharmonic changes have a similar application.

PENTATONISM. The basic assumption of a five-note scale seems to have held a fascination for Debussy, but it is not limited in his music to melodic writing, nor to the five black keys of the piano. It is used as harmonic clusters ("Poissons d'or") as well as in the horizontal flow of themes with diatonic harmonies. The important point is that the variety of pentatonic series used by Debussy completely lays aside the still prevalent definitions which propose only one conformation of this scale, plus one transposition (i.e., to white keys). Returning to the historical and oriental view of the five-note equation, Debussy obtains plurality and differentiation.

It is becoming an accepted theory that pentatonism is a stage of musical development which all civilizations go through before obtaining six, and then seven, and perhaps finally twelve, tones. This theory brings a logical explanation to the extremely diverse sources of pentatonic melodies: from certain aborigines, from central European folksongs, from Celtic folksongs, in a number of plainsongs, and as a highly developed art form in hundreds of varieties in the Orient. It has been said that a proficient classical Chinese musician may know over 115 individual pentatonic series, and these are not just transpositions of a single set pattern, but different scales resulting from the different relations of steps, half-steps, and steps-and-a-half within the compass and in relation to the tone centers.

Debussy's application of pentatonism partakes of this breadth; it gives a new twist to a mode, or to a diatonic scale, or it branches afield as in "Pagodes," in which four completely different such series are used. "Voiles," "Vent dans la plaine," "Bruyères," "Jimbo's lullaby" are among the many typical examples.

WHOLE-TONED SCALE. One would nearly be tempted to call this the "tempest-in-a-teapot" scale, for it has certainly been controversial. It is amazing how such a detail may have fired the imaginations to a point completely out of keeping with the relative place it occupies in Debussy's works as compared to various forms of diatonicism and modality. We will therefore be quite brief in our perusal of this scale in view of the

27

veritable oceans of words which those interested can find on the subject.

Whole-toned series are limited to two in the equal-tempered system; Debussy uses these two series singly, in fragments or complete, and as melodic or harmonic material, and also in superimposition of the two series (a form of bitonality). The equality of the whole tones obviates the possibility of a spatially, or organically, or acoustically, arrived at tonic-dominant relationship, which can then make their use an excellent medium for supple, unichrome pictorial, or emotional, effects. Yet one must not forget that, if the dissonance of leading tone versus tonic is herein obviated, the even harsher possibility of consecutive tritones is wide open. Further, duration, pitch, scoring stresses can so place their weight on certain notes of the whole-toned series to the exclusion of others as to artificially reproduce two enemy camps of three notes each, which will then enter the wide philosophical concept of tonic and dominant families (see "Voiles"). We will also note that the alternation of whole-toned texture to pentatonic texture is a particularly felicitous contrast ("Vent dans la plaine" and "Voiles").

ARABIC SCALE. Though the use of this scale is limited in the works of Debussy, it is still a very pungent essence in the evocation of the Moorish heritage of Spain, of the flamenco art; for its use we refer the reader to the considerations of "Soirée dans Grenade," "La Puerta del Vino" and "Sérénade interrompue."

From the consideration of the palette of tonal patterns one can now quickly note some of the textural usages and chordal aggregates, with no claim to completeness, which would require an entire book and is not here our stated aim.

PARALLELS. In his contrapuntal mastery Debussy did not limit himself to that aspect of counterpoint in which independent voices must also be rhythmically independent, though this usage is quite prevalent in his works. He also accepted the example of organum, of fauxbourdons, of gymel, and their parallelism of voice progression and therefore of intervals, and extended their implication to include not only parallel octaves, perfect fifths, perfect fourths, thirds and sixths, but major and minor sevenths, ninths, seconds, tritones ("Snow is dancing"). The effect of the parallel major third successions on the tonal scheme has

28

already been noted under polytonality, and we find in Debussy's break with tradition and his remarkable use of consecutives, an amazingly widened horizon of harmony, tonality, and counterpoint.

CADENCES. We recommend Debussy's cadential turns to the harmonic "gourmet"; no two are alike; they are a blessed relief from the "masculine" dominant tonic, albeit a sometimes tantalizing one. One finds two tonal elements fighting in the coda, then superimposed in the cadence, or else a third comes in to terminate, or one of the two protagonists wins out. And as for deception and drama, no tumbler could pirouette with such elegance, nor the greatest seducer flirt so charmingly, nor the greatest emotion rend so completely, as do Debussy's cadences. They have that à-propos of the finishing touches of a perfectionist, and the wallop of an apt punch-line.

PEDALS. Though the very widespread use of pedal-points by Debussy is later considered in discussing contrapuntal levels, one must mention them here, for their harmonic life is independent of other elements of the texture and therefore sometimes acutely dissonance-forming. To that extent then, they must be watched in their harmonic color. One will also note that, although they are sometimes employed on tonic or dominant, the classical usage is extended to include all notes of the tonality, and further, to notes belonging to a separate tonality from that of other levels of the piece. Also, these pedals may involve one voice or a whole chord.

We have already mentioned the relativity of chordal dissonance and the extended use of sevenths, ninths, elevenths, thirteenths. It will therefore not be surprising to find the use of tonic sevenths and tonic ninths, as consonances without need of resolution. In other works one will find that a generally less complex harmonic texture will permit the effect of the sevenths and ninths as dissonances requiring resolution. Both usages then are found in Debussy, as are both usages of the second: as a juxtaposition of two sovereign notes (which many call the sounding of the appoggiatura simultaneously with its resolution; see "Golliwog's cake-walk," "La Cathédrale engloutie," or "Jimbo's lullaby"), or as an appoggiatura, stressed and gently slurred to its lighter resolution. It is evident that in the type of texture which we have described, false relations should be frequent and very pungent. Added sixth chords are often used, but particularly found in humorous, or in jazz-inspired, works.

Another peculiarity of chordal usage is what we have called the "gutted chord"; this usage in Debussy is quite typical, and has much to offer in transparency of harmony, in that it omits the third in a triad, or alternate thirds in chords of the ninth or thirteenth, leaving superimposed fifths. Besides the clarity of color it offers through the omission of the acoustically out-of-tune, and opaque third of the triad, it also has the advantage of leaving the modality (whether major or minor) undetermined for the moment, opening two horizons to the listeners' ears.

These are some of the components of the "harmonic chemistry" which already haunted Debussy in his Conservatoire days, and never let him rest during the remainder of his lifetime; harmony was for him a demanding but also a most rewarding Muse, whose exigencies stimulated him to ever-renewed discoveries, whose classicism forced him to logic in the assimilation or rejection of his new compounds, to the minute weighing of each note which was to enter the magic formulae, so dynamic that fifty years later they are yet projecting into the future.

COUNTERPOINT, MELODY, LEVELS

If Debussy ever rubbed shoulders with the "five species"—and there can be little doubt that he received more than a superficial grounding in them, his music is yet entirely devoid of their limitations and bickering parsimony. His counterpoint, which matches its quality and ease to that of his harmonic innovations, has the spontaneity of a mastery so complete as to have become second nature. In so doing, he transcends scholastic formulae, applying a technique perfected to the point of making counterpoint a non-obvious but "sine-qua-non" medium of musical expression.

Few are the canons or imitations in Debussy's work, and of fugues there are none in the piano compositions. His use of augmentation, diminution, inversion, mirroring (see "Reflets dans l'eau," "Hommage à Haydn," "Les collines d'Anacapri," "Doctor Gradus ad Parnassum," as examples) is very telling, but also sparing. It is, then, in a broader conception than that of these contrapuntal devices that we must search.

An indication was given to us many years ago of the direction in which to look. Backstage during a symphony performance, a chance chatting during intermission brought up the subject of Debussy's orchestral works. The first trombonist of the symphony happened to be present and his face immediately lit up. "Ah!" he said. "That is indeed a great composer. In most all the other works, all we do is bfff-bfff every fifteen minutes, but with Debussy—even we trombonists become great soloists!"

Very obviously he was referring to one of the most important aspects of Debussy's texture, the miraculous melodic continuity which pervades each of the many superimposed parts of his complex polyphony. A super-imposition in which equilibrium is so completely achieved between the various elements that are juxtaposed, that it never, except in the very early works, assumes the aspect of an accompanied solo part, or single melody.

Yet this coexistence of levels has a wide range in its forms of independence. In this consideration one must assume that any group of notes contradicting another group of notes means contrapuntal writing; that any groups of notes which display a self-contained life and meaning not subservient to that of another simultaneously heard grouping, also mean contrapuntal writing. We will then find that the independence of levels in Debussy ranges from the interference of the conflict of two differently accented rhythms (counterpoint of rhythm, or polyrhythm) to the extreme differentiation of levels conflicting in rhythm, harmony, tonality, melodic delineation, all at the same time.

What is the nature of the levels which are juxtaposed? They may consist of the parallel evolution of several voices sounding one melody, a form of organum, or fauxbourdon, frequently and erroneously analyzed as chord progressions, but the voice-leading of which gives sensitive proof of the contrapuntal origin (see "Sarabande," "Hommage à Rameau").

They may be found in chord outlining or in arabesques which appear to contain one homogeneous voice, but which on closer examination reveal the formation of both a melodic voice and a multi-voice harmonic progression (see "Arabesques," "Brouillards," "Doctor Gradus

31

ad Parnassum"). And again, a trill at the seventh, in which the spatial usage of the ornament clearly denotes its two-voiced intent.

But even more frequently one finds three clearly delineated levels in the simultaneous presence and independent development of (1) melody or melodies, (2) motifs or ostinatos, and (3) pedal-points. Though these levels may cross, or exchange relative positions or registers, they do not fuse, and their individual characters are clearly recognizable in pitch design, rhythm, harmonic implications, tonal implications, throughout the piece. Their coexistence is then a miracle of equilibrium, in which, in relinquishing none of their sovereignty, they supplement and complement each other; it takes the mastery of Debussy to minutely weigh proportions to obtain the harmonious cooperation of these "rugged individualists."

Although the music itself is by far the most eloquent source of information about these levels, yet we may say a few words about each.

Pedal-points as used in Debussy's works are a study in themselves; placed in the bass, middle voices, or top voices, ranging in harmonic implications from dominant and tonic to the distant friction of chromaticism, or of bitonality, held, or rhythmically very active, pictorial and highly evolved, or simple, they form a veritable lexicon of the genre.

Motifs and ostinatos, which form a midpoint between pedal-points and melody, belonging at times to one and at others to the second, have an intrinsic series of functions in the Debussy compositions. It will be noted that our use of the term "ostinato" infers a short but telling motif, stubborn or insistent in its permeation of the texture, but not necessarily incessant in its usage (though in "Des pas sur la neige" the presence of the ostinato is nearly unbroken). These motifs and ostinatos function much as the germ-motifs in the structural unification of the form; they also partake of the contrapuntal conception of the thorough bass and chaconne, and play an important role in pictorialization.

It is frequently found that their earliest presentation in the piece will set not only their general character, but their exact and immutable pitch as well. In these cases, they are colored by the evolution of the harmony, melody, pedal-points, through which they remain fixed. In other cases too, they may change, evolve, be varied.

Melody, the third level, has been kept to the last as meriting a closer inspection, more particularly in view of the too oft-repeated accusation leveled at Debussy, that he lacked melody. In the face of his songs, orchestral works, piano pieces, it is among the more startling signs of the miscomprehension of his aesthetics.

Melody, let us remember, is a word designating a quantity which is infinitely variable. It should not surprise us, then, that it should mean as many different things as there are different composers, and different works by any one composer. With Charles Koechlin, we would say:

"What is melody? Is it the Italian 'bel canto' of the 19th century? Or that of Bach—or Monteverdi and Frescobaldi? Is it the obvious 'phrase à effet' of the verist dramas, with the high C at the end? Or the Massenet melody? As many original composers and we have as many different forms of melody; to attribute to any of these forms the dictatorial privilege of having determined permanent rules would be a 'dogma.' "

In that case, one must examine what is the melodic range as used by Debussy. In his early period, and later in some specific instances, we will find innumerable romantic, easy melodies of the more conventional design, an organized theme; but the more he asserts his own style the more is developed the long, supple, fluid line of plainsong and of some of the early folksongs, which completely replaces and eliminates the chatter of repetition and development. The single continuous theme, neat and precise despite its suppleness, evolves steadily in long phrases, never returning upon itself. It is compact, and within its lifespan it creates its own deductive development. In this aspect it partakes not only of the Gregorian inspiration but also of the continuous flow and broad flight of the melodic conception of Bach. On this point there is a passage by Debussy, which we quote, because we feel it is so enlightening. He is speaking of Bach's violin concerto in G:

"Yet the beauty of this concerto stands out among the others which appear in Bach's manuscripts; it contains, almost intact, that musical arabesque, or rather that principle of ornament, which is the basis of all forms of art. The word 'ornament' has here nothing to do with the meaning attached to it in the musical grammars.

"The primitives, Palestrina, Vittoria, Orlando di Lasso and others, made use of this divine arabesque. They discovered the principle in the Gregorian chant; and they strengthened the delicate traceries by strong counterpoint. When Bach went back to the arabesque he made it more pliant and more fluid; and, in spite of the stern discipline which the great composer imposed on beauty, there was a freshness and freedom in his imaginative development of it which astonishes us to this day. In Bach's music it is not the character of the melody that stirs us, but rather the tracing of a particular line, often indeed of several lines, whose meeting, whether by chance or design, makes the appeal. . . . It is most noticeable that no one was ever known to whistle Bach. . . . I should add that this conception of ornament has vanished completely; music has been successfully domesticated." *

Debussy never abandons this long line, this organic stemming of each note from the preceding; even when he gives a magic, nearly self-sufficient role to a motif, or even a telling single note, beware of not noticing that contrapuntal underpinning, that pedal-point, that long melodic line from which that apparently lone motif or single note is issued, or to which it is proceeding. Here also a "stern discipline is imposed upon beauty," but we hardly notice it because of its mastery, because of the infinitely varied aspects it is clothed in.

In discerning his intentions in regard to melody, we must then first accept their contrapuntal function.

Now, as to their technical aspects, we will find that their compass is widely divergent, with ranges of a third to ranges of several octaves. Rhythmically, they are non-metric, both singly and in their superimposition. The rhythmic language is indeed a very rich one. Beyond that, one will find that they are highly expressive dynamically, and that Debussy, in order to insure their complete interpretation, has taken care in indicating the stresses resulting from the pitch apexes of the melodic lines, and the further rhythmic, harmonic stresses desired by dots, dashes, or accents. He has facilitated the task of the interpreter in all cases where melodic notes are common to two voices, by giving separate stems to each of the two parts.

With these helps and with the firmly established notion of their long horizontal development and contrapuntal function, there should not be undue difficulty in appraising their delineations. One last thought can be borne, about melody, with Schopenhauer's definition: By its own nature, melody errs through countless roads and perpetually goes away from the fundamental tone. These adventures of melody express the

* *Monsieur Croche*, pp. 55-57. (Dover edition, pp. 22-24)

diverse forms of human desire. To create a melody is to reveal the most secret recesses of human feelings—it is the work of a genius!

1521315

PIANISTIC STYLE AND PERFORMANCE *

Debussy's pianistic style is exacting; its demands on the instrument and on the performer are indeed extensive. It is usually true that those who exert a strong discipline upon themselves, expect it in others, and it seems indeed a logical tribute that Debussy's capacity for work and for thought should be, at least in part, matched by that of his interpreters.

It is rather difficult, after so many years, to describe the all-around pianist he, himself, was; the Puckish array of contradictions on this point form a Sphinxian enigma which, unfortunately, it is too late for anyone to unravel with any degree of certitude. But for two years I had a great many opportunities to be in contact with him, either while accompanying singers whom he was coaching, or playing for him some of his just-published piano works, and I can well remember his insistence on the precision and exactitude of the indications marked on the scores in their minutest details. It is, then, in the works that we find the answer to his pianistic style and demands in performance, and not in hearsay reports of his "violent attacks on the keyboard" or his "constant pianissimo" playing.

In the examination of his piano works, the first consideration is the total exploitation of the piano's resources and the orchestral effects which are called into play by the tremendous variety of techniques of composition which Debussy employs. The compass covers the entire piano, the dynamics fluctuate from FFF to PPPP; one level may be percussive and another singing; all the shadings from staccato, to portamento, to legato are used singly and in combination, subtle uses of the three pedals singly and together, are essential to the projection of the contrapuntal levels and pictorial colors, and finally the ingenious

* In this book, only those works originally written by Debussy for the solo piano have been considered. It was felt that, although much herein contained could apply also to the consideration of the four-hand and two-piano works, yet, these should form a study apart, perhaps a supplemental pamphlet, in which space could be given to the consideration of their chamber-music aspects and their enlarged interpretative horizons.

array of materials (motifs, themes, pedal-points, harmonies, modalities, and tonalities) all contrive to bring out of the piano its maximum diversity.

In his treatment Debussy makes obvious his confidence in the capacity of the instrument for these heightened forms of expression, and endows it with an orchestral palette, frequently even finding equivalences to other instruments in his pianistic texture. Highly personalized references to such instruments as the flute, bells, gongs, gamelangs, guitars, muted brass, horns, drums, crotales, organ, celesta are among some of the effects transmitted to the piano. But it is rather in its tremendous range of expression that the piano now reaches toward the coloristic conception of the orchestra.

The technical virtuosity of this Debussy pianism demands: First, accept the romantic technical dexterity which had brought the piano to its great role as solo instrument. Second, having accepted this basis, renovate it from top to bottom, by discarding its outworn patterns, and keeping a constantly renewed and genially fresh source of materials to challenge the performer. It is proverbial that Debussy's piano works do not "fall under the fingers"; each new work brings a new set of technical problems, a new form of virtuosity to conquer. Third, and paramount, while Debussy calls forth all the pianist's ingenuity as to technique, he also demands of him the thoughtfulness and education of a thorough musician. Like Bach or Mozart, Debussy takes for granted that an interpreter will be a musician first, and a technician of his instrument second. It was to him a constant source of irritation not to find this to be the case:

"X is not from Bordeaux, but from Z. That does not prevent him from having a rather strange understanding of my music. . . . Now, that people should buy my music . . . and treat it without restraints, I see no harm in it, but that those who call themselves 'virtuosi' should continue to spread misconception and desolation in concert-halls—this I continue to find irritating." *

". . . I have ceased being surprised at the frequent lack of understanding which greets my poor music. Without undue dramatization, I assure you it is truly appalling." *

In a lighter vein, but no less meaningful, is his view of the virtuoso and the type of appeal he makes to the public:

* Debussy, *Lettres à son Editeur*, October 17, 1916.

"The attraction of the virtuoso for the public is very like that of the circus for the crowd. There is always a hope that something dangerous may happen: Mr. X may play the violin with Mr. Y on his shoulders; or Mr. Z may conclude his piece by lifting the piano with his teeth." *

Indeed, virtuosity for its own sake is remote from Debussy's conception of the piano or of music in general; it should also be absent from that of his interpreters.

What, then, are some of the basics of interpretation, over and above virtuosity, which form the prerequisites of performance of Debussy's piano works?

A knowledge of counterpoint sufficient for the appraisal of the independent levels and of their continuity, sufficient for a sensitive reaction to voice leading.

A knowledge of harmony wide enough for an enlightened recognition of dissonance in relation to the norm of the texture, and for the highlighting of its presence through recognition of its accrued tension and of the releases of tension which will follow it. This knowledge of harmony then presupposes an intimate realization of the function of each changing harmony to that which preceded and that which will follow, an initiation to the harmonic rhythm of the passage or composition at hand.

A knowledge of melody sufficient so that, whatever tonality is elected, the organic relationship of each note to the other is felt, that those notes which are sensitive degrees will realize their gravitational pull toward notes which are more stable—a realization of the function of tone centers and their satellites. The conception of melody will also keenly realize the persistent attention brought by Debussy to curves in pitch, and to the dynamic fluctuation with which they are supported. It will also recognize the infinite variety of characters of these melodies, for which Debussy has evolved a precise system of editing symbols as to degree of lightness, heaviness, staccato, legato, etc.

A knowledge of rhythm which will first demand the laying aside of erroneous notions of meter, and of the bar-line as other than a measure of evolving time. A conception of rhythm which will not only accept durations as eminently precise, but will go even beyond the letter-

* *Monsieur Croche*, p. 54. (Dover edition, p. 22)

perfect to the live and sensitive in its minute accentuations of stresses brought by harmony, pitch line, scoring, sensitive degrees.

A knowledge of scoring sufficient to realize the differences in dynamics and texture resulting from the number of voices employed (from a single voice to fifteen superimposed), and from the spacing of these voices (widely open, or close together).

A knowledge of time and tempo which will be precise, for in Debussy's interpretation an overabundance of rubato, of arbitrary fluctuations in tempo, has long been current; yet performance metronomically even throughout, in his works, is just as unthinkable. It means that the basis of tempo must be exact for each succeeding section or break in texture, determined from Debussy's indications, and the overall timing of a piece is then the result of the thoughtfully arrived at tempi. In a letter to his publishers, Debussy writes: "You know my opinion on metronomic indications: they are correct for one measure, like 'roses, the span of one morning,' but there are those who do not hear music and who take advantage of this absence (of metronomic indications) to hear still less."

A knowledge of pedaling, which first encompasses the function of each of the three pedals, and further of their combined uses. It means the development of a precise "foot" technique which can use the sustaining pedal for pedal-points, the soft pedal for general level of dynamics, and the forte pedal for an exact recognition of the harmonic and melodic changes, and allowing for no blurring or melting together of unrelated elements, which unfortunately happens so often! It also means, in the use of the forte pedal, acute sensitivity to its use fully depressed, half, or shallow, and its changes in parallel or overlapping techniques. Most of all, though, it makes appeal to the awareness of the many abuses pedaling can lead into.

Debussy held the Chopin pianistic tradition in high esteem and used to mention his early lessons with Madame Mauté de Fleurville, in which she stressed that Chopin wanted his students to study without pedal and only to use it sparingly in performance, as a sort of breathing in speech, or punctuation in grammar. Debussy speaks of this point in a letter, and continues by saying: "The quiet truth is, perhaps, that the abuse of the pedal is only a means of hiding a lack of technique, and then, too, one must make a lot of noise so that no one can hear the music which one is butchering!"

A knowledge of touches in piano technique commensurate with the variety of the demands of the Debussy palette. This, indeed, we remember, as do many others, about Debussy's playing; his variety of coloring was as great in performance as in composition. To his music the mere depression of the key with more or less force is not sufficient. The manner of depressing those keys affects the tone and opens many avenues of coloristic research.

We can take the "slap" touch in my method,* as an illustration. Others will be found in the consideration of the "Études." This "slap" touch, named somewhat improperly but recognized by students under this appellation, is particularly applicable in Debussy for effects of resonance with great carrying power, yet devoid of opacity, and of the clicking of the hammers against the strings, and obtainable in soft as well as loud passages. The "slap" is really the production of tone by the sudden release of weight from contracted muscular units; it associates tone production with abandon of the fingers and results in a transparently resonant tone quality, if coupled with the use of the forte pedal. The impulse given to the key by the relaxed units, with the addition at times of added velocity, sets the strings into vibration and gathers (by a precise use of the forte pedal) the sympathetic response of numerous other strings. Whereas, in articulation, the finger grasps the key to produce tone, in slap the finger suddenly abandons its weight to the key, from which it recoils again in readiness for the next release. With the addition of the impulse, and of a less absorbent finger condition, this touch, which normally is used for all resonant and translucid melodies, can further find its application in the interpretation of percussive, but long-vibrating, effects of gongs, bells, and can be further varied by the uses of the soft and forte pedals. This is only an example, which in the interpretation of Debussy must multiply the means in order to match his demands. In summary, then, the performance of Debussy is demanding, technically and musically. It is precise; its demands are clearly indicated. It cannot be vague and impressionistic (poor excuses for laziness), and neither can it be dry, mechanical, and metric. The flow of

* E. Robert Schmitz, *The Capture of Inspiration.*

expression is free, constantly determined by the texture, constantly reflecting the thought process of a man sensitive and emotional, keenly perceptive, and clearly logical.

INFLUENCES: FROM THE PAST AND ON THE FUTURE

About the influences which temporarily colored Debussy's life, some of them passing briefly, some leaving traces, and again some deeply affecting (by adoption or reaction) his musical aesthetics and technique, much has been written, during his lifetime and in the years since.

Since we have already examined the relation of his music to large aesthetic movements, we will merely cite some of these influences, leaving it to the student to refer to longer discussions of their effects, in the many books wherein they are contained, and to search within the music for their relative intensity of impact, or evidence, if any, for by now it must be clear that plagiarism or slavish imitation will be found nowhere in Debussy, even in the early works. He is the creator of a style, not the disciple. Then let us list briefly, in partial chronological order, these shimmering bubbles in the Debussy sky, some pricked and some cherished, all having come into the orbit of his keen perceptivism:

Chopin, via Madame Mauté de Fleurville, and early piano lessons.
Massenet, Gounod, as part of the Conservatoire days.
Fauré, and the exquisite art of modulation and poetic inspiration.
Pre-Raphaelism and Wagner, around the era of the Prix de Rome and Villa Medici days.
Symbolist poets; a long relationship extending from student days through adulthood.
The expositions of 1889 and 1900: the lure of the Orient, and the wonderful All-Russian festivals conducted by Rimsky-Korsakoff.
Moussorgsky: "Boris Godounov" and the songs.
Satie, and experimental harmony.
The clavecinistes: Rameau, Couperin, Scarlatti, their clarity of patterns, their conciseness of form.
J. S. Bach: the divine arabesque, contrapuntal dissonance, and organ style.

Palestrina, and modal plasticity.

Mozart, in his sensitive use of ornamentation, and the appoggiatura.

The union of poetry and of a new form of realism, in the coloring and pictorialization of the subjects Debussy treats, has achieved a most happy mean between "art for art's sake" and music with an idea, and has uncovered in the study of his creative process the dynamic philosophy of perceptivism.

And if the debt owed by succeeding composers to Debussy is already great, and mounting each day, think, then, of our staggering indebtedness as performers and listeners for the exuberant beauty revealed, the generously shared emotions, the poetry and color, the prodigious gift of the self, so jealously guarded in life, so bountifully entrusted in his music.

His music takes its place among those expressions that stir our depths, in which we hear the echoes of our emotions, in which we are awed by the universality of this unspoken language. There is a description so close to our estimate of Debussy, that in closing we dare quote it:

"Great music is a physical storm, agitating to fathomless depths the mystery of the past within us. Or we might say that it is a prodigious incantation. There are tones that call up ghosts of youth, and joy and tenderness; there are tones that evoke all phantom pains of perished passion; there are tones that revive all dead sensations of majesty and might and glory—all expired exultations, all forgotten magnanimities. Well may the influence of music seem inexplicable to the man who idly dreams that his life began less than a hundred years ago! He who has been initiated into the truth knows that to every ripple of melody, to every billow of harmony, there answers within him, out of the Sea of Death and Birth, some eddying immeasurable of ancient pleasure and pain." *

* Paul Elmer More in "Lafcadio Hearn" in *Selected Shelburne Essays* (Oxford); also recently reproduced in *The New York Times Book Review* and in *The Reader's Digest.*

General Lavine—eccentric

Vase with mænads and satyrs
(First Century B.C.)

2.
Piano Works 1888-1904

DEUX ARABESQUES (1888)

These two early compositions, of the year 1888, are filled with charm —the charm of decorative patterns gracefully adorning objects, monuments, a room, or even the frame of a picture.

Arabesques are defined as the interlacing of figures of flowing fancy, according to the Arab custom, an art particularly developed in a civilization denied by religious beliefs the right to artistic representation of the human form. Yet nothing in these compositions is Arabic, the term arabesque having taken the wider connotation of patterns which repeat themselves in graceful curves, or combine with other patterns in lacy tracery.

These happy, unpretentious, and gay arabesques of Debussy are essentially French; they do not overreach their ornamental purposes. Debussy here uses charming musical designs with the same love and subtlety as the Japanese handle flowers. The fluidity which the composer loved in Bach's "divine arabesque" is at least part of the inspiration for these flowing works, but Debussy sets it into a more elusive and precious harmonic texture, for all its neo-classicism. It is noteworthy how these ornamental patterns are repeated, transformed, and coordinated, and, though the method cannot properly be called interior decoration, it is akin to it—a tonal decorative art.

Yet these arabesques have more than pleasurable significance for us, because, unlike several other early compositions, they already possess in embryo important characteristics of Debussy's individual art. Their use here is almost hermetic in character; whereas most other young composers would aggressively promote their early discoveries, and thus make them obnoxious, here innovation is well-bred.

The delicate use of ancient modal texture is one of the characteristics foreshadowed in the "Arabesques." In the first, the opening measures have a descending series of chords in the first inversion spread in arpeggiato; these chords form a bass melodic succession which progresses from the fifth, fourth, third, and second degrees of the medieval Dorian mode to come to stability on its tonal center F♯ (first degree triad, F♯-A-C♯, measure 3). Then, while this chord maintains the tonal stability, Debussy continues the descending scale through measures 3 and 4. The modality loses itself smoothly in the course of measure 5 into dominant harmony which resolves to E major diatonic in measure 6. Nothing affected in these five measures, the transmutation from Dorian to diatonic is remarkably smooth and individual. This delicate procedure is found several times in the course of the "First Arabesque." An almost identical arrangement is found in the middle section of the "Second Arabesque," although the modal transmutation is not quite as subtle.

Another characteristic is Debussy's regard for proportion, symmetry, and balance in his forms. Both Arabesques are basically ternary, the first A-B-A, and the second with the addition at the end of a coda containing both materials. Yet no flagrant signposts to pompously announce the end of a section, the return of another; already in these early works the art of construction is infinitely beyond mere patchwork!

The skillful use of series of consecutive seventh chords ("First Arabesque," page two, measures 18-20) is so deftly handled into the patterns that they do not weaken the tonal texture.

To come back to the influence of Bach, which is quite perceptible: the "First Arabesque" is basically contrapuntal in texture. For instance, in measures 6-7 in which the weight of the arpeggi of the left hand stresses the first and third beats, while in the right hand the appoggiaturas and initiations of motives stress the second beat. Note also that the typical pattern of measure 6 in the right hand has the nature of a procedure frequently found in Bach ("Well-Tempered Clavichord," "Preludes"), i.e., a melodic arabesque composed of two voices progressing in alternation and united as a single melody. Observe further how the more defined melody arises from the arabesque's texture at measure 17 to continue through the following measures to the end of the section in

E major (measure 38); it springs naturally from the two first measures of the piece, an organic process common to many Bachian passages.

A few errors to avoid and some particular cares to take with the performance of each of these works can be signaled: first, let us repeat from the preface that performances which are untidy "à la romantique" or "vague impressionism" are nowhere welcomed in Debussy. Even in these early works the texture is classic, albeit sensitive and subtle—but sensitive and subtle are not synonyms for untidy and vague!

First Arabesque

The descending progression C♯ to B in measures 1-4 must be homogeneous and even, and a similar interpretation will hold for recurrences of this pattern. Throughout the arabesque one must be clearly conscious that the rhythm is frequently non-metric, and that main accents of the measure may occur on any of the four beats, and not on the so-called downbeats; for instance, in measures 1-2, the arpeggi rise to the third beat in supple contour to this apex. In measures 3-4-5, the sensitive apexes of the melody again are never on the first beat. These examples are only instances of a prevalent factor.

In measures 6-7 and similar passages keep the right-hand arabesques clear and even. The two-voiced texture, as explained above, leading through a number of passing tones, does not permit the use of the pedal any more than in similar Bach patterns. At measure 7, the appoggiatura D♯ must be stressed and linked, decrescendo, to its temporary resolution which in turn must be linked to the ultimate resolution of measure 8.

At measures 13-16, the stringendo and ritenuto are gradual and avoid breaking the continuity of the musical idea. In these same measures an adroit use of the pedal (permissible here since the triplets are composed of chord notes solely) will enhance the temporary but non-obvious animation. In measures 22-24 the ritardando means an elegant unfolding of the embellished echo of the seventh-chord phrase, but not a romantic display of passion and irregularity. The tempo is neatly resumed in contrast as indicated in measures 23 and 26. In this last measure the dominant harmony should be asserted by making the G natural clearly audible.

From measures 29 to 46 inclusive, note that the effect has become more emotional; it is rich in abandon, swaying impulses, tenderness, and fantasy, provided all points of harmonic tension are set into proper value. Do not separate resolutions from the appoggiaturas that precede them, and give the two their sensitive meaning by properly stressing the appoggiaturas and lightening the resolution as an abandonment of tension.

Note, in measures 47-49, that the phrasings of the right-hand and left-hand passages are in contrast to each other. The majesty of measures 63-66 turns back to the clearly defined style of the opening, at measures 67-71.

Second Arabesque

The "Second Arabesque" is less lyric in character than the first one. Its patterns have sharper outlines and its rhythmic pulsations are more active. The overall effect is brighter, with occasional sturdiness, quite in contrast to the supple delineation of the "First Arabesque."

From the onset the rhythms of the small ornaments of the right hand must be timed exactly; the triplet of sixteenths must balance properly with the ensuing eighth-note. This treatment is within the organic balance as shown by the slightly different version of measures 66-71, where unevenness of consecutive eight-notes would not be acceptable. This peculiarity of the patterns and the added danger of blurring the neat progression induce a careful use of pedal. Recommended is a pedal of eighth-note duration, not more, on each beat, and holding the left hand exactly as indicated.

Do not hesitate to place a sharp stress on the appoggiatura of the second and third beats in measure 8. It is necessary for contrast, as evidenced in recurring forms.

In measures 15-16, observe the accent and tenuto of the second beat of measure 15, then render the ascending scale intelligible to set into value the successive dominant-seventh (measure 16, first beat), with appoggiaturas, then tonic-seventh (measure 16, third beat), followed by the ninth, which is the apex. This increasing harmonic tension is

Poissons d'or

Lid of a canopic jar
(about 1500 B.C.)

Greek dancers: frescoes of the First Century B.C.

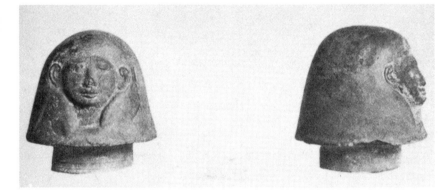

Canopes (lids of canopic jars)

Greek dancers (the center one plays the crotals)

**Bas-relief showing
players of crotals
(background, right)**

"GENERAL" EDWARD LAVINE

ONE OF
BELLE
HATHAWAY'S
SIMIAN
PLAYMATES

neral Lavine—eccentric

Japanese pagoda

Japanese pagoda

Gamelang orchestra (Bali)

Pagoda in Burma

The main entrance of a Japanese temple

extremely effective by its own nature, provided the performer does not ignore it.

The section of measures 28-35 is sturdy and should not be robbed of this character by preconceptions as to "delicacy" in Debussy. In measures 38-62, note carefully the tenuto harmonies under the arabesque pattern, sometimes staccato, and sometimes slurred by twos. In measure 39, the upper voice should remain staccato to the end of the measure (the four dots on the last four eighth-notes are missing). In measure 40, the upper voice should be slurred by twos. Compare these measures to measures 46-49, which are accurately phrased. This central section is more supple and less exteriorized than measures 28-37. Measures 82-90 may be played at ease. The almost idle harmonic state on two pedal-points creates an impression of suspense, but this indecision does not mean that the timing should be rubato.

Measures 90-100, note the contrapuntal clarity. The four imitations must enter in a precise and almost impulsive manner, leading to the sturdy build-up by contrary expansion.

In general, this arabesque is intended to convey a sense of active but classic buoyancy, with an occasional dance-like sturdiness.

SUITE BERGAMASQUE (1890)

This suite was composed in 1889 and published in revised form in 1903 (Lockspeiser), yet dated on editions as of 1890, with the Fromont copyright originating in 1905.

The word "Bergamasque" itself evokes an antique setting, a world of adventures, and it is indeed such a world one encounters in the devious meanders of its etymology—a very amusing course, for one finds dances called "bergamasche" in the suites of the Italian musician Girolamo Frescobaldi, a native of Ferrara near the Adriatic. Again one runs across references to the tapestries called "bergame," originating in the city of that name, a very ancient settlement, older even than Rome, and located forty kilometers northeast of Milan. A further investigation brings us closer to our goal, for we find that "bergamasque" refers to a region of Bergamo and of its inhabitants. The character of these inhabitants is famous in all Italy, for upon their characteristics of rusticity and clumsiness were built a series of dances and, further, of them was born Harlequin, the prototype of the antique Italian comedy. Egotistical and shrewd, under an apparent simplicity, Harlequin originally satirized the "jargon" and defects of the Bergamo peasants. He was the buffoon of the comedy, with a face smeared with soot and clothing sadly patched up with all kinds of colors in crazy-quilt patterns.

By the seventeenth century the cast of characters of the Italian comedy was well known throughout Europe, popularized by troupes of excellent actors. During more than a century this was nearly the only form of theater in Paris. The personages included: Scaramouche, Pulcinella, The Doctor, Arlequin, Pantalon, Scapin, Beltramme, El Capitan, Mezzetin, Pierrot, Isabella, et al. These personalities found their way into the court representations, and later endured in the art of puppetry and through the literary fascination they exerted in the nineteenth century.

That Debussy should have known them in all their guises is certain, for once interested in the word Bergamasque Debussy's inquisitive mind, tempted by the unknown, would not rest until satisfied, but the initial impulse, or rather the first cause, of the suite must be sought in the vaporous, fugitive verses by Paul Verlaine (d. 1896) in *Fêtes galantes,* of which Debussy had an intimate knowledge, and more specifically in "Clair de lune":

> "... *que vont charmant masques et bergamasques*
> *Jouant du luth et dansant et quasi*
> *Tristes sous leurs déguisements fantasques* "

In his tribute to the seventeenth and eighteenth centuries Debussy is nearly as explicit as Ravel in his acknowledgment of heritage from the clavecinistes as to many points of style, and as to the dance suite form—a classical suite in which the "Clair de lune" takes the place of one of the slow dances.

In its harmonies, which bow in passing to ecclesiastical modes, in its refined and elegant melodies, its style and ornamentation, its keyboard aptness, its baroque art of chiaroscuro, its precision of contours and clarity of form—all enhanced by a boldness of colors born of the intervening centuries, this suite is indeed a precious blend of innovation and tradition.

PRÉLUDE

In this prélude there are already many of the characteristics of Debussy's style. In his treatment of the form Debussy retains its original character of an introductory, improvisatory, and brilliant first movement, while endowing it with the completeness of sonata form, a step in the direction of the independent, complete pieces which form the series of préludes still to come.

The rich and somewhat daring harmonies move inconspicuously to support the freely developed arabesques and passages rich in anticipations, and retards lead to stronger, squarer passages scored in four, five, six voices moving simultaneously. A tonal texture, fresh in its melodic, harmonic, and rhythmic elements, bears witness to an already highly individual style.

The first ten bars in "tempo rubato" (first material of the first subject group) possess a rapidly evolving and broad range of expression, improvisatory in style. The brilliant surge of measures 1-2-5-7-8 are opposed by the supple elegance of measures 3-4-6-9-10. The two last measures use chords of the tonic ninth in an exceptionally subtle way to lead to a deceptive subdominant tonality. One feels the expression of a romantic soul, unshackled, but sensitive without preciosity. The choirlike episodes in stricter tempo (second material of the first subject group) at measures 11-14 are again tempered by the ease of measures 15-16, to resume with nobility and a certain formality in the closing measures, 17-19.

Then a new, pellucid texture in the Aeolian mode (second subject, measures 20-29) brings an archaic atmosphere, almost fragile, balanced by the return to four-part writing at the opening of the development section, measure 30. The contrast of the second subject in its modal color to the pure diatonism of the first subject group is genial in effect. These diverse aspects of texture bring great richness of expression to the piece. They already embody the Debussyan ideal of music "as much melody, as rhythm, as harmony—and modality free." Measure 44, a resumption of the choral texture, receives added character through its increased harmonic expanse into graded tensions and releases, and brings, at measure 52, an almost ecstatic stability of translucid filigree over pedal-points.

The recapitulation, concerned only with the first subject group, begins at measure 66 and leads directly into the coda, measure 76, in which Debussy makes a brilliant, albeit classical, use of the arabesque patterns answered by the choral groups.

PERFORMANCE. In the performance it would be a sharp misinterpretation to play the arabesques of the first ten measures in a metric-monotone timing, since it is marked "tempo rubato" by Debussy. A brilliant sturdiness in the first measure, a clear enunciation of the first beat of the second measure, leads to an acceleration through the second measure to stabilized tempo in measures 3 and 4, but with the second halves of these measures benefiting from a slight rush. The first two beats of the fifth measure express enthusiasm, building to the apex of the major-seventh chord on the second beat; an easy-going elegance in the successive texture allows for a rallentando at the end of measure 6 to give full expression to the ultimate appoggiatura and resolution. A similar interpretation holds for the repeats of this theme.

At measure 11, the timing becomes regular with a broadening at the end of measures 12, 14, and through measures 17-19, conveying an atmosphere of archaic grandeur. From measures 11 to 19 the voices must be dynamically equal and performed exactly together.

From measures 20, a sensitive stressing of appoggiaturas and slurring to their resolutions will set alive the delicate texture. For instance, in measure 20, B is to be stressed and slurred to its resolution on A. This treatment will also render intelligible the non-metric, free rhythm of measure 23. With the same functional observance of natural phrasing, measures 26-29 are replete with appoggiaturas which must be intimately linked to their resolving notes.

The section of measures 30-36 must be treated as in part-writing, with regard for the independence of phrasing of each voice and the balance of all the voices in relation to each other.

In measures 44-51 the choral style of writing demands careful observance of held notes, i.e., observe the note values and hold them as

50

indicated, each and all voices legato, but not blurred by abuses of pedal. Stress the expanding tonal texture of the third beats of measures 45, 47, 49, 51.

In measure 52, a skillful catching of the B♭ triad, with the sustaining pedal, will permit the maintenance of the pedal-point, while affording the limpid quality needed in the rest of the texture. The same process can be applied to measures 56-60, where the dynamic build-up begins toward solidity and power. The recapitulation and the coda will find further applications of previous indications.

MENUET

As will happen so often in classical suites, and in Debussy's music, the title is more indicative of the contemplation of the menuet's spirit than expressive of the intent to compose music for dancing purposes.

We are very far from the tradition-confined daintiness and "menu" steps of the court menuet. We are also quite beyond the limitations in scope of the classic-period menuet.

It has been suggested that it is like a reflection in a mirror—a menuet in the distance seen through the windows from a garden. It is rather the expression of varied moods as stylized in the imaginative mind of the musician. The enriched synthesis of many a menuet, and of the feeling that each may have harbored or instigated "extra muros."

While preserving in a subtle way the traditional ternary meter with a second-beat accent, such peculiarities of form are delicately hidden in a fanciful array of rhythmic, scoring, pitch, and harmonic accents, like a charmingly diffused survival of tradition. Here the logic of the music itself leads more than the pre-established idea of rules, as it does also in the form in which a sonata outline substitutes for the menuet-trio-menuet alternation. The rhythmic subtlety is matched by the "tantalizing flirtation between modalities," even though sections are stabilized into tangible tonalities (for instance, measures 1-2 in Dorian); but a permanence of the Dorian would tend to stifle the freedom of this constantly live texture.

Measures 1-18, the first subject and its repeat, are simple and elegant, but measures 18-21 affirm a more marked rhythm, and the transition in measures 21-25 brings a transformation to a warmly lyric, almost romantic, period, the second subject (measures 25-41).

The development section opens at measure 42 with the initial subject for a short and still more refined statement. From measure 50 a sturdy development acts as contrast, built very classically on a rhythmical augmentation of the first subject. At measure 58 a development blending the two main subjects returns to a beautiful lyricism akin to songs for several a capella voices, rising to very sensitive expression.

At measure 73 a period of stretto-imitations, or sequences, over a B♭ pedal, acts as a condensed recapitulation of the first subject, followed in measure 81 by the great lyric phrase of the second subject, which ends in a perfect masculine cadence at measure 96. Here a short coda of eight measures, built on motifs of the first subject, brings us a mischievous alternation of cadences toward a C-major ending versus an Aeolian ending. The latter wins, of course.

PERFORMANCE. A good performance of the menuet demands ability to produce the contrast of phrasing and pianistic style necessary to render perceptible the varied effects of its diverse sections.

The first thematic pattern (measure 1-3) is non-legato (but not spiccato); it must be even, and by this evenness it will afford contrast in the occasional slurred notes (appoggiaturas slurred normally to their releases). The reciprocally counterbalanced rhythms (for instance, at measure 4 and 7-9) need gentle stresses on long durations with a legato style. The fluid light legato is to be found at measures 5-6 as an example, and, while demanding the legato quality, could not bear pressure to insure it. Skill is required for absolute togetherness of the double-thirds, and preservation of the ornamental lightness of the 32nd notes. A light staccato, punctuated by solid accents, is found in measures 18-21. The eighth-note on the first beats of these measures is held for its full duration and should not sound staccato.

For the lyric second subject a sustained legato, extreme legato style, with sustained choral effect, is best. But despite these differences in styles of playing, intended to distinguish the various moods of the composition, the unity of the whole is to be maintained and the tempo to remain steady. The work is replete with delicate values which need exact phrasing and minute attention. As examples, let me point to:

(1) Measure 1: The first beat: The melody is A-B-C-D in sixteenth-notes; these notes are to be stressed slightly more than the harmonic notes D-F-F-A in the same group which function as accompaniment. It would be atrocious to perform the melody of that group as consisting of A-F-C-A.

(2) Measures 5-7: Note that over these measures the phrasing signs indicate clearly that the subject-units are like four-and-a-half measures in 2/4 rather than three measures in 3/4, so do not sin by strong first-beat accents.

(3) Measure 58: The legato sign is from the dotted eighth-note to the sixteenth-note, not conversely. This type of phrasing is typical of Debussy, and absolutely intentional when so marked. The sixteenth-note has an effect of lift, not of a stressed appoggiatura.

Many more examples could be given, but these remarks may help the interpreter in his attitude and desire to read exactly and understand the emotional intent.

CLAIR DE LUNE

The extraordinary popularity obtained by this composition should not induce the musician to underrate its importance. After all, not all that is popular is trivial. Humanity still raves at the beauty of sunsets, or of dawn, and of the moon rising . . . and yet their magnificence endures, unaltered by popular appreciation. Furthermore, this "Clair de lune" is one of the most frequent "dramas" of the musical scene; it is slaughtered in public more often than revealed! Perhaps its utter simplicity of texture, containing true glory of subtleties, is the reason.

Filled with delicate, romantic feeling, it conveys through its precious harmonies the silvery atmosphere of the moonlight. Its elusive before-the-beat and after-the-beat yearnings spirit us away from the matter-of-fact reality of noontide and its vertically blazing light.

The impression of the landscape in the opalescent light takes precedence in Debussy's estimation over the romance on earth. Nothing here can better convey the atmosphere than what Debussy writes about music in a more general way, in saying: "It is inscribed in Nature. It must be in intimate accord with the scenery."

53

It is a piece in half-shades and half-lights, with the peaceful abandon that the scenery establishes. Its anticipations and retards of rhythm create suspense, but, as proven by some famous virtuosi, the inexact timing of such values can easily dispel the mystery. Under such brutal assaults the piece becomes vulgar, distorted, and sometimes very Hollywoodish! The moon is now made of pasteboard, and the light is crude, a klieg focused by a machinist . . . it is a poor substitute!

In the second half of page 16, the agitation may be in the foliage of the landscape, but then it is a lovely breeze and the light is casting countless shadows. Then on page 18, the breeze has subsided, the peace has returned, but the light is now more iridescent than ever.

In the first measure of page 19, the novel introduction of the C♭, resolving on B♭ in the second measure, is like a sigh of regret and premonition of the fading moonlight. The three last bars of the second line of page 19 are like the parting greetings, hesitant and imploring. In the last three lines, the subject vanishes into immaterial abstraction.

Debussy could harbor a love for the beauty of nature quite comparable in intensity to that bestowed by the greatest lovers in history upon the most entrancing women! But such love of nature is humble and religious in quality. Its reward is in its expression of beauty bequeathed to the world.

Possibly the most important requirement for a good performance of this work is to insure that no "bench-in-the-park scene" be part of it. It must be contemplative and trustful. The time of literary connotations, such as one finds in Schumann's "Promenade" (Carnaval, Opus 9), where the presence of two lovers is so precisely indicated by the transference of the melody to the low register (the boy), then to the soprano register (the girl)—that time has long since passed. The moods reflecting nature in the music of Debussy are of a mystic essence—the worship of beauty, the feeling of hands joining together submissively in the attitude of prayer.

The peace of the transparent and soft light must not be disturbed by brusqueness in rhythm. The harmonic progressions must evolve in a constant murmur in the background through a perfectly smooth legato in voice leading. Yet one must avoid opacity, which is contrary to moonlight, and creeps easily into this piece if the pedal is used without due regard for harmonic changes. One frequently reads, or hears people saying: "The music of Debussy must always maintain a background of vagueness." How misleading! Debussy never wanted to hear that which he had *not* written, but he did want the complete tone-fabric of what he had created. His fabric is full, rich, complete here. Do not punch holes in it, but do not make blots on it either. Do not confuse the harmonic colors, but instead pass gently from one to the next with the subtlety indicated by the texture. Do not tear the fabric into separate fragments, but do not mar it by wrinkles or deface it with strange admixtures of unwanted colors either. It is silvery silk; therefore, let us not wear its surface to the thread! Let us have the shimmering light reflected by it.

As to sensitiveness of relation of melody and harmony, I shall give only one example. If the performer does not find a way to sustain the vibration of the double-third, Db-F (measure 1, seventh beat), so that this resonance may encounter the new harmony, Gb-A natural (measure 2, first beat), then the subtle tension has not taken place, its subsequent resolution is meaningless, and finally from moment to moment the precious texture is vandalized, becomes trite, vulgar, and utterly spoiled. This same example can be found fourteen times on the first page alone.

PASSEPIED

The "Passepied," of the four pieces of the suite, is that which is closest to the style of the French clavecinistes. Its tempo, however, is quite distinctly slower than that of the passepied of the seventeenth century, and its time signature is a departure from its ternary character. Originating in French Brittany, the passepied maintains the precise rhythmic characteristics of all dances of Bretagne. It was extremely popular in Paris in the seventeenth century, running a close second to the menuet, with the added charm of the syncopations not permitted in the latter. Accordingly, it is natural that its character be permeated also with that of court elegance and a Parisian lightness of texture which tempers the countryside sturdiness.

One of the most marked features is the constant activity of the non-legato accompaniment, which is uninterrupted throughout the piece. It is like a light and most perfect canvas upon which varied embroideries express varied moods. Upon the regularity of the delicate canvas, rhythmical dance episodes alternate with more lyric passages. The dance is tempered by these romances.

The Aeolian mode is quite fully the principal modality, but at moments some reverberations of Phrygian are also felt. Measures 3-7, the quaint melody (the principal theme of this rondo-sonata form), is almost like a cantus firmus. In measures 7-8 a third voice gently adds its timid color to the texture. The cantus-firmus style is resumed at measures 10-14, but the duet is subtly reintroduced (measures 14-18), and will continue with increased lyricism and gentle syncopations, until it reaches its emotional goal (measures 24-28), in which the duet melody has evolved into a fully harmonized melody enriched by the "measured rubato" and its touch of romanticism. Note the triplets of quarter-notes set on groups of four notes in the accompaniment. The initial texture is resumed (measure 30) and is gradually and organically transformed from measure 39 to become harmonically rich in its complexity and emotionally intense, the sensitive degrees in voice leading creating inner stresses within the texture. This section evolves to measure 59, when a return to quite unsentimental dance accents, rhythmically strong, expresses straightforward "joy of life." It is also one of the returns to the Aeolian mode. The dance and healthy mood proceed to measure 74, where an enharmonic change brings a secondary melody of lyric character. The sturdy episode of measure 59 is now repeated fragmentarily, as if already a distant vision. By measure 95, it is absorbed by a bridge which wavers intently between distant tonalities, creating a charming suspense. The unrest is appeased as it resolves at measure 86 in the recapitulation of the first theme. A troubled lyricism, conveyed again by "measured rubato" (3 against 4) and tonal suspenses, returns at measure 105 and leads to an ultimate return of the opening theme in a faint, ethereal scoring.

After a typically Debussyan cadenza (measure 123-127), the composition concludes with a coda of ten measures in medieval Dorian. This piece is remarkable for its constant life-stream, uninterrupted feeling of motion, obtained with such simple and gentle materials. It forever embodies some of the finest qualities of Debussy—the freshness of youth, its humble admiration but clairvoyant perception of true elegance. Never loud, it yet possesses the strength of that which flows freely.

PERFORMANCE. Perhaps the greatest difficulty in performance of this piece is the maintenance of the "constant factor," i.e., the accompaniment in eighth-notes in its double function of neutral canvas and unobtrusive constant motion, while the various melodies express varied moods, and at times are gradually troubled (rubato); the lyricism, the rubato, the sturdiness, as well as the simpler accents of the dance as expressed by the first theme, must never affect the canvas upon which they are embroidered.

One marvels at the ultra-acute sensitiveness of Debussy to the most minute tensions in texture, that makes the study of this piece fascinating for the true musician. Such phrasing indications as those at measures 7-8 are of the utmost importance. Slurred notes (measures 15, 16, 17, 19, 21, etc.) should induce the performer to a full sense of the stress of appoggiaturas and the softness of their resolutions (the absolute rule of Bach as transmitted to us by C. P. E. Bach). Dashes as found at measure 24 do not mean accents, but distinct pronunciation, just as if each note told a different syllable, a necessity to the full expression of the rubato.

Such accents as are found in measure 36, the third beat, are needed lest the C♯ fail in directing the logic of the modulation. The legato signs (for example, measure 38) express the fear of the composer that the texture may be chopped by groups of two notes. Occasionally Debussy, not unlike Bach, omits slurs over appoggiaturas and their resolutions. Perhaps he, like Bach, assumed that the performers would possess sufficient musical knowledge not to betray such fundamental tonal functions. (Measures 51-59!)

The dashes and dots in the section, starting at measure 59, indicate very concretely the dynamic conception at two levels.

Notice the delicate section found in measures 86-90: the uninterrupted flow of motion must continue, the lower voice (measures 86-89) must sing legato, the first theme must preserve its phrasing, and the right-hand part (measures 86-90) must lead smoothly to the left-hand part at measure 90.

The held notes in the left-hand part (measures 114-118) are necessary to the fullness of the cadence. One must perceive the chord of the seventh moving successively from the seventh degree to the second degree, Aeolian determination.

One arpeggio and not two must sound through measures 123-124, and again at measures 125-126. Through the coda, a delicate stress on the first beats of measures 128, 130, and 132 will enhance the "medieval Dorian" conclusion.

RÊVERIE (1890)

It is strange to consider what trick of modern fate has made hundreds of thousands of people know Debussy through this single work. "Rêverie" was published by Fromont many years after Debussy had given it to that firm for publication, and without informing the composer. Debussy wrote: "I regret very much your decision to publish Rêverie. . . . I wrote it in a hurry years ago, purely for material considerations. It is a work of no consequence and I frankly consider it absolutely no good." *

If he felt thus about "Rêverie," a charming and melodically delightful piece, what indeed must have been his sentiments about the continuous printings of "Ballade," "Mazurka," "Nocturne," and "Valse romantique"!

The very beautiful principal melody of this piece should have sufficed to silence the numerous critics who denied that Debussy wrote, or could write, a melody! To the contrary, it is above all a most excellent melody. Its shape is at times well-centered within a small range, and again at other moments it conveys all the relaxation and yearning of a true song of love in the expansiveness of its tonal range.

It is truly a dream-song, and ideal in the sense of immaterial; the impression is preciously guarded by the long periods of modal suspense, by the fluidity and breadth of the melodic line, by the supersensitive ability to avoid any gross evidence of hackneyed patterns in the accompaniment.

As an example of the modal suspense and delicately fashioned har-

* Dumesnil, pp. 229-230.

mony, one would cite the opening in which the sensitive fourth degree peacefully holds us in suspense for six measures, creating a strong feeling of distance, that historical distance at which the medieval Dorian is from us. In the next two measures one resolves to a diatonic F major, but Debussy does not allow us to settle comfortably; through measures 9-10 he sways us from the sensitive sixth degree to the dominant, and in measure 11 further sways us by the chord of the ninth and that of the sixth degree. It is simple, but so is a perfect jewel. Many other examples could be pointed out. As to the breadth and fluidity of the melodic line, its tenderness, trust, and abandon, which we mentioned above—it has the simplicity and naturalness of a free fluidity, enhanced by the subtle avoidance of a note-against-note accompaniment. It is classical counterpoint. The very complete tonal ranges (see measures 11-18) nevertheless escape melodramatic expressions.

The accompaniments of simple melodies can be terribly trite or pompous, particularly in placing tangible roots on all first beats. Chordal, or harmonic, rhythm can be wearisome when too regular. Over-definite harmonies can be commonplace; but here we have none of these defects. There is already a wonderful sense of texture. Consider, for example, measures 11 and 12; the ninth chord is poised for a measure and a half, followed by a minor triad of the second degree; upon this the melody is completely pure, no passing tones, no appoggiaturas—this is wise spacing of the effect of tension. Note also the suspense of the central section on dominant pedal-points.

A few points of interpretation need to be mentioned. In the nine first measures, one should set into value, though delicately, the left-hand pattern as it builds to the third beat, then abstract it through the fourth and first beats. During the six first measures the B♭ in the bass must vibrate over the tie to ascertain its first-beat harmonic relation to the melody in the right hand. Note the setting into value of the harmonic tension of the first half of measure 5, and the appoggiatura in measure 7. In measures 9-10 set into value the motion of inner voices from the sixth degree to the fifth degree and integrate this progression as leading to the root at measure 11.

The best use of the pedal in measures 11-12 is based on harmony; pedal for six beats and then for the next two beats. This harmonic rhythm is repeated in measures 13-14 and 15-16, but in measures 17-18 the harmonic motions, and therefore pedal treatment, are on the first and third beats. In measures 19-22 the harmony is static and unified; avoid unnecessary total pedal changes. Notice that in early publications there is a misprint in measure 19; the last note should be E♮ instead of D♮. The mood remains one of dreamy quietude, but at measure 23 a first ascending appoggiatura (first beat) builds emotionalism, via further tension at measure 25, to the ultimate harmonic and emotional apex at measures 27 and 29. These are hyper-romantic surges of feeling, lost in the section of measures 30-34.

A second melody introduced in the tenor (measure 35) is like an answer to the first melody. Stated first in a four-measure period, it is then restated and developed to reach again a harmonic emotional tension (measures 39-43) and a release to measure 49.

The note A in measure 50 is an anacrusis to the following motive. The break in style in this section is very complete. From a melody accompanied by harmonies in arpeggio form we now have four-part writing, choral-like. The equality of balance between the four voices is necessary, no voice being stronger than the other. Note that some printings have an error in measure 54; the first beat should be a B natural.

From the end of the motif of measure 58, Debussy builds his central section, still choir-like, but on dominant pedal-points which do not resolve as conventionally prescribed. In measures 60-61 the three upper voices give support culminating in the soprano, but from the last beat of measure 61 through measure 62 the tenor part is the emotionally expressive, dissonance-creating factor to be gently brought out. The texture must be translucid in measures 70-71, and great care must be taken to maintain the continuity of the melody when it passes from the left hand to the right, between measures 71 and 72. Do not chop it in two!

From measure 77 the varied recapitulation of the first melody must not lose its proper stresses and continuity, despite the skips necessitated in performance.

When the choral texture is resumed (measures 93-94), note that the harmony is really a dominant-seventh chord on the fifth degree of D minor and that here the chord that might appear as a chord of the fourth degree, finds its full meaning not as such but as an appoggiatura on the dominant-seventh (B♭ and D resolving on the second beat to A and C♯ respectively). This is further emphasized on the fourth beat of measure 95 when the appoggiatura B♭ is embellished.

The phrasing of these early works by Debussy does not compare in accuracy with those of his later years, but the texture is elegant, and dictates the proper treatment. In such a case as that of measures 93-94, the chord of the fourth degree *is* a dissonance upon the chord of the dominant-seventh.

DANSE (TARENTELLE STYRIENNE) (1890)

Highly creative and individual from the standpoints of melody, voice-leading, harmony, and rhythm, the "Danse" is already definitely stamped by Debussy's personality. Perhaps not as pungent as to orchestral instrumentation as later works, it was nevertheless suggestive to Maurice Ravel, who transcribed it in 1925.

As is frequent with Debussy, the stimuli are diversified, but each, shedding its autonomy, blends in the formation of a new and integrated driving force which is no longer literary but tonal.

It is thought that the tarantella originated on the shores of the Ionian Sea at Taranto, and that its animated dance rhythms had an early medicinal value; citizens bitten by the tarantula spider fell victims to a powerful drowsiness which had to be fought against by energetic—not to say, frenetic—action. This even led to the use of the phrase "bitten by the tarantula" as an idiomatic expression designating overly agitated or excited people. There is indeed no doubt of the rich rhythmic contrasts and vitality of the dance. While the tarantella became the national dance of the Neapolitans, this particular one, under its initial name of "Styrian Tarantella," is transposed to the land of Austria, but strongly affected by the Serbs and Croats. Hence exotic modal tendencies, not within the imprint of ancient modes.

It is of no great importance in itself to situate the piece geographically, but it is vital to notice how deftly and continuously Debussy abducts us from scholastic cadences, formulae, harmonies, and rhythms. He already clearly indicates that he intends to be free to create according to his impulses, but he also proves that his impulses already have an amazing sense of balance in the coloring of all musical elements.

A brilliant composition, enriched by beautiful melodies, contrasted by the translucid, filigree-like middle section, it is hardly a texture in which confusion, romantic rubato, or impressionistic vapors would be at ease. A detailed account of the interpretation becomes superfluous if the performer has understood its basic elements of tension and release. These can be summarized briefly:

RHYTHM. The meters of 3/4 and 6/8 are almost constantly contrasted or alternated in the opening section (measures 1-29), and again in measures 44-51, and similar passages in the recapitulation. When these meters are in contra-distinction, the second beat of the 3/4 is contradicted by the four eighth-notes of the 6/8, and the two rhythms should be kept individually perfect. Further, in the episode starting at measure 62, the syncopated chords bring a new rhythmic complexity in groups of four measures. The central section of the piece has the restful stability of a slow harmonic pulsation (with changes every four measures), upon which the melody moves with graceful freedom and tender elegance.

MELODY. The melodic elements of both the opening and central sections contain apexes of phrases which are not in agreement with the dreary conventional metric accentuation, but "batteries" in 6/8 produce here an effect quite parallel to that of the even pulsation of the foot of the jazz players—setting into value the syncopated stresses. In this respect rhythm and melody are remarkably cooperative.

HARMONY. One can consider a few measures at random. Note the tension in measure 1 of the encounter of the F♯ in the left hand, with the second chord in the right hand. In measure 13, the relation of the double third B natural, G natural in the right hand, to the next E♭ in the left hand, creates harmonic intensity. A similar coloring is obtained in measure 44 when the bass changes from consonance to dissonance on the fourth eighth-note of the measure. Considering these typical instances, one finds that the harmonic tension often coincides with the rise of the melody and the purely rhythmical conflicts, creating an overall texture rich in excitement, life-motion, unbound by conservative formulae.

The performance would be impaired seriously by an application to this work of the erroneous notion that the music of Debussy is always delicate or impressionistic! In the opening section he is buoyant, full of life. In the middle section the harmonies are full of tension and releases; the sensitive melodic progressions must retain their clarity of expressions, without opacity of neglectful pedals, or of unclear conceptions of the harmonic changes and voice-leading.

One must not fear brilliancy in the dance proper, and translucence in the quiet central portion.

VALSE ROMANTIQUE (1890)

There is no accurate way of discovering the exact date of the composition of this piece, but its texture indicates a very early time, perhaps even earlier than any of the other pieces herein considered. It is somewhat experimental as to harmonic color, but not very felicitous as to inventiveness, particularly in the slim and repetitious melodic material, the many passages in rather neutral chord outlining.

The influence of Chopin is to a certain extent present, but missing is the lyricism even of some of the other early works. But, after all, early sketches are not what one judges the future creative giant by; a cursory glance is sufficient, enabling us the better to realize the magnitude of the future by the puniness of the past. We would feel, then, that the "Valse" has no claim to representing Debussy except for purposes of study.

BALLADE (1890)

Despite the publication date of 1890, everything in this piece, as in the "Nocturne," indicates that it was probably written much before the "Rêverie," the "Petite suite," and "Arabesques." In fact, it may have come soon after the "Mazurka." In verifying the date of his first trip to Russia, which could furnish the obvious stimulus to a Slavic ballade and to many of its earmarks, one finds that the summer of 1881, or that following season, is a more probable date.

The "Ballade" contains the embryo of the theme Debussy was later to use in "La plus que lente." Chromatic progressions which he was to shun later as such, and to make very specious use of, are here quite obvious. The evidence of concern to purify harmonic texture and melodic flow toward cohesion which one finds in "Rêverie" is not evident in the "Ballade." Just as the "Nocturne," the "Ballade" unveils early experimentation but also unconscious subservience to certain aspects of Russian melodies and to Fauréan formulae of modulations and pianistic instrumentation.

Melodically the "Ballade" is unduly repetitious, a procedure which Debussy was later to reject and almost despise. He soon considered that a melody should continue to expand, flow, but without repeating itself "with ill-mannered insistence," just as if the listener were deaf or too "thick" to perceive anything before having been told repeatedly. Several writers have remarked that "some of the arpeggio figures here are to be found later in the toccata of 'Pour le piano.' " I fail to understand this statement; while some of the arpeggi of "Rêverie" and even perhaps of the "Arabesques" are truly forerunners of those in the "Toccata," neither the harmonic stresses nor the voice leading in the "Ballade" seem to have any kinship to later works. His treatment here of the antique minor is remote from the subtle modal technique soon developed.

Since this work is obviously not one of which Debussy was especially proud, I shall give more attention to other works. It is good to have the "Ballade" in one's musical library for enjoyment and for study purposes, but it is hardly fair to represent Debussy on any concert program with this early sketch.

MAZURKA (1890)

While this work again shows the embryo of some of the harmonic predilections of Debussy, it is decidedly immature and justifies his later attitude, when he wished these early works had not been printed. He considered them worthless; they are not truly so, except by comparison with later works. But then one does not try to find maturity in so early a work. It is good to remember here the "Capriccio" written by J. S. Bach when he was twenty-one years old, for the departure of his beloved brother. That was very immature, too, which is only natural.

This "Mazurka," published in 1891, was probably written around 1880. It shows Debussy as yet under the first spell of his study of piano with Madame Mauté de Fleurville, a pupil of Chopin. Debussy was deeply impressed by her evident insight into the style of the famous Pole, and acquired himself great and enduring love for his music, hence this early attempt to follow the path and compose a mazurka. Later, Debussy's respect for Chopin, and his own highly personal aesthetics, transmuted such influence.

The modal texture tends to experiment a little, but very timidly. Anyone who understands the greatness of the mature accomplishments of Debussy generally refrains from playing these early works, but a study of the piano works of the Master would not be complete without mention of how "the infant began to walk." The answer is "very normally, i.e., awkwardly, as with all infants"!

NOCTURNE (1890)

We are here examining a chrysalis—or the immature seed. Yet the seed already contains some of the elements which in later years will germinate, take form, and produce amazingly beautiful flowers.

One does not approach such a work as this—a youthful attempt to embody into sound the aspirations and feelings of a young soul—one does not contemplate such a work to find in it the ultimate attainment but rather to become aware of the first signs of a life which is to be rich in music.

"Nocturne" shows us Debussy in 1890, or earlier, just beginning his search—his search for beauty. Already the desire to escape materialism induces his refusal of conventionality: a persistent use of deceptive cadences, a refusal to establish the "expected" tonality, the displacement of tonal centers away from the predictable, are among the many traits seeking freedom, but they also show his hesitancy toward a definite goal.

After a short introduction which possesses the necessary notes to lead into at least half a dozen different tonalities, Debussy carries on in a neo-Fauréan vein. Eventually, after a graceful bridge of eight measures, passing successively through the tonalities of E♭ minor, D♭ major,

G♭ major, A major on a dominant pedal, D major also on a dominant pedal, Debussy creates a texture which altogether conveys stability and a sense of archaism—a process of which he was to be the unique master later on. In this entire middle section, there are three distinctive features: the long pedal-point in chord progression which wavers between F major and D minor, a melody quite freely evolved in ancient minor or Aeolian mode, and a 7/4 meter.

The form is conventional with the return of the first part as the third unit.

A few notes on the performance: After the "ad lib" introduction, the "a tempo" marks the start of the Fauréan passage, in which, while the spirit is romantic, the frequent modulations need to be clearly understood and not blurred by the pedal. In the central section, it is quite necessary to produce the tonal effect of two places in the texture: the limpidity of the Aeolian theme (marked "dans le caractère d'une chanson populaire"—"in the spirit of a popular tune") is necessary; it is not to be overpedaled. The use of the sustaining pedal to maintain the independence of the bass chords from the melody is highly desirable. The intent of instrumentation is quite evident; an investigation of some of his orchestral works will show many such examples of the simultaneous presence of two or more tonal planes, akin to the idea of two independent choirs, and not to the notion of an accompanied melody. The contrapuntal freedom is then to be preserved.

Even if this composition is technically immature and its individuality is in "search of its own means of expression," it is already quite French and requires unobtrusive tonal clarity.

SUITE POUR LE PIANO (1901)

Composed in 1901 and premiered by Ricardo Viñes at the Société Nationale.

Over ten years had elapsed, with no writing for the piano, when under the modest title of "Pour le piano" ("For the piano"), a suite appeared which is a major landmark in the history of piano literature, and perhaps one of the most significant masterworks in this form written from the middle of the nineteenth century to our day.

The suite crowns the piano's liberation from limitations of texture which had crystallized over three-quarters of a century, stifling all possible survival. Its music is freed from empty mechanistry, stuffy display, but does not fall into license. It seeks the hard discipline of Bach and of the early French and Italian keyboardists, and at this limpid source recaptures gaiety, fluency, and charm, an untrammeled rhythmic life and novel harmonic energies. Yet, despite its backward look to the harpsichord and organ ancestry, this suite today is an outstanding contribution to the expression of the total resources of the modern concert piano. Its achievement is gliding unassumingly but with mastery over the piano literature of three centuries, integrating their musical resources into a new fabric which reflects this vast space of time without the slightest affectation or embarrassment. Meticulously balanced, the new wealth of melody is matched as lavishly by the proportionate development of the harmony and rhythm. It is a full-fledged work, vital, possessing its best attributes unified by the unostentatious but telling style, now in full bloom, of the great French master.

Prélude

In this prelude one cannot escape noting the heritage from the German organ school and more specifically from J. S. Bach. All the bravura brilliancy of the organ toccata, the repartition of the pedal passages and pedal-points, the moods are basic eighteenth-century organ art; the first theme and final cadenza remind us of the D-minor "Toccata" (and "Fugue"), and the lyrically passionate and stormy second theme is a cousin of the "Fantasia in G minor." Not only in the spirit, the thematic materials, the pedal technique are we reminded of Bach, but in the broad scope of the work, in the patterns, in the freedom of harmonic succession over the static pedals, we recognize an extension of the German master's contrapuntal virtuosity—bringing us harmonic aggregates of elevenths, thirteenths, an agitated harmonic texture suddenly encountering the staticism of whole-toned passages. It is baroque art in its co-existence of mutually antagonistic elements, in its terraced oppositions of extremes in dynamics and coloring. Yet its constant motion is close in conception to the "divine arabesque of Bach," a divine arabesque set into value by periodic upheavals in harmonic motion.

A rapid survey of the form shows us a more complex structure than that which usually exists in preludes, or toccatas, in its richness of contrast and development of the two main themes. Yet, neither does the form fit the loosely woven fabric of the fantasia—the design here is more sober:

Bars 1-6. First subject.

Bars 6-23. Second subject and its development.

Bars 24-26. Transition.

Bars 27-38. Repetition of the twelve first measures of the second subject.

Bars 39-42. Transition, similar to measures 24-26.

Bars 43-57. Development of the first subject, in heavy scoring, modulations.

Bars 57-59. Transition.

Bars 59-71. Development of the first subject, under a measured trill, leading to a shortened deformation and transition built on this.

Bars 71-96. Development of the second subject, very soft, over the same trill and an A♭ pedal, with frequent jocular interruptions of motifs of the first theme in triplet rhythm.

Bars 97-118. Recapitulation of measures 6-26, second theme, and transition.

Bars 119-127. Recapitulation of measures 43-51, first theme in heavy scoring.

Bars 127-141. Two short developments on the first theme, opening the coda.

Bars 142-147. Transition built on a huge contrary-motion scale passage; in thirds, in the right hand, and octaves in the left.

Bars 148-163. A fermata chord, which, in the traditional manner, ushers in a virtuoso cadenza, to which six measures of cadential chords are added in strict tempo to conclude the movement.

The modality of this piece at times borders on polyphonic Aeolian. The underlying tonality in harmonic turmoil upon a pedal-point is that of A minor until measure 43. Succeeding materials include a C-major episode, measures 43-51, a rich transmutation to a first warning of the whole-toned texture, measures 57-59, and a chromatic passage, measures 61-71, where stability on a pedal-point of A♭ initiates a "musical clock" passage in whole-tone, which lasts twenty-six measures. At measure 97, the recapitulation brings back the A-minor assumption, interrupted at measure 134, for a short period of whole-toned texture. The segment beginning at measure 142 resolves the tonality to Aeolian and ushers in a very original cadenza, in which constant comparison between scales in whole-tones and scales in the ancient minor produces a kaleidoscopic effect. The concluding, broad chords restate the principal harmonies which created the texture of the early sections of the piece, highly modulatory but concluding in Aeolian.

The contrast of whole-tone and Aeolian has a telling effect upon the musical materials. The simple patterns, which conveyed at first (Aeolian) the impression of an organ toccata, are transformed in the whole-toned passages. They acquire an entirely new meaning, having lost their soul as they lost their significance in voice leading of sensitive degrees. They temporarily sound like the tinkling of a musical toy, but later regain their expressive life. Remark the gradual construction to an apex of harmonic wealth (measures 6-17) and how integrated are the factors of harmony, pitch, instrumentation, scoring, all closely unified in purpose.

A strong sense of continuity and long-range breadth in this piece can be in large part ascribed to the well-concealed but strong interweaving of the voice leading in the horizontal plane; passages, such as that of measures 14-23, are essentially four-part writing on a pedal-point.

In the performance of the prélude the sharp contrasts in its texture reflect sharp contrasts in interpretative objectives. It is sturdy (measures 1-5; 43-57), it is strong in close-knit texture (measures 6-43), it is riotous (measures 51-57), surprising in contrasts of immobility and motion (measures 57-59), mysterious and agitated (measures 59-71). It is again immobile, and we listen to toy music (measures 71-97), but the sturdy and strongly knit section returns (to measure 134), a delicate suspense (measures 134-147), a return to exuberant, riotous glory which is majestically crowned by the end (159-164).

A few remarks concerning the most frequent weaknesses in perform-ance may help young pianists to liberate themselves from misunder-standings.

(1) The clarity and completeness required in classical music are equally desired in this neo-classical prélude. Confusion of the patterns, running together of the harmonies, are both evils to be avoided. The texture has all the harmonic richness it can afford without careless mergings of its progressions.

(2) The first theme and its returns (measures 1-6, 43-57, 119-134) must be powerful, steady in time, non-legato, martellato. Its variations of scoring (haloed by arabesques, or reinforced by overlaid chords) do not change its basic character of masculine virility and sharp har-monic color; it is a compact motif, resonant in its emphasis of fifths and use of augmented triads.

(3) The passages that strongly point to this prélude as a sturdy grandchild of the great organ toccatas of J. S. Bach (measures 6-43, 97-119) must realize the organ's capacity for completeness and yet clarity of levels. The singing voice in quarter-notes must be legato without blurring the pedal which changes after each quarter-note. The pedal-point A must keep on singing at the utmost depth of the texture; by taking this A with the sustaining pedal at measure 6, and "feeding" it through the repartitions which start measure 9, the effect of the pedal-point can easily be obtained. The arabesques in sixteenth-notes must be heard in their completeness, akin to violin patterns. Their harmonic and melodic tensions fluctuate so that some patterns are stressed and others resolve the stress. A keen awareness of the harmonic life and voice-leading of these patterns is necessary to make their progressions intelligible.

(4) The whole-toned sections (beginning measures 71) must receive absolute, clock-like precision of interpretation and, until measure 97, must remain free of romanticism, affectations in dynamics and tempo.

(5) The cadenza of measure 149 is beyond the traditional arpeggio and assumes a deliberate character of free improvisation, yet remains well defined in all its details. The last six measures of the prélude are bold and courageous; their eloquence depends on the dramatic clarity of their declamation.

Originating from the Spanish "Zarabando" (or "Zarabanda"), and also from the Persian Serbend dance, the sarabande was at its maximum vogue in the seventeenth and eighteenth centuries, as a court dance and a steady member of the dance suites. It is a dance of grave character, not as imposing as the pavane, but slower than the menuet, though also in ternary time. It could be likened to an austere menuet. The theory is also advanced that the sarabande originated with the Saracens to whom the chaconne is also attributed. Both dances came to Europe, it is fairly sure, from Spain, and to Spain very probably from the Arabic invasion. The sarabande was originally danced to the accompaniment of castanets.

This particular "Sarabande," though it is dated with the rest of the suite (as of 1901), seems to originate, according to most information, from earlier versions, dating back five to six years before the "suite." Published in a Parisian magazine, the early version is described as a slow movement, serious, elegant, in sarabande tempo, rather like an old picture, or a memory of the Louvre gallery.

This might indicate that the original stimulus for the present "Sarabande" may have been the contemplation of some Spanish portrait, in which the fatuous appearance of the court of Philip II would suggest the stately majesty of the Spanish court dance. That such a portrait could create a rich "chain reaction" in Debussy's mind is a normal assumption, in view of his methods of creation and in view of the elaborate and varied ceremonial dance, true to the Zarabanda, which the present score exposes.

The broad, fatuous conception is conveyed by the successive changes from choral six-part writing to unaccompanied solo, to accompanied solo, to widely spread chords (a baroque trait, but also a typically Spanish conception). The vision conveyed is of large choirs answering each other from opposite locations; it has widened the stage into palatial dimensions. At times imposing in its simplicity and antique character, it is, at other times, rich in scoring and harmonic texture—countless colorful brocades being moved slowly from one incidence of reflected light to another—a noble bouquet of parallel, then contrary, melodies.

71

As middle movement and contrast to the "Prélude" and "Toccata" of this suite, it expresses a solemn stability in the midst of the aerial lateral structures of the other two movements.

Some musicologists in considering this "Sarabande" deny paternity rights to that incorrigible bachelor, Eric Satie. Satie's "Sarabande No. 1," which contains an amazingly varied array of novel chord successions, was composed in 1887, and it is presumed that he and Debussy met in 1888 or 1891.* It is not a question of estimating the degree of inventiveness of either composer, for we are well aware that such is not the true means of evaluating the beauty of music. Yet I feel Debussy would never have condoned a viewpoint necessitating a belittling of Satie's gifts for the sake of enlarging his own; history has shown Debussy's gifts to the future to be sufficiently awe-inspiring.

From the standpoint of the tonal color of this piece, it seems an over-simplification to acknowledge C$\sharp$ natural minor (transposed Aeolian mode) as the tonality of this piece, although it is this color which gives the ultimate cadences and reposes of the end of both the first section and the last section. Its extensive exploration of other transposed modes should be taken into consideration much as the passing modulations of a diatonic composition, which give it piquancy and richness, and lends to the return to the home key the desired freshness of a familiar scene seen after a long absence. In passing, one may mention a few of the tonal colors as an illustration:

Bars 1-8. Phrygian with G$\sharp$ as tonic, modulating in the second phrase to Mixolydian with B as tonic.

Bars 9-14. Modulation from Mixolydian to Phrygian with D$\sharp$ as tonic. Note, measures 11-12, the four lower voices in whole-tones.

Bars 15-22. Phrygian with G$\sharp$ as tonic, modulating to Aeolian, with C$\sharp$ as tonic for full cadence.

Bars 23-26. An insistence upon the notes F$\sharp$-A-B-C$\sharp$-E, and the open

* While Satie was verily extremely eccentric in his opinions, it is nevertheless quite evident that his early musical essays (1886–1895) were not imbued with a desire for mystification but were a true expression of revolt against academic rules that had become obsolete. During that early period he was the only daring musician friend Debussy knew. His influence may indeed have been much greater than that of the reactionary-minded colleagues of the Villa Medici. The fact that Debussy later orchestrated Satie's "Gymnopédies" (a rare tribute in Debussy's life) and his enduring friendship for Satie would tend to confirm this assumption.

fourths lend a near-pentatonic sound to this passage, yet the overall aspect is of C♯ (Aeolian). A detailed contrapuntal analysis brings out a bi-modality built on the two axes B-F♯, and C♯-G♯.

Bars 27-32. Transpositions of the above section (sequences) bring a cadence in Mixolydian on E.

Bars 33-41. Aeolian (F♯ tonic) leads in measure 35 to a passage in Dorian (still F♯ tonic).

Bars 42-46. Phrygian (G♯ tonic) with the accepted lowered fifth, leads as in the opening to Mixolydian with B as tonic.

Bars 50-72. Phrygian with D♯ as tonic leads to the tonal center of G♯ again, and to the cadence on C♯ (Aeolian).

PERFORMANCE. A good performance of this piece is one sensitive to:

(1) The nobility of behavior of the sarabande—"its grave and slow elegance."

(2) Its harmonic texture, i.e., its tensions and releases.

(3) Its melodic, beautiful straightforwardness—expressive.

(4) Its significant scoring, or orchestral pianism.

(5) Its textural form, which underscores its formal aspect.

About requirement 1: Observance of exact value—peace in the steady timing, total absence of rubato, but constant presence of sensitiveness in phrasing and appropriate tone legato.

About requirement 2: First and above all, the ability to preserve what is a tension in the midst of a brocade (texture), so rich that one may confuse the usual with the unusual. To preserve this point the performer must become fully convinced that successive chords of the seventh may move in such a way as to create the effect of chords moving into their successive inversions (positions), and therefore create a smoothly consonant feeling of stability. This is true for example in the relations of chords 1, 2, 4, and 5 in the first measure, but it is not true in the relation of chord 3 to chord 2 or 4, as chord 3 functions as an appoggiatura with all the proper implications of stress on appoggiatura, slur to the resolution which is to be softer than the appoggiatura, and with a coincident pitch apex to emphasize this accent. However, as a converse use of the chord of the seventh, when it occurs in measure 6, on the third beat after two triads, it represents a comparative increase in tension (which also coincides with melody rise and broadening of tonal range) and therefore the third beat of that bar with two consecutive sevenths is the most intense moment of that bar. A similar effect is at bar 9 with a different type of scoring, but the chord of the seventh here supports and gives the impulse upward to the melody (soprano). The superimposition of the fourths, G♯ to C♯ and F♯ to B, in the middle section (measure 23) brings a more dissonant aggregate and resonant swing (muted trumpets). The above indications about significance of harmonic texture are given as a key example of the method of perception to be used.

About requirement 3: All its melodies must be expressive through a careful observance of their rises and falls. Also it is necessary to acknowledge what is melody, and, conversely, what is harmonization of melodies. For example: Measures 1-2-3-4 are six melodic-part writing, equal in importance. Bar 5 starts unison melody which through bars 5-7-8, collects additional voices. Bars 9-10-11-12 are a solo embellished melody, supported by harmonies with a semi-neutral expressive quality. Bars 13-14 are four-part writing, all melodic, going to bar 23. Notice that dots are placed upon chords indicating their not quite legato character, but these dots *do not* affect the middle voice which sings the important melody fully legato. Then notice that, at bar 28, more voices are to be melodically sustained, until all voices are sustained at bars 33-34.

This much should be sufficient to lead the eager student to penetrate deeper into the soul of the music by respectfully acknowledging its symbols (writing).

About requirement 4: The significance of scoring is in acknowledging:

Its degree of mass (great number of voices equals great body of sound, even if subdued).

Its range (great or smaller).

Its texture (low—deep; high—transparent).

The position of chords (closed or open)—for comparison, the chords of the seventh in bar 1 are smooth as the relation of degrees 1-7 is open, but the chords of the seventh in bars 38-39-40-41 are intense, sharply dissonant as the relationship of the degrees 1-7 has been brought to a close position.

About requirement 5: Observing the piece in a broad appraisal of its form, we have three sections: section one from bar 1 to 22; section two from bar 23 to 41; section three from bar 42 to 59; coda, bar 60 to end. This form is set into remarkable evidence by the disposition of chords, which in sections one and three are disposed generally for lyric smoothness, whereas in section two many similar chords are disposed so as to produce a growing dissonant effect.

Toccata

This piece is again a remarkable example of neo-classicism and of its effect upon the rich harmony of an ultra-sensitive perceptivist. It gives a new life to the simplicity of patterns of the early clavecinistes; without loading its elegance it exalts its sensitiveness. It has all the youthful, carefree impetus of the arabesques of Scarlatti or Couperin, but it has the strength of a rich harmonic canvas which is completely personal to Debussy. Imbued with the daring rhythmical freedom of the contemporary age, the "Toccata" successfully blends its long central section in lilting syncopation with the balance and clarity of design of the classic—a modern offspring of the brilliant showpieces which toccatas have been through the ages.

An intense spirit of life emanates from the activity of all the musical elements. From the reports of the theories of the groups of poets, writers, painters, who composed the inner circles in which Debussy shared so much during his years immediately after the Prix de Rome, it is evident that the idea of realizing a form of art integrating the feelings of poetry, color, architecture, and sound haunted these artists. As a parallel to this trend of thought it is not surprising that Debussy should have sought the ideal musical texture in an intimate and balanced integration of melody, harmony, rhythm, contrapuntal concepts (but not schoolbook counterpoint!), and instrumental coloring, while preserving an architectural sense of form. The realization of this ideal is evident in the "Toccata"—for those willing to perceive it.

Considering the melodic aspect, one must not here expect the obvious melody with accompaniment. The melodic trend permeates all horizontal motions of the texture without imposing its dictatorship or making the other musical elements its oppressed slaves. Its constant patterns are really elegant arabesques bearing a melody importance.

The harmonic aspects of the texture have the same quality of unobtrusiveness, and yet offer a rich and infinitely varied harmonic life, which quite entirely offsets any possible monotony which could accrue from the repetitions of similar patterns. Its pedal-points establish the stability which counter-balances the quickly evolving harmonic changes. We may mention here a few of the tonal colors employed, more as an indication of the variety and as a starting guide than as a complete analysis, for it is far from such for which a volume in itself would be required: Aeolian with C♯ as tonic (measures 1-6); transition to Dorian (measures 7-8); Dorian with F♯ as tonic (measures 9-12); E major (13-20); C♯ minor evolving toward B major (measures 21-25); modulatory sequences ascending (measures 26-41); tonal sequences descending (measures 42-45; 46-49); subdominant pedal with pentatonic alteration of subdominant element (measure 50), leading to dominant (measure 61) and to resolution on Aeolian (measure 62).

A repetition of the opening material in Aeolian leads through its transition toward the Dorian, but resolves deceptively to F natural, as tone center of a Lydian passage (measures 62-78); the large middle section opens with this F as pedal (measure 78), acting as subdominant to an evasive C major of which the startling color comes only after numerous meanders (measure 104); B minor (measures 157-166) is interrupted by a chromatic passage (measures 167-169), resumes with the surprising interpolation of a measure in B♭ (measure 173), and the chromatic interruption beginning at measure 178 leads into a modulatory section to measure 197. The first theme returns with C♯ as its tonal center but not in Aeolian, or ancient minor, but in the major diatonic at measure 198. It is, however, succeeded by Dorian with F♯ as tonic at measure 206, by E major at measure 210, and by C♯ minor and modulations, at measure 218, as in the opening section. The last statement of the opening theme is in C♯ major, but goes through the coloring of B minor (measure 240), chromatics, and the dominant seventh of C natural before obtaining its flamboyant cadence in the various positions of the tonic C♯ major chord.

Rhythmically the spirit of this composition ranges from the classical, precisely carved monoline pattern to an extremely rich fabric of controlled syncopated stresses (middle section starting at measure 78, also at measures 173-197. The twentieth-century excitement is yet brought back into the clarity of design of the seventeenth century.

The contrapuntal concepts may be perceived most easily through the contradictory stresses between the moving terraces of sound, counterpoint of rhythm, and counterpoint of the superimposed thematic motifs, arabesques, harmonic progressions, and pedal-points.

The instrumental coloring is prodigious in its range of registrations, and its precise determination sets into remarkable relief the full capacity of the piano, at times as a percussive instrument, but also as a singing instrument of great resonance. The fugitive nature of many of the modulations, which seems to merely lightly touch tonalities as it passes them by, and the varied use of harmonic tensions, melodic apexes, and durational weights—not in coincidence—all create life and keep this music in constant rapid pulsation.

The architectural aspects of form are essentially classic; a ternary form in its large sections (A, measures 1-77; B, measures 78-138; A, with variants, recapitulation, and coda, measures 139-266), it includes also some of the features of the sonata form, namely, the exposition of the two main materials, development sections, a very complete recapitulation of the first material, a coda on this material. Further, in its details, it achieves a happy balance of these two large forms with a detailed recurrence close to that of rondo form:

Main theme: In four materials, measures 1-8, 9-12, 13-20, 21-25.

Episode: Development on two of the main theme materials, 26-61.

Main theme: Restatement of the two first materials of the main theme, measures 62-77.

Episode: Based on second theme in four successive developed statements, measures 78-93, 93-114, 114-127, 128-138.

Main theme: A transition and development based on fragments of the first theme, measures 139-154, 155-170.

Episode: Based on the development of the first theme in the previous section with the addition of a new motif of two measures, which is concurrently developed, measures 171-197.

Main theme: Complete recapitulation with only minor addenda of the opening 25 measures of the prélude, i.e., the four materials of the main theme, measures 198-220.

Episode: A rapid recapitulation of part of the first episode, a development of the first theme, measures 221-227.

Main theme: A restatement of the first two phrases of the main theme, with the addition of the motif found in the episode of measures 171-197, opens the coda at measure 228, which leads to cadential progressions concluding the composition at measure 266.

An extremely well-balanced form, elegant and sober in spite of its overflowing vitality, which ends like a fanfare of joy. Not one of the component elements of the "Toccata" overpowers the others. The integration of melody, harmony, rhythm, counterpoint forms a classical balance, and the daring realization of sonorities as yet unknown and of modern syncopation embroidered on the classical canvas of elegant arabesques forms a daring alloy.

In the performance, the general requirements to watch are the perfecting of a classical clarity of all the patterns, steadiness of tempo, and exactitude of all the note durations as marked. A further important point is the precise projection of harmonic stresses (dissonance to consonance) and rhythmical stresses in the independent voice to which these belong.

Let us examine a number of detailed points of performance, from the beginning:

Bars 1-2. The pattern is single-voiced. No metric accentuation, nor notes held over.

Bar 3. The pedal-point on G♯ is harmonic; the melodic succession is in the left hand.

Bar 4. Similar to measure 1.

Bar 5. Similar to measure 3.

Bars 6-7. Similar case to measure 4.

Bars 9-12. Because of the chordal aspect, a most precise but light stress is given to the fourth eighth-note.

Bars 13-16. The use of pedal should be restricted to a short sixteenth-note duration on each beat. The main weight (stress) of the texture is syncopated on the half-beats.

Bars 17-20. The chordal weight is in even eighth-notes but the stress is created by the right hand, on the second sixteenth-note of each beat.

Bars 21-25. The texture must not overlap and become chordal; it must remain melodic in opposition to measures 26-34.

Bars 26-34. The effect of harmonic tension (sustained) on the first beat obtains its softened resolution on the second beat.

Bars 34-42. The same chordal characteristics are present as in the preceding section but enlivened by the introduction of the seventh on the second beat; there is tension at the right hand on the first beat and tension exclusively in the upper voice of the left hand on the second beat. This begins the syncopated stresses, essentially a contrapuntal concept.

Bars 42-45. Clarity of pattern is present, but brilliantly underlaid; the open sevenths are somewhat massive.

Bars 46-49. Same harmonic texture as in the preceding four measures but enlivened by chord stresses on the second beat (syncopated).

Bars 78-80. Outline clearly all sounds of the ninth chord and establish the proper balance of stresses by which the first eighth-note is stressed at the bass, the second eighth-note is stressed in the tenor, and the third eighth-note is stressed at the apex of the right-hand pattern. This establishes perfectly the character of the syncopation of the entire middle section. It is suggested that the left hand hold the quarter-note with the finger, and the pedal be used only on the second beat, to magnify upper stresses. An abuse of the pedal can make this entire section insignificant.

Bars 81-106. The texture remains as above, but the entrance of the second theme adds an element which must be expressive in its rises and descents without stifling the continued effect of syncopation, and neoclassic clarity.

Bars 106-115. The texture builds up in a less syncopated rhythm, in two-bar units, to and through a dominant cadence to the powerful repeat of the second theme. Ample brilliance and sustaining is required with the pedal used for lengths of two bars.

Bar 113. The power is at a maximum, yet the arpeggio must remain precise in its outline. The syncopation has shifted to the fourth eighth-note of the measure.

Bar 128. Note the additional stresses marked in the arpeggi, as a trebling of the melody, and which the performance must take into account. The section retains the broad character of the longer arpeggi (two measures) and of the reduced syncopation.

Bars 137-154. Do not overlook the sudden break from FF to PP and leading to PPP—a deceptive cadence—a return to the single-voiced arabesque, clear and simple.

Bars 155-159. The passage must be timed very exactly. The left hand must now be almost inaudible, *una corda*.

Bars 159-166. Utter precision, dry and PP, and clarity for the little portions of the first theme which surreptitiously prepare the restatement.

Bars 167-169 and 178-198. Observe that the contrary chromatic progressions (three- to five-part writing) demand utter clarity lest they degenerate into mere noise and thereby reduce the kaleidoscopic modulating excitement to nothingness.

Bars 198-249. This section is rich in all the materials already discussed, but note, besides, that the motif used first in measures 175-177 reappears at measure 182, and affirms itself steadily to measure 193. This idea becomes the controlling factor of measures 236-249. The motif has the character of a fanfare and must be interpreted with the precision of the trumpets in Debussy's "Festival" for orchestra. No confusion is permissible.

Bars 249-258. One must bring into evidence the syncopated character of the broad chord phrase of the left hand. The main stresses are on the chords found on the second beat of measures 250 and 252, and on the first beat of measure 254.

Bars 259-266. The final portion of the "Toccata" must sound like a glorious fanfare of victory. The diatonic major resolves the classical turmoil of modulations and syncopations!

A few misprints remain uncorrected in the printings of this work. In measures 13-17, the accents. In measure 236, the first note in the bass should be F♯ instead of A♯. Measure 242 should be identical with measure 240.

D'UN CAHIER D'ESQUISSES (1903)

This sketch was not really intended as a piece. It is a study, in many ways comparable to those made by great painters and architects, as they experiment during the gestation period preceding the final expression in a work of magnitude. It is as though embryonic ideas were set into turmoil and in their agitation sought to unite into an integrated and wider expression of their own intimate effects.

Laloy finds here "a music in which echoes of legends call to each other"; it is a poetic figure, and indeed the work already seems to skim the candid and yet symbolic language of "Pelléas."

It is a very rich sketch, all proportions kept to these few pages from the notebook of a genius. When Debussy wrote it, he was under the captivating charm of "The Sea," and, truly, the earnest student will not fail to find here many of the tonal impulses which are at the core of the score of "La Mer" ("De l'aube au matin") and contain many of the seeds of the thematic material of the great orchestral poem.

On April 20, 1910, Maurice Ravel paid homage to Debussy by playing this sketch as a première, at the Société Indépendante in Paris. It is an indication of the great importance attached by outstanding musicians, such as Ravel, to this sketch. Its value resides not so much in its use as a piece to be played but rather in its embodiment of a most significant moment in the history of music—that moment of potential energy which heralds the birth of an all-time masterwork, "La Mer," and possibly even of another giant composition, "Pelléas et Mélisande" —though the relation of this sketch to the latter work is less cogent.

A later diminutive work, having the same character of a sketch, a spontaneous waltz called "Page d'album," appeared in the *Etude* of March 1933. Maurice Dumesnil suggests that it was written in 1915 for an auction benefit, perhaps for "Le Vêtement du Blessé," a war benefit for clothing for wounded soldiers.

ESTAMPES (1903)

Completed, July 1903. First performance, January 9, 1904, at the Société Nationale by Ricardo Viñes.

For those who have followed the development of the tonal texture of the preceding compositions and have perceived its ever increasing richness, the ability of Claude Debussy to transform into music the most abstract vision must seem amazing. Finding under each new stimulus the exact modal color, the exact rhythmic counterpoint, the most telling architecture to compel us to share his vision to the utmost, is a technique which could not by-pass the temptation of musical *estampes.* Estampes, images printed from engraved copper or wood plates, are so designed as to set the image in strong perspective.

To apply this process in his tonal texture was a natural sequel for Debussy, enhanced by the challenge to his imagination of the particularly elusive and complex pictures he set out to stylize: the life-tempo of an oriental city of pagodas, an unpredictable evening in the warm night of Granada, a stormy afternoon with Parisian children. Years of gestation purified these visions to the pungency of an essence.

PAGODES

Nature: According to many books, the initial stimulus for "Pagodes" was Debussy's entranced hearing of the Javanese gamelang orchestras at the International Expositions in Paris in 1889 and 1900. This would infer twelve to thirteen years of maturation, and a transmutation from the delight of the gamelang, and the first contact with the Orient, to the creation of a symphony of sounds transcending the Javanese scene and typifying any one of a hundred widely spaced oriental cities.

The subject matter: Pagodas are consecrated temples of the Orient and are found in India, Burma, and Indo-China as well as in China and Japan. Their architecture exhibits the same general tendency as do oriental dances. A stabilized and sober base gives rise to movemented, ornate, sinuous, and shimmering superstructures. In looking at the score, you see this tendency reflected, and it is full of meaning to those who have traveled in the Orient.* It embodies the oriental sense of fixity as well as the incredible teeming surface of the population.

You will recognize the pentatonic atmosphere of oriental music of the past, the grace of the dancers of classic drama, the very design of the pagoda roofs, embodied in the arabesques of the music. You will hear the multiple counterpoint of the bells, gongs, chimes, and street noises.

* The author toured the Orient extensively in 1930 and was greatly impressed by the charm and pictorial beauty of the countries he visited: Japan, China, Indo-China, Siam, Malay Peninsula, Java, Bali, Ceylon, etc.

Debussy once said that "even Palestrina's counterpoint is child's play when compared with that found in Javanese music." How indicative this statement is of Debussy's advanced conception and use of rhythmic counterpoint as being on a par with melodic counterpoint! Yet the amazing sense of proportion and balance, so characteristic of the art of Debussy, reigns. It is still French clarity in its precise grasp of oriental atmosphere, and it is essentially music, despite all literary connotations.

Before we consider its delicate requirements for performance, it is necessary to understand the nature of the four aspects of its texture, namely:

The gamelang aspect—the art of chanting percussion and rhythmic counterpoint.

The scale aspect—pentatonism, four distinct such scales being used for different thematic materials.

The oriental aspect—shimmering golden surfaces, feline grace of dancers and people, the infinite fixation underlying the surface barocity of noises.

The Western aspect—evolution of a sonata form, with its increasing tension, and final denouement.

The gamelang orchestra is almost entirely composed of percussive instruments, with the exceptional use of a two-stringed viola. This, however, is not the only instrument capable of a melodic effect. The modulating small gong once struck may rise as much as a major third in pitch, producing an effect similar to a slide on high trumpets. Otherwise, the gamelang includes clappers, gongs of varied dimensions and ranges, tuned drums, kettledrums, bells in great variety of range. The musicians of this orchestra are the most remarkable masters of intricate rhythms, the basis of the complex nature of their music. The themes are extremely concise, but are reiterated persistently with a constant variation of their parts and their rhythms.

The harmonic aspect in "Pagodes" is one of fixation on the pentatonic scales, of which four different ones are used. It is important to be aware that the omission of two scale degrees within the span of the octave creates a definite transparency of texture. Just as the pagodas are relatively small in body, but spread in ornamental roofs, this music is small in basses but vividly spread in ornate tonal superstructure. As the roofs of pagodas curve upward with grace, so does the general melodic line and the oft-repeated motif, G♯-C♯-D♯. The pedals and inner voice progressions, which seem to infer a bitonal structure (diatonic versus pentatonic), are so chosen as to be subservient to the pentatonic progressions.

We will now look at the structural aspects of this piece:

Bars 3-10. The first subject is really the ostinato or pervading material of the entire piece, undergoing infinite changes and variations of rhythm and of function. It is in the pentatonic on black keys, C♯-D♯-F♯-G♯-A♯, a widely known form in occidental neo-orientalism.

Bars 7-10. The second material (tenor) uses a pentatonic bordering on modal, D♯-C♯-B-A♯-G♯.

Bars 11-14. The third material, entering under a partial augmentation of the first theme, uses a pentatonic made of B-G♯-F♯-D♯-C♯. This is in the nature of a second subject.

Bars 15-18. Return to the first pentatonic form, related to the first subject also, in its design.

Bars 19-22. A development of the second subject.

Bars 23-26. Development of the first subject "à la Netherlands School," the motif being so juxtaposed at the two voices as to permit contrary motion both in the melodic counterpoint and in the rhythmic counterpoint, i.e., the beginning of the motif in triplets superimposed upon the end of the motif in two's.

Bars 27-30. The first subject remains as right-hand accompaniment to the second subject in the left hand.

Bars 31-36. Bring in the fourth material, a second part of the second subject on a still different pentatonic group, G♯-B-C♯-D♯-E♯.

Bars 37-44. A development of the first and second subjects together, the first in diminution acting as accompaniment.

Bars 45-53. Conclude the development with the fourth material.

Bars 53-72 are an exact recapitulation of bars 3-22.

Bars 73-77 restate bars 11-14.

The coda begins at measure 78. The thirty-second notes embody a further rhythmic simplification and diminution of the first subject, which is placed under this in its original form (bars 80-83), followed by the secondary material originally stated in bars 7-10, which is followed in turn by the second subject from bar 88 to the end, the coda serving as a second recapitulation.

INTERPRETATION. From all these observations one can surmise that at no time should the texture be played to convey opacity, or dullness. The rhythms must be independently executed in perfect timing, and their alternating stresses well organized in superimposition.

The tempo should remain almost unchanged throughout the piece except for those short ritenutos of one-beat duration (bars 4, 6, 8, and later in repeats), which are to be like the addition of one eighth-note, and for the two periods of general accelerando, which are measured acceleration. In no case should these slight fluctuations in tempo be disorderly, i.e., rubato!

The playing at all times must have a light percussive quality, not massive, but highly resonant. The clarity of pattern is necessary, and at times their myriad brilliant strokes must convey the play of the sun on the golden roofs, the vibrations of gongs in the air.

The use of the sustaining pedal to affix the underlying tonal pedal-points is highly advisable as it permits the use of the damper pedal effectively for the transparency so necessary to a good performance. Do not fear to reach the unparalleled vibrance of the double forte. When Debussy wrote double forte, he really meant it.

SOIRÉE DANS GRENADE

Nature: One evening in the middle twenties, Manuel de Falla, my dear friend, was sitting with Mrs. Schmitz and me at the Fouquet on the Champs-Elysées in Paris, and I remember asking him which was the pianistic work he considered the most expressive of Spain. De Falla answered, without any hesitation, " 'The Evening in Granada,' which contains in a marvelously distilled way the most concentrated atmosphere of Andalusia." This opinion he stated officially in the *Revue Musicale*:

"The power of evocation integrated in the few pages of the Evening in Granada borders on the miracle when one realizes that this music was composed by a foreigner guided by the foresight of genius. There is not even one bar of this music borrowed from the Spanish folklore, and yet the entire composition in its most minute details, conveys, admirably Spain."

To this must be added the fact that Debussy never visited Spain, as he never penetrated it further than San Sebastian.

This "Estampe" is richly endowed with multi-faceted musical materials evocative of the kaleidoscopic nocturnal life of Granada. Notice the silvery bells of the dwarf donkeys; the sinuous and languid melody of the Moorish heritage of Spain; the prevalent rhythm of the habanera, which unifies and permeates the whole piece and is here treated through correct phrasing, better than by most Spaniards, conveying faithfully its rhythmic anticipation of the second beat and its secondary stresses of the fourth eighth-notes; a series of melodies, some boisterous, some languid, some rubato, some strict, all characteristic in their roles.

A materialist might be arrested by the attractive task of counting the numerous patches of music as they happen, and thus come to a rough understanding of how to adjust the puzzle, but the overwhelming thing is that the fragments of the puzzle fit so intimately that the impression is one of complete integration. It is as though we were in Granada and our contemplation of so much to see, so much to hear, so much to witness and to feel, would force our perceptive senses rapidly from one charm to another, but with the deep feeling that it is all there at once.

One image obliterates another, but those are the incidents, there is but *one* image, Andalusia. Its tone-color is reddish like the Alhambra's bricks, its pulse is that of the habanera—even in the dissolving texture of the last few bars, it is still present in the upper octaves.

INTERPRETATION AND STRUCTURE. First, it is important to accept the meaning of Debussy's initial indications. "Mouvement de habanera" does not mean a standardized tempo, it means far more. It means "in the motion of a habanera." Debussy further unveils his desire by writing, "Start slowly in a rhythm nonchalantly graceful." This is a *slow* habanera (just as there are slow waltzes) which will only assert an exact tempo, nearer to the "usual" habanera tempo at the seventeenth measure. The basic tempo of these sixteen first bars is generally taken too fast. The same remark applies to the sections starting at bar 67 and again at bar 122.

86

Notice that the rhythmically sinuous nature of the habanera is easily crippled when the performer fails to perceive the true rhythmical stresses and replaces them by unwanted metric accents. To make this more intelligible let us take two of the most typically habanera-like passages. At bars 17 and 18, the stresses as represented by the scoring and the harmonic points of tension, as well as by the evaluation of comparative durations, rhythm, and melodic formations, should be on the first beat of bar 17, then on the fourth sixteenth (anticipated second beat), then on the middle of the second beat (strongest point of harmonic tension). In bar 18, stress the second beat. A stress on the second beat of bar 17 destroys this rhythm.

Our second example is even more decisive, as here Debussy has taken great care to make his intent known. At bar 38, the dash on the first beat as well as the weight of the chord confirms its sturdiness, but again it is the last sixteenth of the first beat which is to be stressed (as indicated by its slur) and possibly minutely elongated. On the second beat proper, it is a lively lift not a down (notice the dot on A), and on the fourth eighth-note of the bar, the stress and sustained quality indicates it as a down, not a lift. This basic characteristic of the habanera is further confirmed by the innumerable centers of harmonic and melodic tension as found in bars 8, 15, 16, 17, 19, 30, 32, 33, 35, 38, 39, 40, 41, 43, 45, 46, 47, and so forth.

The six first bars must assert the C♯ pedal-point more by its transparency than by force. The passing from one octave to the next at the right hand must be almost surreptitious.

At bar 7, the languid Moorish melody must be hypersensitive (the appoggiaturas ever so slightly dropped but resolutions *always* softer than the appoggiaturas). Note that C♯ is the tonal center of this so-called Arabic scale made of C♯-B♯-A-G♯-F♯-E♯-D descending, a more evolved form than pentatonic.

Bars 14-15. Do not break the continuity in the motive as it passes from the left hand to the right hand.

Bars 17-21. The tempo giusto (not tempo primo) must be live and precise. This new idea, reminiscent of the rasgueado (strumming) technique of the guitar, is transitional modally, part "Arabic" and part whole-toned. It can be likened to transition passages in classical forms.

Bars 21-22 are a return to the initial texture, a bridge to the next musical idea starting at bar 23.

Bars 23-28. The "rubato" is to be enhanced by a full realization of the indefinite character of the whole-tone texture. Observe its relief, like a fresh gust of breeze in the midst of the strongly sensuous atmosphere. Structurally this new motif with C♯ still as tonal center, acts as a second idea of the first-subject group in a classical sonata form.

Bar 29 brings back the exact tempo (tempo giusto), acting again as a transition to the next musical idea and establishing the tonal center of F♯.

Bars 33-36. Study very precisely the phrasing and rhythms of the right-hand part while starting to affirm the habanera pattern as gradually overpowering the preception of all other expression. Note in the right-hand part, the chromatic successions formed horizontally in the inner voices, C to C♯, A to A♯, G to G♯, etc., which give the chords marked by dashes the value of appoggiaturas resolving on unaccented chords. These, in turn, are congruent with the notion of F♯ as tonal center (relative to the following section) and establish this section as opening the second subject group.

Bars 38-60. We come to the second subject in A major, full habanera.

In bars 38-41 do not hesitate to build a powerful rhythmical crescendo upon which the main theme of the habanera must enter quite explosively (it is double forte—no less).

From bars 42-57, obtain a sustained quality on the second eighth-note of the melody. Do not make the diminuendo of this section too early as there are fully twenty bars (41-61) to evolve gradually from double forte to piano.

Note in bars 59 and 60 the unifying use of the initial C♯ pedal.

Bars 61-66. Whole-toned and identical with bars 23-27. They act here again as transition, to the last material to be exposed.

Bars 67-77. A further idea of the second-subject group revolving around F♯ as tonal center. Remark that it is in the slow initial tempo, not in the tempo giusto, further it is the initial tempo "with still more abandon." The character of this section must be extremely tender, persuasive, sinuous; the two contrapuntal parts of the right hand must be heard as such, and the harmonic stresses created by the encounter of these two parts are frequently in syncopation with the bass which continues in the simpler form of the habanera rhythm.

Bars 78-91. The return of the transitional material originating in bars 23-27, but this section is no longer whole-toned. F♯ major and D♯ minor are the tonal centers, and the section acts as the beginning of the recapitulation from which the Moorish first subject is withheld until later.

Bars 92-97. Recapitulation of 17-20, the subtle return to a "distant" tonal texture gives the effect of the habanera rhythm vanishing into the distance. As it becomes fragmentary, you gain a sense of space, as in a landscape of which one feels the presence without being able to see the forms clearly.

Bars 98-108. Recapitulation of habanera in A major.

Bars 109-112, 115-118. Here the rhythm of castanets interrupts the recapitulation. These must be precise, as indicated, the beat being twice as fast.

Bars 113-114, 119-121. Condensed recapitulation of bars 67-77. These interrupted sections must not convey the impression of consecutive events, but rather of a continuous presence of all of them, of which our perception selects one, then another. Avoid materialistic neatness of tone.

Bar 121 to the end. Recurrence of the Moorish first theme of bars 7-16. The tempo primo taken from bar 119 (slower than the regular habanera) must emphasize the lascivious, languid character of the melody, conveying the night, the heavy perfumes, the warmth, the poly-sensuous dreams of the Andalusian night. The slight recalls of secondary musical ideas must remain in an almost intangible background.

JARDINS SOUS LA PLUIE

Nature: This "Estampe" brings us back to France, after our imaginary but vivid visits to Asia and to Spain. Choosing segments of two of the nursery rounds most popular with French children, Debussy unerringly paints the French scene, and includes in it the presence of youth. The story? It might be the games of children in a garden, interrupted by a storm, at first in the distance and finally confirmed, and the final victory of the children resuming their games under the final raindrops falling from leaves. It might also be nap-time. Children asleep in the nursery, lulled by the mother's singing, "Dodo, l'enfant do, l'enfant dormira bientôt" ("Sleep, child, sleep, the child will soon be asleep"). The heavy atmosphere of a leaden, sultry Parisian sky. A few raindrops, a far-off rumble, the storm gathers force, a nearby tree bends and moans in the wind, its branches crackling ominously against the wall and the windowpanes. The children, awakened by the storm, are frightened, the mother sings to them and they join in, but a sudden strident thunderclap drowns out their voices. Mother resorts to another song in her effort to conquer the inner panic of fright, "Nous n'irons plus au bois, les lauriers sont coupés" ("We'll not return to the woods, the laurel trees are cut down.").

At last the storm subsides, a last distant lightning, a far-off rumble. "Is it all over, mother? Why, of course, my darlings!" Once again relieved gaiety reigns complete. A rapid glance through the window. Yes, the rainbow is there framing a laughing sun, gaily smiling about his victory over the storm.

The great painter Manet, a friend of Debussy, once said, "The principal person in a painting is the light." Regardless of its story, you will find this is true of the "Gardens in the rain." The remarkable play of lights is effected by the alternate uses of four modal materials: minor, major, whole-toned, chromatic. The somber color of the opening portion is attributable to the minor modality. By the same token, the sparkling brilliance of the end, and of several fragments of the diminishing storm, is attributable to the major tonality. The whole-toned idiom (section beginning at measure 56) and the chromatic idiom (section beginning at measure 64), used in close contrast, portray the mounting force of the storm.

Structure: As to structure Debussy again couches this image in classical architecture.

Bars 1-56. A large opening section states the first theme ("Dodo, l'enfant do"), developed at length as a whole and in fragments and taken by transition passages from E minor to a modal segment, to F♯, then to C minor and to D flat minor.

Bars 56-75. Transition, whole-toned passage, chromatic passage, and G♯ trill acting as dominant pedal to the ensuing passage.

Bars 75-83. The second theme ("Nous n'irons plus au bois") softly, like raindrops falling from leaves. (C♯ major.) This material ends the exposition of this sonata form.

Bars 83-90. The second theme is interrupted by a return of the first theme, whole-toned in texture with E as tonal center but under the accompaniment of the second theme.

Bars 90-100. The second theme reasserts itself, again in C♯ major.

Bars 100-112. Transition, whole-toned at first, but soon forms ascending series of dominant-seventh to tonic sequences.

Bars 112-116. First theme in B minor.

Bars 116-126. Transition in the form of a violent outburst, descending in pitch in the color of diminished seventh chords, yet strangely close to pentatonic groups.

Bars 126-133. Fragment of the second theme in B major.

Bars 133-136. Second theme in E major under submediant chord and opening with an outburst reminiscent of measures 116-126.

Bars 136-140. First theme in the bass, G♯ minor.

Bars 140-143. Second theme in E major.

Bars 143-147. First theme in G♯ minor which concludes the long development of the two themes.

Bars 147-151. A coda which takes the place of the classical recapitulation, or which forms a highly condensed recapitulation, begins with the first theme in B major.

Bars 151-157. First-theme fragment in the right hand, with the second theme in the left hand, in the tenor voice, and in augmentation. Cadence in E major.

INTERPRETATION. From a general viewpoint it must be remembered that rain seldom begins in sheets of water (particularly in France). It is gradual in its momentum and decline. After the storm the sun seems more brilliant because of its reflection on many wet surfaces, while raindrops still fall from leaves and flowers. Thus, the texture demands at times great clarity in performance, non-legato (opening section and again at bars 27-37), and at other times a close integration of all patterns in a fluid atmosphere, linked by the pedal but not to the point of destroying the natural transparency of water, or of mixing harmonic progressions. The first sixteen measures are to be non-legato, with practically no use of the pedal. Notice, at bars 8-15, that the consecutive fourths included in the texture sound remarkably well if the passage is not allowed to acquire a chordal opacity.

Notice also that pitch and harmonic intensity throw the main accent of the measures 10-14 on the second half of the first beat, with the phrasing starting each measure at that point.

From bars 16-22 avoid giving the left hand on the second half of the beat the usurped importance of a quarter-note. It is part of the sixteenth-note arabesque and not part of the lower progression. At bar 24, observe the foreshadowing of the impending storm with a greater use of the pedal, but in the two succeeding bars return to a semi-dry texture. The interplay of major and minor on the two themes in the following section must be translated by clear-cut opposition in the performance, i.e., light and clear for the major. Study this passage (bars 37-43), and realize that there are three levels of melodic activity each with its own stresses, phrasing and texture, which the performance must respect. Bars 64-71 convey the turmoil, but observe that the lower voice alone is in quarter-notes and legato.

Also verify that in some of the printings of this work a number of misprints remain. At bar 66, the fourth quarter-note in the right hand (A) is natural, the same in bar 67. At bar 68, the third quarter-note in the right hand (F) is natural. The unison is very pure, forte and strident, but as early as bar 73 its brilliancy diminishes rapidly to give way to the F♯ ringing above. Throughout the ensuing section this trill must not be metric, but instead a very diffused background to the two melodies. From bar 103, note the intended accent at every two bars which heralds the thematic return and builds the tempo toward it.

Play the cadenza (bars 116-122) extremely rapidly and brilliantly, but it should be interpreted as a single line, and not loaded by the overlapping of sounds. The trills are more and more subdued. At bars 126 and 130, lightning flashes. The B in the bass and the upper G♯ of the arpeggio must be stressed, then an immediate drop in dynamics brings a soft but very rapid trill, which in bars 131 and 132 builds in the general crescendo. Oppose the color of the first theme, now boisterous and solid, to the second, which is gay, mischievous, lighter, and non-legato. From bar 147 to the end a steady building of the dynamism and gaiety, portraying the glory and confidence of the victoriously returned sun.

MASQUES (1904)

This piece, which was probably a much earlier composition than the publication date would indicate, has been listed as primarily intended as a part of the "Suite Bergamasque." It is indeed probable that it was composed as early as 1890, as shown by its style of writing and the comparative lack of textural resources. It is, nevertheless, a piece which has much freshness and youth, and somewhat parallels Verlaine's inspired "Fantoches." It is obviously imbued with thoughts of the personages of the Italian comedy, and one finds in it the mischievous characters of Scaramouche and Pulcinella, and also the amorous seduction of Zerlina.

It is interesting to note the neo-classic interest brought by Debussy at different times of his life, and in different works, to the seventeenth-eighteenth-century Italian comedy with its masques and bergamasques. Not only in the "Suite Bergamasque," already considered, but the "Fêtes galantes" (for voice), the present sketch, in mood, the prélude "La terrasse des audiences du clair de lune," a ballet projected in 1909, of which only the libretto was completed under the title of "Masques et Bergamasques." *

In 1915 the theme was still a powerful stimulus to the imagination of Debussy, and he considered a work for the theater based on Verlaine's *Fêtes galantes;* like many other projects of his last years, it could not be fulfilled.

A Parisian reviewer wrote of the present piece that, although this music "attracted him as some forbidden pleasure, some vicious habit," he was nonetheless fond of it!

The piece is not difficult; it is direct and should express the vivacious alertness of carnival spirit, and by moments the light coquettishness of

* Debussy, *Lettres à son éditeur,* pp. 78, 83.

93

Zerlina. Its belated publication should not mislead us. Its texture clearly indicates its early composition and its anterior conception to that developed in the "Suite pour le piano."

L'ISLE JOYEUSE (1904)

One of the most extroverted of Debussy's compositions, "L'Isle joyeuse" is also one of the most orchestrally conceived piano works. In its more modern texture it represents an equivalent to the Lisztian endeavor in piano literature.

It has been suggested that the initial stimulus to its composition might have come from the contemplation of Watteau's painting, "The Embarkment for Cythère"; it is indeed imbued with the gaiety, animation, and sensual atmosphere of the Watteau painting, but music is alive and does not abide by the momentary fixation of canvases. The play of rhythms is relentless, truly Bacchanalian. It is no longer "The Embarkment for Cythère," but rather "The Revelry *at* Cythère" around the temple of Venus. The enchantment of the "land of love" pervades the music, culminating into triumphant dance rhythms, a glorious fanfare in honor of the goddess. It is veritably the isle of joy and its homage to the Deity of Love never becomes dulled by even the slightest shade of morbidity—Cythère, one must remember, is not an island on the Rhine permeated by legends of the Nibelungen!

Completed in August 1904, at Dieppe, the work was given its première in 1905 by Ricardo Viñes at the Société Nationale in Paris, but by 1917 the distinguished Italian conductor, Bernardino Molinari, could no longer resist its lure and made an orchestral transcription of merit.

To evaluate the relative difficulty of the work, we may quote from Debussy's own letter to his publisher, J. Durand, dated September 1904: "But God! how difficult it is to perform . . . that piece seems to assemble all the ways to attack a piano since it unites force and grace . . . if I dare to speak thus!" While Debussy was right in this statement, he was yet to compose far more difficult works in subsequent years.

The main melodies have the exultant simplicity of folk songs, and the infectious carefreeness of Mediterranean tunes, a color they share with those of "Collines d'Anacapri" ("Préludes"), and the dotted rhythm in alternation with triplets is always a sign of gaiety, whether sly or outspoken (See "Puck," "Pickwick," etc.)

The harmonic color is no less vivacious than the varied rhythms. Opening with a recurrent cadenza in successive polytonality, one explores diatonism, whole-toned series, chromatic passages in kaleidoscopic alternations.

The form, a complexly woven sonata structure, gives us in turn: an introduction (measures 1-6) in the form of a free cadenza which will serve as unifying link in the several guises its recurrences take (measures 28, 52, 246); a first theme exposed and developed (measures 7-19), to which a secondary episode of importance is added at measure 21 with development and returns of the cadenza, bringing the entire first-subject group to measure 66, inclusive; a second theme (measures 67-99). The development section, of which some aspects have already, as is frequent, been included in the exposition, considers the first subject (measures 100-117), adds the second subject without break in texture (measure 118), and develops their elements simultaneously to measure 145, inclusive. The next development superimposes the first theme and the secondary episode mentioned above in alternate and simultaneous development. A cadenza (measures 183-186) and a muffled drumbeat ushers in the condensed and varied recapitulation with the first theme (measures 189-201), secondary episode (206-209, 214-221), second subject over brass fanfares (measures 222-245), opening cadenza or introduction (measure 246 to the end).

As is quite usual in the tonal texture attained by Debussy around this period, the performance demands great variations in style of interpretation. Certain sections (such as measures 7-19, 25-52, 64-67, 100-117, 146-148, 161-167, and 187-198) demand lightness, precision, elegance, clarity, careful sobriety of pedaling. To the contrary, diffused suppleness is desirable in the whole-toned passages (measures 19-25, 122-123, 126-127, 130-133, 138-142, 149-158, 167-187, 198-202, 206-210, 214-218). The expressively undulating rubato starting at measure 67 demands a perfect legato with a sensitive stressing of the melody upon a canvas made of very regular five-note patterns; this section is pervaded by tenderness and love. The brilliant, boisterous joy of some sections (measures 1-4, 25-27, 48-67, 138-167, 202-206, 210 to the end) calls forth all the vibrance of the resources of the instrument, unguarded and spontaneous with an ever increasing exultation, yet clarity of texture; a precise use of the sustaining pedal, starting measure 222, to hold the pedal-points is recommended.

Within these large considerations of the general interpretation there are also many smaller details to consider:

In the introductory cadenza measures (1-7) the free, improvisatory character is kept during the first six measures. Do, nevertheless, observe the crescendo ending in a deceptive nuance, and do not be shy about the forte at measure 3, nor about the percussive accents (measure 6) which establish the exact tempo basic to the next section, and which must be precise from measure 7.

The first theme (measure 9) must be timed very exactly as to its dotted rhythm and triplets. Do not slur the short values to the long durations.

In the section beginning measure 19, create a sense of tonal fixity by clearly enunciating the pedal-points G natural and A in the bass. Over these pedals, the triplet patterns form a delicate canvas so that the motif starting at measure 21 can be set into value despite its soft dynamic content. No break should occur in the transfer of the thematic material from the left hand to the right hand (measures 24-25).

In the section of measures 28-52, the texture is light and translucid, harpsichordian in clarity, yet allowing for a non-massive gradual crescendo to the joyous outburst of measures 52-54. This outburst is interrupted by the turmoil of measure 55, resumed again, and interrupted again; it finally rescinds through measures 64-66, to reach the extremely captivating sinuosity of the second theme.

The second theme brings the contrast of the rhythmically neutral left-hand part and of the subtle variations of rhythm of the right-hand part. The degree of rubato is already indicated by the note-durations and should not be added to, or subtracted from, in the danger of destroying the rhythmical abandon, lyric and expressive, but with aspirations!

A dance-like precision is resumed, measure 100, in contrast to the song-like flow of the second theme.

From measure 136, the suspended-life mood of the whole-toned texture is now awakening and building to the explosive diatonicism of measures 142-146. But, immediately, the dynamic level drops to allow a rebuilding of excitement to the animated first theme (measure 161).

From measure 167 whole-toned suspension is returned to, and forms the basis of a long crescendo, very effectively cut, PP subito, measure 187, for the entrance of a distant march with muffled drums. Deceptive crescendi occur in measures 195-199, but the crescendo of measures 200-201 is conclusive and brings the glorious trumpet fanfare of the next four measures. Whole-toned texture and suspenses alternate with fanfares, but from measure 222 the performance demands an organization of its various levels for utmost clarity and brilliance in this superimposition of pedal-points, brassy trumpet figures, and yet an exultant upper theme which must not lose its character of abandon. The final section is of turmoil and exuberant joy, of pagan libations.

Pagodas in Burma

3.

Piano Works 1905-1910

In the following sections, we will consider successively the two sets of "Images," which were composed in 1905 and 1907 respectively.

These images, as a group, are considerably more abstract in their inspiration and design than were the "Estampes"; here imagery is a function of objects upon the mind, creating metaphors to enliven these ideas by lending them a hypersensitive form. Continuous free variation is the technique which translates the continuous musical impulse which they contain.

The first set of three works, dating from July-August 1905, is mentioned by Debussy in a letter to his publisher, J. Durand, of September 11, 1905:

> "Have you played the 'Images' . . . ? Without false pride, I feel that these three pieces hold together well, and that they will find their place in the literature of the piano . . . (as Chevillard would say) to the left of Schumann, or to the right of Chopin . . . as you like it."

It is strange to reflect that only three of the six "Images" are performed with any degree of frequency and that even these do not enjoy the remarkable popularity which they should. There are certainly a number of reasons for this slower ascendance, one of which is the aforementioned abstractness; demanding more imagination and a greater transmutation from ordinary events, their appeal is the richer, but also the less easily accessible. Time and thought can remedy this factor, as it will undoubtedly do so also in the case of the "Études." Another factor is, of course, the difficulty of performance, which we feel is more apparent than real in comparison to other oft-performed works of Debussy and to works which the twentieth century has brought into the normal repertoire of most pianists. A last consideration, which applies to "Mouvement," "Cloches à travers les feuilles," and "Et la lune descend sur le temple qui fut," is the question of their non-adaptabilty as to content to large crowds and to concert halls. In an era in which a tremendous intensity is, in the overall, directed to immediate gains in fame or fortune, the art of peaceful, thoughtful performance of music for a restrained number, in a small room, is no longer generally in vogue, and precludes the infinitely rewarding exploration of more diaphanous or complex musical expressions. We hope, though, that time will again, in its amazing cycles, bring back to pianists their heritage and birthright of being musicians first, and circus performers second . . . or, better yet, last.

It is interesting to note that with the second set of "Images," Debussy seems to have acknowledged the need of making his musical intentions even more evident, since so many failed to see the melodic continuity of voices in his texture. In this group, he starts using three staves, which better enable him to precisely indicate the terraces of sounds, also making more absolute his indications of nuances and phrasings.

Obviously, his concern about exactitude had been somewhat ruffled, as indicated by a letter to his publisher (January 1907), in which he begs him to "induce his engraver to respect the exact place of nuances." He further mentions, "It is extremely important."

It is a well-known fact that engravers, being generally non-musicians, may attach more importance to the graphical aspect of a page than to its musical significance. This aesthetic concern through the ages has surreptitiously moved many a sforzando from one note toward another, at times so dangerously close that the error has been accepted as tradition, hard to explain but followed blindly.

Such displacements of accents are noticeable even in reprinting of recent works.

One wonders how many such insidious practices have obscured the works of Beethoven, for instance, as one peers over "illegitimate" stresses which a tenth of an inch to the right or left would make absolutely logical! It is indeed a field of study . . . but now let us turn our thoughts to "Images."

100

One could say that what Debussy saw in the water was the reflection of his own love of subtle design—a very characteristic French admiration for the amazingly varied opalescence of play of light and water, and the diaphanous deformations of realities viewed through these two fluctuating media.

This composition marks one of those tense moments in Debussy's evolution when his imagination leads him anew to unexplored fields. It is at once full of creative genius and yet affected by the restlessness of the new research. The resultant creation is fascinating even though the integration of musical ideas in some aspects remains of an improvisatory character, unsettled. That Debussy felt a certain uneasiness in working with this medium is brought out when he wrote his publisher, J. Durand, in August 1905, in answer to the latter's inquiry about the completion of the work: "The piece does not please me much, so I have resolved to compromise on new ideas and according to the most recent discoveries of harmonic chemistry."

What are the component elements of this harmonic chemistry? A subtle interplay of diatonicism with whole-toned series and short passages in pentatonism is the tonal medium enriched by a "chordal" conception which in truth is made of minute contrapuntal movements of patterns superimposed, crossing each other, complementing or supplementing each other in their delineations, and in their freedom bringing the rich by-product of dissonance, i.e., of simultaneous sounding of intervals basic to the harmonic progression and of notes alien to it.

The form brings an alternation of treatment of the two main themes in the following sections:

> A: measures 1-15
> Transition: measures 16-24
> B: measures 25-35
> A: measures 36-43
> Transition: measures 44-48
> B: measures 49-71
> Coda, containing recalls of both A and B: measures 72-95.

But this rondo-sonata alternation is only a canvas to a rich ricercar variation technique in which the two themes, in fragments or whole, undergo all the developments of the Netherlands School fame: mirroring, inversion, augmentation, diminution, imitation, but not as ends in themselves, though the fascination in abstract is already very great; here these techniques are used in strict subservience to the pictorial purpose at hand, to the poetic-emotional climate of the composer's conception. They are, therefore, unobtrusive in forming a unified basis for the kaleidoscopic effects of water and light, the reflections of clouds or trees, the concentric ripples of drops in the water, the nearby forest from which a distant horn call is heard toward the end.

In the first eight measures, the harmonic patterns of the right hand are full of concentric fascination as are the successive undulatory circles created in the peaceful surface of a pedal-point by the dropping quarter-notes of the theme (Ab-F-Eb). A perceptive comprehension of the right-hand patterns will reveal the mirroring of that theme in diminution. This effect is even more evident in the variant of measures 36-44, where the arpeggi unfold the embellished melodic impression.

The pictorial shades are almost infinite as Debussy opposes the aquatic fluidity of the contrapuntal texture of measures 1-8 and 36-44, to the troubled and drowsy opacity of the chord progressions with chromatic undertones (measures 9-10, 31-32, and so forth), to the flickering reverberations of surface shimmer (measures 9-11), to the translucid pentatonism and consecutive fifths of measures 16-17, to the immensely spread and almost intangible reflectory surface ripple (measure 24-30) under which the suspense of the whole-toned theme lends a depth of agitation, soon reflected in a gradual return to temporary diatonism (measure 36).

The tremendous variety of shades is intimately pervading, imbuing the listener with its rich pictorial gamut. Charmed by an aspect of nature, the sensitive artist recreates its geometry of motion as he yet portrays its poetry, simplicity, and ever-changing animation.

It is evident that the performance or reprojection of such a texture will make strong demands upon the pianist. We would like to indicate some of the trends, some samples of the problems of interpretation.

Since we have already pointed out that the right-hand part of the first eight measures hides, under its appearance of chordal formations, a contrapuntal fabric, it means the treatment in performance must recognize the melodic fragments as they traverse each other, in full legato, and also the tension created by certain notes must be gently brought to the fore (for instance, in the first measure, the C of the second chord; in the third measure, the B of the second chord, and so forth). A supple, singing tone quality, and the use of correct fingerings will insure a three-part legato sensitive to the harmonic evolution. In these same measures, two other levels need consideration: the pedal-point, which is singing but essentially soft, and the three-note theme in the middle register, brought out by absorbent fingers with speed of action for brilliance (what we term impulsed slap touch).

In measure 9-10, the voicing of the chords has melodic intent but the descending arpeggi play within the resonance of the chord preceding them.

The pedal effect (B♭) maintains the continuity of the main melodic line through measures 11-13 and ends only after the resolution of measure 15.

Measures 16-17 have a limpid progression; the crescendo of measure 17 is designed to emphasize the fourth sixteenth-note, but does not affect the extreme upper and lower chords of the third and fourth beats which are maintained PP.

In the cadenza-transition of measures 20-24, one must avoid opacity, for within each group there are harmonic changes or spreading of the tonal texture, an enrichment which opacity will neutralize.

In the section beginning measure 25, the arabesques must be fluid and of rhythmical evenness, and in the timing of the left hand, care must be taken not to make the sixteenth-notes faster than their actual value.

Note that from measure 28 a stronger character results from the changes of whole-toned texture to dominant harmony, vitalizing the second theme. Observe that the nuances indicated in the half of measure 31 and 32 bring an F to the last chord, but not to the A♭ pedal which remains at a much softer level.

In the section beginning at measure 36, the interpretation of the left hand remains as in the opening section, but for the right hand emphasis is laid on translucidity, very light yet legato.

There should be no break in tempo at measure 44; the animato is gradual through measures 44-50; it is like an accelerated, broadening ripple, with the right hand clear and even, and the left hand legato and very exactly timed. In contrast, observe that the sudden return to tempo (measure 51) makes the left-hand arpeggi more than twice as slow as the preceding arpeggi in the right hand; further observe again exact timing of the melody in the right hand.

The basic tempo remains steady despite the acceleration of the arpeggi (harmonically assertive, measure 53-54), their broadening again (measures 55-56), and their acceleration in triplets coupled in brilliant major harmony (measure 57). These variations of speed are clearly given their exact timing by note durations.

In measures 58-59 do not hesitate to give its full impact to the declamatory lyricism of the thematic motif, followed by a very gradual rallentando and diminuendo evenly distributed from measures 60-66. The lyric quality must be retained in measures 66-72, but with arpeggi glittering as on a transparent water surface.

The imitations (mirrored augmentations) of measures 67, 69, 70, and 71 can be set into value by stressing the anticipated third eighth-note, and other syncopated entrances of the three-note motif.

From measure 72, a sense of great calm and distance pervades the musical texture, yet the high treble recalls of the opening theme must have a luminous purity and resonance, and the recall of the second theme (end of measures 79-81) must have the soft pungency of a distant muted horn call. From measure 82 the agitation fades even more completely, but an exact timing must be maintained to insure the difference between binary and ternary motives; in this section, the sustaining pedal can be used to excellent effect in maintaining the chords while allowing clarity for the first motif.

In general, exactitude of timing is important throughout this piece, since a disorderly sense of tempo and of durational relations will destroy the transformations of the fascinating surface designs which evoke so charmingly these reflections on the water.

The opinions of musicographers concerning this piece are widely divergent, and range from considering it one of the most beautiful pieces written for the piano since the last sonatas of Beethoven, or a most magnificent funeral offering, to finding it rather stiff and unrelated to Rameau's musical personality.

It is a well-known adage that one must never discuss of likes and dislikes in art: "Des goûts et des couleurs, il ne faut point discuter" . . . but as to its fittingness as a tribute to Rameau, it is another matter.

One cannot doubt Debussy's genuine attachment to the art of his classic forebear. His effusive expression of joy and emotion in thanking his publisher, J. Durand, at two separate times for the gift of special collections of Rameau's work, has the fire and conviction of a profession of faith, a sincerity which permeates this work, as does the tender sadness of a disciple paying tribute at a great distance.

There was no particular anniversary of Rameau's birth or death in 1905, the promptings then were those of an accumulated desire to translate admiration and affection into some tangible form other than the article written some years before.

In Debussy's character of these maturing years, plagiarism was an utter impossibility; he could not, or would not, have written a work in slavish imitation of Rameau's style, an attempt he would have (to the contradiction of his own disciples) considered insulting to the memory of the man he was honoring.

He could, and did, imbue this work with the alternating austerity, passion, and deep affection for the old master, and with a refined and transmuted eighteenth-century style, rendered piquant by a freedom of progressions in which the harmonic-conscious Rameau would have been delighted.

In selecting a slow sarabande, Debussy pays homage to Rameau's affinity for the classic dance forms while yet obtaining the noble and grave tenderness of which this particular dance is capable.

In exploiting extreme contrasts of scoring from single voice (declamation, recitative) to single voice accompanied by chords (aria), to contrapuntal sections of several independent voices, Debussy places his offering within the baroque style of Rameau's period and also emphasizes the latter's various styles of texture. And if there are sections, as in "Pour le piano" that remind us of organ style, one remembers that Rameau was an organist of long professional standing. What more apt tonal medium than that of medieval modes, to denote the great distance in time and the great distance in death, as a psychological factor? A modality full of freedom with no resemblance to the painfully mastered technique of student textbooks, but a live, evolving melos fluctuating from its Aeolian to its Phrygian axis, and with infinitely precious harmonic gems. A texture foreshadowed in the "Suite Bergamasque," and in the "Sarabande" of the "Suite pour la piano," and now reborn in this matured "ancient" style.

Note the thematic answers at the fifth, for instance, measure 1 answered by measure 10, and measure 5 answered by measure 6, a play on the plagal and authentic ranges of the mode. The masterly use of opposed forms growing out of various developments of monophony and polyphony give this piece the quality of a great "fresco," and the absence of a pedantically exact schematization preserves the charm of a carefree flight of music into wider spaces, carrying an emotional message which transcends the mere gesture of man to man.

The opening mood is one of reverence, but in its development come great sorrowful tenderness (measure 14 and on), a first glorification (measure 24), and a rescinding towards a most seductive tenderness (measure 31).*

The texture gradually builds again in a pageant to the second apotheosis (measures 51-53), which is little by little calmed by sadness (measures 53-57), returning to reverence through a concise restatement of the first section, and attaining an almost religious peace in the coda in which a series of chords descend the degrees of the Dorian scale—as if to Rameau's tomb!

In performing this composition it is helpful to imagine, but with due respect to the evidences of scoring, the opposition of (1) homophonic style, which generally is periods of incantation, against (2)

* In such sections the simultaneously sounding melodies form a polyphony which is like a modern mirage (evocation) of that of Palestrina.

purely decorative sections, which tend to situate the scene in neo-Greek atmosphere (viz. Rameau operas), and (3) polyphonic passages scored for many voices of equal interest and independence, which twice culminate in powerful and yet concise declamatory statements of tragic expression. The treatment is that of soli, choir, declamators, and orchestra, with effects of a veiled but yet percussive nature.

The homophonic chant of measures 1-4 must be played strictly together at the two hands; it is expressive and emotionally intense in conjuring the memory of a departed musician.

Note the archaic effect of crotals (measures 5-6), soprano voice, gently percussive but silvery over imposing chords stepping quietly along the ladder of the Phrygian mode, unemotional but decorative.

In measures 7-10, the homophonic statement in Hypophrygian mode is again an appeal, the repeat of the initial incantation a fourth lower, but it now develops into polyphonic terraces through measures 11-13. Then, a tender section, polyphonic, and expressive as of ancient mourners, proceeds through various pedal-points, unceasingly animated in its lamentations and polyphonic building, to bring the dramatically homophonic statement of the initial four notes of the incantation (measure 24), repeated like an echo (measure 25), and rescinding to the conclusion of the first section at measure 30.

Note the interesting change of harmonic texture, quite considerable, quite polyphonic, and yet ethereal in scoring by the spreading of the texture (measures 31-37); the passage is luminous and translucid.

A processional begins in measure 38. The left hand must sound like veiled drums answering the appeals of the mourners. Measures 43-51 bring a gradual acceleration not only of tempo but also of tension, culminating in the tragic and desperate reiteration of the second material (first introduced at measure 31). The sentiment of tragedy is here virile, gripping; it must not be weakened by wrong preconceptions of effeminate interpretations of Debussy!

Observe in measure 57 the rich restatement of the opening theme in polyphonic treatment. In measure 65, the coda is reached; it is a noble statement of faith and peace, and the chord progression must carry through with absolute continuity to measure 75, with all recalls of themes made subservient in dynamics to this long line. Remark at measure 72, the interesting progression of chords descending with submission and resignation into the depth of the glorious past.

MOUVEMENT

As we have remarked already, one of the most confirmed characteristics of the music of Debussy is the ever inquisitive challenge of the new, the insatiable urge to create and not repeat. Debussy seldom composes a piece in close similarity to one already highly and successfully integrated as to its typical mood. This applies to the style of the texture also. In a piece such as "Pagodes," he enclosed his most clairvoyant perception of the ambient life around these temples and of the nature of the gamelang orchestra. In the "Evening in Granada," another mood, another humanity is distilled in the most concentrated essence of Andalusia; Spain will twice again be his entrancing inspiration, but it will not be the languid and sentimental Spain. In "La Puerta del Vino" the mood will be almost coarsely tragic, and in "Sérénade interrompue," picaresquely humorous.

It is this attitude of totalness within conciseness which makes each work of Debussy irreplaceable, even by another work of his same pen. Composing for him was not a routine task of the daily schedule, but the answer to mounting surges, to the demands of always renewed imaginative fields.

With this appraisal one can approach "Mouvement," a composition of a basically abstract nature, despite the very human charm of its central theme; an uninterrupted moto perpetuo of triplets in sixteenth-notes, punctuated by steady eighth-notes, conveys a mechanical inexorability which is the herald of the "machine age," and for all its delicate texture embodies an early expression of the rhythmic dominance which inspired many composers during the first quarter of the twentieth century. The impression is that of a delicate wheel running at high velocity, repulsing and then again attracting strange harmonic elements, as though these were microscopic animalcules, at times absorbed by the irresistible centrifugal force of gyration.

Though abstract design is not solely represented by this work in

Debussy's compositions but is to be followed by "Les tierces alternées" and the twelve "Études," yet "Mouvement" is unique in its particular incursion into the curious world of perfected mechanics. Its predominance of rhythm does not achieve its power through elemental force, but, on the contrary, through the delicate persistence of the machinery of a Swiss watchmaker.

It elects the neutral harmonic canvas of C major (a favorite starting point in many excursions into dissonance of the last fifty years) and, from this base of operations, excursions in successive and simultaneous bitonality tense the fabric, resolve to the neutral canvas, again invoke the friction of another set of positive-negative poles . . . a whirring richness of tonal molecules which the whole-toned coda suspends to a final cadence in—you guessed it, C major!

A strict structure is maintained, ternary in its large sections, but the unifying rhythmic impulse, or rather compulsion, carries through and over the landmarks of sectional analysis.

In the performance the prime requirement is the understanding and acceptance of the premise of a precise and unified tempo throughout the piece. It does not allow for rubati at any moment; further, and contrary to the opinion expressed by some commentators, the central section is not slower. Debussy here merely demands the avoidance of an accelerando. Once the inexorability of the tempo has been accepted the next requirement is to maintain great precision, and clarity, in all patterns, a regularity of the three semi-quavers respectively. One may then convey the strong effect of unimpeded motion.

The use of the pedal must be very sparing in measures 1-30. At measure 30 it is best to affix the pedal-point (C-G) with the sustaining pedal in order to use the damper pedal without clogging the mechanism of this machine of precision with a "mud of passing tones." In measure 34, the low G can also be taken with the sustaining pedal. From measures 42-53, a limited amount of pedal is permissible as the left hand sings unaffectedly its gentle, lyric theme. In measure 53, clarity is again desired, as is the use of the sustaining pedal for the pedal-point. In the section of measures 67-79 the machine runs smoothly, but the pedal must respect all chordal changes as they also coincide with the upper melody.

In measure 63, the triplets in the right hand are very light whereas the call in the left hand is very violent. From measure 79, the triplets are precise, but one must set into value gently the lower melody.

From measure 89 to the strident apex of measure 109, there should be no loss of tempo; the theme moves freely with stresses in its melodic ascents and descents, but avoiding wrong accents on downbeats which would make it lifeless.

In the recapitulation beginning at measure 115, the recommendations of the beginning remain the same, but from measure 157 to the end, perfect timing must continue with, however, a deft use of pedal rendered permissible by the whole-toned texture. There is no cessation of motion—it merely becomes inaudible, invisible.

CLOCHES À TRAVERS LES FEUILLES

A literal translation of the title of this first "Image" of the 1907 series would be "Bells (heard) through the leaves."

Opinions are again in conflict about this piece. Louis Laloy, who knew Debussy well, writes that he related to him the touching habit of some French villagers, of sounding the church bells (as a knell) unceasingly from All Saints' Day until time of the Mass of the Dead on All Souls' Day. The nostalgic vibrations of the bells permeating the forests from one village to another, from sunrise to evening, is, according to Louis Laloy's claim, the stimulus which suggested the idea of this composition to Debussy. A contradiction comes from the remarks of a man who seems to understand a great deal about Debussy, Leon Oleggini, who feels that these are not chimes which constitute the pedal-point upon which the harmonies and melodic designs are supported.

Personally we feel that this work is one of those to which literary connotation adds little. I would agree that it is full of chime effects, but also that the whole-toned texture is the real pedal-point that supports the harmonies. The texture is generally extremely transparent, and does not have the morbidity and desolation of a knell; in fact, it is much less expressive of these moods than are "Des pas sur la neige," for example, or even "Hommage à Rameau." We are really in the presence of a play of sonorities and their combined resonances; an atmosphere of suspense like mist, is clarified by the limpid section of semi-pentatonic texture, followed by the return of diffused whole-toned texture.

To all those who love delicate perfumes—to all those who have religiously sipped an old brandy—to those whose eyes have become moist at the solitary contemplation of a peaceful but lovely sunset—to all those who through the senses of smell, taste, sight, receive the greatest impacts of life, who have awakened senses, and can hear, this piece will bring the enraptured feeling of a gentle intoxication by sounds—by sounds alone, echoing the most subtle and refined moods of their "vie intérieure" (inner life—psyche?).

The performance of this work in large concert halls should be avoided, for it is like the beauty of the clavichord, abstract and delicate, and can only be fulfilled and perceived in intimacy and utter silence. Such requisites are never found in human beings any more and most assuredly not in concert halls.

Playing this piece for oneself, with all the introspection which befits it, one will be entranced by the incredible perfection of the spacing of sounds in time as well as in pitch relations.

A good performance will convey the absolute regularity of rhythms, will avoid mixtures of chords that could mar the transparency of the tonal patterns. In short, a purified classical style of performance and an unconcerned quietude of the individual's soul will allow this fragile mezzotint to carry its impersonal tonal sensation into one's inner peace.

ET LA LUNE DESCEND . . .

It must be considered, above all, that the abstraction of this sketch makes it futile to try to situate the scene in any determined locality, in any positive physical setting. Its title suggests a "descent of the moon upon the temple which used to be," inferring that the moon, here a divine symbol of soft and transparent light, is resting its beneficial influence upon a dream of that temple which is no more. The title, however, was not the program, but rather an attempt to convey with words the impression created by the music.

111

Again the tonal "gourmet," Debussy, is like an artisan setting rare gems in precious metal and enjoying the beauty of their radiant fires.

In the opening series of chords and their later usage, the sounds may have been those of consecutive chords of the ninth, displaced upon the degrees of a constant and very gentle melody, but the craftsman has purified these chords of the ninth by abstracting the third and seventh and placing them in second inversion; the result is very melodious and softly scintillating.

The entire piece is the work of a "tone-alchemist." Its inherent qualities include the conveying of the immobility of ancient things, the transparency of buildings, hollowed and gutted by time, the poetic tenderness of the sensitive artist toward the mysterious past and his contemplative simplicity. It has the serene severity of "organum," but the moonlight softens even this aspect.

An exhaustive analysis of the work would show that the tonal texture is freely but minutely evolved at times in Aeolian mode, then Hypodorian, and Myxolydian, with short sections in a diagonal chromaticism resulting from the alternated contrary position of consecutive chords of the seventh.

Note the reminiscences of the texture of "Nuages," measure 31. It conveys the impression of great space and contemplative silence.

In the performance, the aim is to convey a sensitive transposition of something unseen in nature, yet present in a dream.

In the first five measures, one should work toward the cohesion and perfect legato of six violins, expressive but pure.

The dash (−) on B (measure 6) indicates a continuation of the dominant feeling established in the first five measures. It establishes a tonic-dominant pedal-point from measures 6-11. The chords moving above it are very sensitive if one acknowledges the delicate harmonic tensions caused by the major seventh succeeding the major or minor triads, which are so presented as to convey the parallel dissonances of organum. When the chords have a dash and a dot above them, they need a gentle percussive quality, as of a SFZ-PP.

In measure 14, the two rhythms superimposed must be very exact and with no rubato. The crosswise chromatic progression of measures

16-17 must be smoothly heard, and in measure 18 the syncopated F-natural needs to receive its normal stress.

In measures 27-28, the upper pattern must be very fugitive, and fluid. The section beginning measure 29 must show very exact rhythms, and at measure 31 an utter legato of both voices must be obtained, but without chord-mixtures through ill-use of the pedal.

Most of what follows demands the same care as is here suggested.

While consciousness of the modality is eloquent in helping the realization of phrasing, stresses and releases, the overall requisite demands a study of the work similar to that accorded fugal style. It should be read with the horizontal vision of counterpoint, seeking melodic continuity, and avoiding the tonal opacity which would result from holding notes beyond their duration through a misuse or abuse of pedals.

For example: In measure 39, hold the first beat F-G with the right hand until the left hand has played the low B♭; then, holding just those three notes, affix them with the sustaining pedal as the clearly sounding bass. One should be conscious of the fact that G is the most stressed, not B♭.

In looking attentively through this score, you will discover many such important subtleties, the sum of which can make or destroy the aesthetics of the performance.

POISSONS D'OR

On the exact stimulus for the composition of this work, there is a real field-day for musicographers, and a remarkable lesson on "how history is written," for out of a number of otherwise rather reliable and/or complete sources on the works of Debussy, one gets the rather puzzling, not to say hysterical, statistics below:

The inspiration for this piece is:

(1) A piece of embroidery.

(2) A number of goldfishes in a bowl.

(3) At least two goldfishes in an open-air pool, with stones.

(4) A Japanese print ("Estampe").

(5) A panel of black "Chinese" lacquer on which are designed two fishes in gold and mother-of-pearl.

(6) A crystal bowl supposedly located on Debussy's desk and containing goldfishes.

(7) General love of nature.

Finally, two sources agree that it was a piece of Japanese lacquer owned by Debussy, showing one goldfish and its reflection in the water, a photograph of which is found in Maurice Boucher's book, and the original of which is well remembered by the habitués of Debussy's studio. This object lesson in documentation only proves that once the original stimulus has acted, Debussy's transmutation evades the specific and concentrates on the universal aspects—in this case, of goldfish.

Indeed, for those who understand symbolic tracery, the multiple characteristics of an imagined scene are amazingly conveyed; the delicate finning of a goldfish maintaining an almost stationary position, then its rapid impulse of fins and fast gliding, the sudden changes of direction of its capricious motions, its colorful brilliancy and the iridescence caused by the glancing of sun-rays through the water on the shining gold of its scales, the feeling of its weightless nature, the scintillating gleams of its undulating metallic coat, the delicately stirred surface of the water in the wake of its motions—all these variations are contained in this piece, yet it never describes a fish; its subject matter is motion and the interplay of gold, sun-rays, and water.

The ending and beginning emphasis on F♯ are only passing bows to the key signature in a tonal and harmonic texture which is as capricious in its changes of directions and colors as the subject matter. The treatment of diatonic passages places rhythmic and reiterative emphasis away from tonic and dominant in an apt escape from capture, the further bichordality and bitonality of numerous passages bring a rich friction of poles; chromatic progressions tense the fabric, which wholetoned portions then suspend, in a hide-and-seek game with pentatonic clusters. We are in constant pursuit, and are constantly pursued in this miraculously colorful palette, to the details of which only a major thesis could do justice.

The structure elects rondo form for its general delineations, as follows:

Bars 1-7. A, first theme.

Bars 8-9. Transition.

Bars 10-17. B, second theme.

Bars 18-21. Transition, based on opening motif of A.

Bars 22-29. A, first theme.

Bars 30-45. C, interrupted at measures 32-33 by a portion of the first A section, of which the bass melody forms a complementary curve, or answer, to the two opening measures of C.

Bars 46-55. A, repeated three times but very varied as to rhythm, and with alternation of diatonic and whole-toned colors.

Bars 55-56. Transition.

Bars 57-79. D, originating in rhythmic pulsations, its bass melody is born at measure 64, and worked out in sequences to measure 72, then in alternation with a rubato phrase, measures 72-79.

Bars 80-93. A, followed by a coda at measures 94-105, in the form of a cadenza, bitonal, and non-thematic.

Before performing this work it is important to be convinced that the body of a goldfish is luminous and almost transparent, and that it displaces itself quite suddenly by dashes of rapid timing. It is also important to realize that goldfishes live in clear water, which is easily stirred by their motions, and that light is affected by its incidence on agitated water surfaces. One can then approach the work with the intent of obtaining transparency, precision, elegance, and lightness of performance, avoiding opacity and the mistaking of a goldfish for a whale, or even an old carp.

Section A: The tremolo in thirty-second-notes of the opening measures and in frequent recurrences, must be timed exactly so that the interplay of the two parts may form a clear trill, for instance, between A♯ and G double-sharp in measures 1-2. As indicated by the composer, this trill must be "as light as possible." In measures 3-4, the iambic thirty-second-note to half- or eighth-note in the upper voice must be like a jerking of the fins, clear and rapid. Note the marking of Debussy: a slur and two accents, one of pitch on the thirty-second-note, another durational and harmonic, increasing on the second note. The upper voice is marked P and "marqué" (marked), but the two lower staves remain in their original nuance of PP. There should be no rubato in the transition of measures 8-9.

Section B: In measures 10-11, the rubato is created through the strict observance of the groups of five sixteenth-notes set against the binary rhythm of the right-hand part. In measures 14-15, the bass pedal-point can be taken by the sustaining pedal and the damper pedal can then be changed for each of the right-hand chords; the arpeggi are rapid, light, unobtrusive, but the last one (end of measure 15) in true timing asserts the crescendo. In measures 16-17, the left-hand trills (all on major seconds) must have the dynamic nuance of Sf to PP subito. Note in measures 18-22, the difference between notes marked with dashes which are held, and those marked with dots, which are short and light.

Section A: Earlier discussion applies to this return of the opening section.

Section C: The motif presented in this section is much more capricious than those used previously, yet it obtains its continuity within its own dynamic level. The arpeggi should be clear, rapid, and light, and one should avoid maintaining their resonance over the ensuing quarter-note. The grace notes should not be blurred with the chords, which they ornament; played at the ultimate moment, they yet remain detached from the ensuing cluster. It is interesting to note the fact that the grace notes are chromatic to this section in which whole-toned and pentatonic fragments coexist. In measure 45, the appoggiaturas of the arpegietto must be gently stressed, and the chord outline rendered clearly intelligible.

Section A: Again in this section, one notes the dynamic preference given to the upper staff with MF, whereas the lower two staves are indicated as P. This means that the agitation and rapidity of the thirty-second-notes must in no way compete with the sonority of the theme. In the transition, or episode that interrupts the section (measures 48-50), note the interesting effect of bipentatonism; the dotted notes on a black-key pentatonic series in friction to which the short-durations are on a white-key pentatonic. Note the slurs, yet do not hold the short durations over the longer ones. At measure 51, the considerations of the opening of the section are resumed. In measure 55 build the onrush which impetuously seeks the luminous climax of measure 56.

Section D: The strong C♯ pedal of the opening of this section (measure 57) gives way to a very precise, measured texture, non-rubato. Note the differentiated use, once again, of dashes and dots. The crescendo of this section is built steadily, but not with an accelerando. It attains its first peak in measures 72-73, a frisky agitation of golden glimmer, and a second peak in the legato, rubato, turbulent, and troubled texture of measures 74-75. A repetition of this contrast is contained in measures 76-80.

Section A: The return of the first theme is flashingly dramatic; its fin motions are violent; the texture remains climactic and turbulent to measure 86, where the lightness of the initial statement is recaptured in even greater transparency.

Cadenza: The opening of the cadenza "à la Liszt" is very free in its acceleration, but its poly- and bitonal effects must remain perceptible. One pedal for each group of five notes is unthinkable! Note that from measure 98, the friction resolves itself to the superimposition of the F♯ major tonic and the C major scale. Measures 103-104 return to measured timing and to a peaceful dynamic level, despite the continued bitonal friction and the colorful minor to major outlining of the F♯ chord in the two measures. The major form wins out in the final measure.

CHILDREN'S CORNER (1909)

How often in paying spontaneous tribute to another does the person who writes reveal his own sensitive qualities, aspirations, understanding. One reads in Debussy's own words (*Monsieur Croche*, p. 42-43)* his evaluation of Moussorgsky's children's song cycle ("The Nursery," composed 1868–70) and through his warm appraisal of the humanity of the Russian genius, to whom he has more than one point of likeness, one glimpses Debussy's own deeply abiding tenderness:

"Sometimes, too, Moussorgsky conveys shadowy sensations of trembling anxiety which move and wring the heart. In the *Nursery* there is the prayer of a little girl before she falls asleep which conveys the thoughts and the sensitive emotions of a child, the delightful ways of little girls pretending to be grown-up; all with a sort of feverish truth of interpretation only to be found here. The *Doll's Lullaby* would seem to have been conceived word by word, through an amazing power of sympathetic interpretation and of visualizing the realms of that special fairyland peculiar to the mind of a child. The end of the lullaby is so gently drowsy that the little singer falls asleep over her own fancies. . . . All these little dramas are set down, I repeat, with the utmost simplicity. . . . We shall have more to say about Moussorgsky; he has many claims to our devotion."

* Dover edition, pp. 19-20.

Indeed, through an "amazing power of sympathetic interpretation and of visualizing," Debussy also composed the series of musical gems, "The Children's Corner," in 1908, for his daughter Chouchou, then five years old. The titles were in English, a form of humor, alluding to Chouchou's English governess.

Great artists are often accused of being too egocentric to care for various members of their family, but, in the case of Debussy, it is a well-established fact that for his only child he experienced a very tender love. "The Children's Corner" is as though the great composer had bent his own stature to donate the best of his art to the infant child. When Chouchou was still very young, her father would bring her some delightful little toys (as most fathers might well do). But then he would ponder over their real significance to the child (few fathers might still do this); it was not merely toys he wanted to give Chouchou, but an incentive to Joy! And so, he conceived that she could really derive joy from the toys when induced to make the little elephant walk and go to sleep, when she would have a serenade to play to her doll, when she would hear the little shepherd play some tunes on his reed and dance, and when she would make the Golliwog, the little Negro puppet-doll, dance a cake-walk, during which he would take those sublime and grotesque postures that only the greatest dancers, or the articulated toys, can perform. So came the inspiration to write the finest music to complete the make-believe universe of his beloved Chouchou; a music that would inspire her to play, to imbue her playthings with joy and life; it was a real labor of love, binding his consummate skill, his orchestral wizardry, to the miniature music for his adored child . . . a gift of love and humility. "To my beloved little Chouchou, with the tender excuses of her father for that which follows," reads the Dedication to "Children's Corner." Little did Debussy dream then that ten years from this date, he would be separated from his daughter, to be reunited only a year after, through her own untimely death.

DOCTOR GRADUS AD PARNASSUM

In his letter to his editor, J. Durand, on August 15, 1908, Debussy says: " 'Doctor Gradus ad Parnassum' is a sort of hygienic and progressive gymnastics; it should therefore be played every morning, before breakfast, beginning at 'modéré,' and winding up to 'animé.' I hope that the clarity of this explanation will delight you." The mischievous humor underlying this brief program is the keynote of this charming take-off on solemn and pedantic piano exercises "à la Clementi or Czerny?"

It is up to the listener to decide whether Debussy is here encouraging Chouchou to a rebellion worthy of her father's Conservatoire days, or whether he is merely observing her struggle with these tyrant exercises . . . a struggle begun in all earnest, but soon departed from for more imaginative patterns, returning to the lesson at hand, yawning, slowing down, in daydreaming and distractions—a fly on the ceiling can evoke such a series of delightful adventures—and brilliantly concluding, with the bogeymen vanquished and laid aside.

Debussy makes no concessions in harmonic color; he realizes the child's immense capacity for uninhibited colorings, a ready adaptability and delight in varied palettes which preconceived notions have not yet marred.

From a basic C-major assumption, which returns several times, and closes the composition, the harmonic scheme romps through modal sections, series of chords outlining juxtapositions nearly bitonal in their essence, a number of diatonic schemes, and successive polytonality in his approach to the orthodox cadence.

Using the strict exercise as a refrain, this rondo emphasizes its free episodes by the contrast they offer in harmonic coloring rather than in rhythmic or melodic contour. The augmentations of the refrain in the third page serve admirably as a central slowing of the "perpetuum mobile" character of this piece, and emphasize its structural strength. A few points may be noted on the performance.

It stands to reason in a rapidly evolving harmonic series, of which the patterns form the chord outlines, that the running together, or blurring, of successive harmonies is undesirable in projecting the richness of their evolution and departures. Further, out of these chord outlines is born a melody, which, by the very markings of Debussy, is assigned the independence of a separate voice, in counterpoint with the moving bass, and must be given preference over the other components of the chords. Marked "without dryness," the interpretation automatically forbids the use of brittle, percussive touches, staccato and unphrased, for even in the strict refrain Debussy's humor remains subtle.

Note that the harmonic rhythm of the opening measures and successive similar passages encourages the assumption within the large phrase of a secondary phrasing of two groups of four notes together, the first of these groups receiving as a whole (not by one note at a time) a slightly greater strength than the second. For instance: In measure 1, the first phrase building up to the E and resolving to D on the beginning of beat 3; the next phrase building up to the F on the fourth beat and resolving to the E on the first beat of the next measure, etc. Though this phrasing must not be overdone, it foreshadows the texture of the next line, and renders more explicit the preparation for the independent voices.

It is suggested that on the opening bass note, its resonance be held by the left hand, and not the sustaining pedal, which would then lend some of its resonance to each C heard in the patterns—and destroy their harmonic value. However, in passages such as measures 7-10, the use of the sustaining pedal is quite in keeping with the harmonic construction.

JIMBO'S LULLABY

Jimbo, a little velvet elephant, pudgy and soft, one of those favorites of Chouchou's allowed to partake of the ceremonials of her own bedtime; but the little elephant, too, must have *one last* story, *one last* song before entering the land of Nod, with his charming little mistress.

The opening melody (measures 1-9, 21-28, 63-70) is true to the slow, awkward gait of the little elephant, with the modal-pentatonic delineation suggesting the mystery and exoticism of his "genre." A second material brings us the lullaby per se; using again the well-known and richly associated children's lullaby, "Dodo, fait dodo . . ." (also in "Jardins sous la pluie"), the mood is at first only suggested (measures 11-14) but later becomes explicit (measures 39-46). A third material, first heard at measures 29-38, has a plaintive, insistent quality (more noticeable in its later chromatic descent and sudden, marked skip up).

120

Is it Jimbo or Chouchou who is pleading for a little more singing, some way of stalling for time before going to sleep? Or perhaps reacting to a scary episode from a fairy tale. The material returns after the lullaby (measures 47-62), then it serves as the counter-subject for the first melody (measures 63-67), and finally ends the piece, reduced to its last thirty-second-notes, and slowed down gradually into the oblivion of slumber.

It is a rich structure in the alternation of these three materials and their interplay, and a rich harmonic color ranging from the pentatonic series on a modal scheme, through diatonic bitonalism, and chromaticism to a final cadence which reconciles all these elements with the B♭ tonal center, now a common denominator.

In the performance the first thing to notice is that the dynamic range is from P to PP to PPP and shadings between; its soft character must be maintained as a general level within which the various dynamics of the materials can be calculated to be in correct proportion to each other.

Note that the melodic materials which have a greater expressive life than the various pedal figures, harmonic or contrapuntal notes that accompany them, are frequently in middle voices, and oppose their sonorities to the surrounding materials. The first melody and the lullaby are legato in character, whereas the third material is partially but lightly detached. In the pedal figures one will also observe some legato and others lightly detached. A close observance of these changes in touch in their relation to each other, and of the phrasings proper to each material as marked by Debussy, will bring a rich interplay of the varied personalities of these sonorities.

In the last eight measures the retard is made within the musical texture by the augmentation and should not be added to by a change of tempo in which the musical material (motif of the third theme) would be lost.

SERENADE FOR THE DOLL

This serenade was published separately in 1906, and may have formed the early basis for the entire series.

A favorite doll, a companion who shares the play and confidences of

Chouchou, perhaps battered from wear, but none the less loved by its owner. What is more natural than to wish for a special piece for this most important friend?

As in the préludes, the thought association to a serenade immediately conjures the tones of a plucked guitar or banjo, adding its whimsical patterns and touch to this light and graceful miniature.

The opening material, an ornamented melody, opposes its pentatonic quality to the steady E-major pedals above or below it, for although its component notes are well within the E-major scale, its tone centers do not capitulate to this assumption except at the cadences of its main phrases. Another charming capacity of this main melody is the ease with which it answers itself a fifth above (measures 3-7 versus 9-13), a capacity put in sharp relief by the last statement of this material in which the opening three notes of the melody answer each other P and MF at the two ranges (measures 106-114).

A first episode (measures 14-30) has a sequential character, chromatic in a gentle way yet bringing a tenser dynamic level. A return of the first material (measures 30-34), more heavily scored, brings a freshness of decided syncopation which foreshadows not only the character of the ensuing episode but of the middle portion (measures 66-83), a jazz-inspired dance, intricate in its displacement of accents and sinuous polyrhythms within the miniature field. A scherzando whimsy is brought in the final episode (93-105).

As to performance, Debussy's recommendation that the soft pedal be held during the entire piece, even in the places marked with an F, apparently hints at keeping the child-scope of this dynamically move-mented serenade, which could easily, through its rhythmic and melodic variety, assume very adult proportions. It may also protect that plucked (but soft) sound of the guitar or banjo, as well as the overall character of lightness and charm asked of the performer at the beginning.

The rhythmic elements and the dynamic sharp contrasts, within the general level adopted, are the two elements recommended to the performer's close attention, with the contrasts of legato and staccato also, which offer much of the charm of this piece.

How many children, kept home from the cold, have watched at the window, their foreheads glued to the glass, the enchanting fascination of falling snow? Gentle flakes falling softly, gradually multiplying, bring an undefined nostalgia and uneasiness of this world, lost in white, but the wind lashes the bits of ice against the windowpane, the snow's dance whirls dervish-like, diminishes, and gradually returns to the poetic charm of single, floating flakes.

In this exquisitely fashioned piece Debussy reflects more than the snow, or the astonishment of the child at this wonder of nature; he places his craftsmanship at the disposal of his own deep understanding of both nature and childhood.

It is interesting to note how the opening measures of this work form the pervading material, integrating the whole. Prominent at times, underlying other sections as ostinato or accompaniment, faster or slower, recalling the first material or blending with a contrasting section, this unifying motif is a subtly tenacious "germ motif." Its first presentation is not without tonal as well as pictorial significance. In a D-minor assumption, it ascends from the second degree to the fifth of the scale. The whole notes (measures 3-6) add the sixth degrees, then the lowered seventh, finally the raised seventh, so that the tonic, which starts a series in contrary motion at measure 7, has the value of a long anticipated resolution. Consecutive tritones in the middle voices and the nature of the melody with its opening diminished fourth (measures 22-29) bring much of the bleakness felt in this second portion of the opening section.

It foreshadows the even more affirmed dissonance, and rhythmic tortuousness of the swirling middle section, ominous in its windswept iciness (measures 34-52). Evolving basically from Dorian to F minor, and E♭ minor the section is rich in friction of pedals (repeated or trilled), ostinato motifs, and agitated melodic levels.

A chromatic transition ascending (measures 53-56), despite its very nature, serves to bring back the peace of the opening section which closes the composition with one last but very subdued reference to the middle material (measures 67-69). The opening ostinato serves to ap-

123

proach the final cadence which, through its minute oscillations, gives uncertainty even to this final D-minor assumption.

In the performance observe and safeguard the differentiated interpretation of the notes marked by dots, lightly detached from each other, but generally soft, and the notes marked by dashes heavier and held legato. In the middle section the repeated notes which begin one of the important melodic motifs should build a gentle crescendo to the three notes with dashes that succeed the repetition. In this section great attention to exactitude of rhythms is demanded by the polyrhythmic superimposition of pedals, ostinato, and melody.

The use of the forte pedal should be more conspicuous by its absence, or very slight usage, than by its presence. A slightly absorbent touch in the detached notes will guarantee the soft roundness desired by Debussy. The long values held by the fingers, in the first page at least, will guarantee that the pedal is unnecessary and will not need to come and melt the snow!

THE LITTLE SHEPHERD

How best to characterize a little shepherd? Of course, by the simple but delicately expressive melodies of his reed instrument, at times thoughtful, at times joyous, but always flowing and free in the rhythm of its improvised cadenzas. A single voice in the clear air to which the restrained accompaniment lends a passing depth and emphasizes the harmonic color of its overtones, echoed by nature.

The rhythmic freedom and variety of this flowing melody remind one of the unfettered delineation of plainsong, to which the very secular dotted rhythm brings the contrast of a dance-like gaiety. Though all the cadences are diatonic and definitely indicate A major, it is only a sophisticated turn of the Phrygian and Dorian modalities of the majority sections of the charming pastoral in ternary form. Note, in measures 24-25, the echo effects in the return of the first section.

The key to the interpretation is a soft and expressive simplicity, sensitive freedom of the melodic line, and only a slight rubato. A tighter interpretation naturally suits the passages in dotted rhythm. An effective arrestation of motion and peace comes from the dying off of

124

resonance at the fermata of the fourth measure and in each of the cadences. Do not rush through these quiet periods, so effective in the overall charm of the composition, so necessary to place in relief the sinuosity of the melodic line. The slight retard (five measures from the end) is yet commented with "en conservant le rythme" ("while conserving the rhythm") of the dotted motif.

Golliwog's cake-walk

Golliwog, the little black doll created by Florence Upton in 1895, and whose name is possibly derived from "polliwog," was sure of immediate success with all children—and many grownups. His hair standing on end, a large red smile and round eyes, and his disjointed stances, supple and grotesque, were titillating factors in his immense popularity, insured in Europe by his simultaneous appearance with newly imported and sought-after minstrel groups.

No modality here—our jazzy playmate is diatonic basically. But, in electing the keys of E♭ major and G♭ major for the two main materials of his dance, he still spices them with altered ninth chords, added sixth chords, chromatic passages, appoggiaturas sounded with chords, passing bitonality; a syncopated harmony to match the rhythmic dexterity of our friend's supple cake-walk.

Humor in quantities is brought by sudden halts, sharp accents, dynamic contrasts, as the vertiginous virtuosity of the little puppet takes us through an array of dance steps, of grotesque poses, tumbles, recoveries . . . and Debussy gets in his ironic fling in an interrupted passage of the middle section, a delightful take-off on the prelude to "Tristan and Isolde," "with great emotion."

After saying so many do's and don'ts, it is a joy to be able to say that this is one of Debussy's least misinterpreted pieces. It is probable that its very direct appeal and infectious gaiety win out over any possible misconceptions.

HOMMAGE À HAYDN (1909)

In 1909, the centenary of the death of Haydn was celebrated by the S.I.M. (Société Internationale de Musique) in the form of a special issue of a collection of musical tributes by living composers to the memory of Haydn; works by such composers as Vincent d'Indy, Paul Dukas, Maurice Ravel, and so forth, completed the volume for which Debussy wrote this delightful piece. In speaking of it to his editor, J. Durand, he explains that it has no other purpose on this planet or any other but to pay homage to Joseph Haydn.

Fashioned on the letters of Haydn's name it reminds us of the German fashion of deriving fugue themes from the letters of the names of famous men, or places. In this particular instance, the all-pervading motif is B-A-D-D-G, arrived at by starting with the German appellation of B, i.e., *H;* one continues with *A* in its normal position, then the first *D* must be found three octaves higher, where in continuing the alphabet through it would be *Y,* the next *D* is taken in normal scale order, and the G is transposed one octave to where it would give *N* by again extending the alphabet. Though this crossword puzzle may seem more apt to a book on cloak-and-dagger decoding of secret documents, if one derives a certain amusement from it, one will then not forget that Debussy was sensitive to humor and often gave proof of his own rapid wit and prankish, though fleeting, moments of fun.

The short piece is a veritable lexicon of the usages one can make of the aforementioned motif; a true ricercar, or research, it marries into a tightly woven whole the techniques of counterpoint, of variation form, and even of the Lisztian principle of the "metamorphosis of themes," with the highly Debussyan freedom of harmony and tonality, the levels of pedal-points, evolving inner voice harmonies, and the treatment of ostinatos. Such condensed richness in the simplicity of this work should give any student a field day.

In the slow waltz opening section, the motif appears late on the already well-established texture of the opening melody and its characteristic harmonies; here it partakes of the expressive and soft character, a complementary soprano answer to the opening bass melody. But in the last measure of the section (measure 22) its first diminution engenders the opening of the second section (measure 23). This second section brings in also the contrast of the motif in augmentation and in choral passages first in the bass (measures 31-35), in the soprano crescendo (measures 43-47), and finally in the high treble, fragmented and stac-

126

cato (measures 53-56). The third section brings to the motif a martial, animated, and querulous portent; gradually it is tightened and diminished rhythmically, while accruing a heavier scoring, and its chromatic bass, which starts by an evolution every two notes, is in effect also tensed later as a straight chromatic passage.

An accumulated tension converges to the apex of the entire piece in the two measures in $3/4$ in which scoring, broad augmentation, and harmony all work to the exaltation of Haydn's name! The dynamic level quickly drops and this last big section ends with high echoes of the first three notes of the motif over held pedal-points. A genial two-measure return to the opening slow waltz sets the scene for the last fleet arabesque on our motif, a surprise twist which serves as a charming hyphen (trait d'union) between Debussy and Haydn.

It is obvious that the primary duty of interpretation will be to preserve in each section the character of its mood and to set into sharp relief the adventures of the Puckish motif; yet the relation of the tempi and of the sections has a classical unity which an overall caution must adopt as canvas, or else risk losing the charm of this quasi-serious, quasi-humorous composition by making it patchy.

LA PLUS QUE LENTE (1910)

"Let us think of cabarets, let us think also of the numerous 'five o'clocks' where the beautiful feminine listeners of whom I thought, meet." With this light touch Debussy wrote this charming waltz, sometimes so sensitive as to betray a youthful romantic earnestness, and at other moments impulsive and frivolous, a turn which makes one wonder if Debussy's tongue was not a little in his cheek! The very popular melodies are yet given freshness by subtle harmonies. It may be the inspiration came from the New Carlton Hotel in Paris where Debussy went with his wife, Emma, to be charmed by the gypsy fiddling of a violinist named Leoni, to whom the MSS was given by Debussy. A very popular tune in Paris at that time was "La valse lente," hence the humorous title of "La plus que lente" for the present work. The work was orchestrated by Debussy for the tympanon. It is music definitely meant for a wide appeal, and not really a stylized, super-sophisticated take-off on the popular genre; it maintains a sensitive balance, even in its passages of humor, devoid of grotesqueness or grossness sometimes found in later parodies of popular tunes.

In the performance, subtle amounts of rubato, allargando, and contrasting animation must follow Debussy's indications and the multiple curves and allusions of the melodies without losing the basic, and most danceable, waltz spirit.

Puerta del Vino

4.

Piano Works 1910-1915

Book I, "Twelve Préludes," published in 1910; Book II, "Twelve Préludes," published in 1913.

We choose at present to consider Debussy's twenty-four préludes, published in two volumes, as one work, in that the two books are a natural sequel to each other in their musical texture, moods, techniques, subject matters. That the second series should at times prove more advanced in its musical language, more difficult in its interpretations, and perhaps tending toward a more abstract treatment of its literary connotations, is only a normal evolution, not a break in style. The last préludes of the second book pave the way for the "Études," give us a brief preview of the style to come, and of the steps in its achievement.

In writing préludes, Debussy continues the natural evolution of this form: from its classical position as preliminary movement or introduction to the main body of a composition. Chopin gave it the completeness of a single, independent movement, and endowed it with a rich, poetic, and imaginative role. A number of romantic composers followed the fashion set by Chopin in series of préludes for the piano. To this evolution of the independent prélude Debussy added a complexity of materials and a completeness of form, which, without losing its essential characteristic of brevity, brought the prélude to its highest point of development.

In the fashioning of these perfect miniatures Debussy has paid the highest compliment to the performers and the public, for he has entrusted to their care his intimate thoughts, his reactions and impressions to a multitude of varied and delightful subjects, sharing many moods, bringing not only the realism of his sharp etching of his subject matter, but also his personal comments—and with the additional compliment of a compactness, of a concentration of material, an absence of repetition which reminds us not only of the oft-quoted "Brevity is the soul of wit," an apt application here, but also of the birth of a century devoted to the exploration of explosive, deceptive minutiae (viz. the A-bomb and vitamin pills).

There is nothing desiccated about the préludes; the full rich flavor of each subject is there, a rapid view of the ensemble, a few telling scratches of the pen—the picture is complete, unmistakable, so much so in fact that independent commentaries on the préludes in dozens of different countries, by dozens of different people, have a coincidence of tone and matter which is indeed a tribute to Debussy's precision of suggestion.

The pianistic style of the préludes again evokes Debussy's heritage from Chambonnières, Rameau, Couperin, in the etched contours, the clarity of style, supple melodies, rhythmic precision, and simplicity of form. The structure, basically ternary and frequently in rondo-sonata form, is yet not a preconceived framework, but is generated by the materials, by the palette Debussy elects—waves of engendering waves, an unbeatable logic within the structure of which the end product, under Debussy's control, attains on all points the demands of classical aesthetics.

In placing the titles of the préludes at the end of each piece, Debussy avoids the coyness of those who have a subject and won't say what its program is. He also makes clear that the music is of first importance, and the stimulus to its added enjoyment is only an afterthought, a helping hand for those who need it, and a confirmation for those who are wavering, and of no importance for those who have found their own thoughts so completely in the music as to need no further suggestions.

Only a man who had Debussy's mature technique, of sharpened and tested tools, could express himself so perfectly. But only a man with a magnificent wealth of knowledge, of experience, of intuition could use these tools to characterize so sharply and so briefly the infinite array and range of subjects of these twenty-four works, which whirl through legends, literature, vaudeville, painting, architectural landmarks, archeological objects, natural phenomena, a multitude of scenes and of personages, each individualized, crystallized, in the moment of Debussy's creation.

In opening these albums of préludes, one wonders at the wisdom of giving them further commentary. One nearly halts in one's task to say, with Debussy: "Give ear to no man's counsel; but listen to the wind which tells in passing the history of the world."

DANSEUSES DE DELPHES (BOOK I)

NATURE. Delphi is the name of a city of Ancient Greece, and is located at the foot of Mount Parnassus, the site of the Temple of Apollo (God of Oracles, Poetry, and Arts). In this temple the oracles of the Pythia were rendered. Although we doubt that there were female dancers in Delphi proper, this dance evokes dignified religious and languid motions. The stimulus for its creation came more probably from reproductions of ancient sculpture, rather than from the exact history of the ritual of the Apollo festivals.

In such sculpture, or on certain vases, one may see the images of young maidens dancing and playing musical instruments. In this prélude, Debussy has added the exotic sense of mythological characters, of incantations and incense, of the plastic symmetry of Grecian art, and the sharp contrast of its percussive musical accompaniments.

There is a graveness and sustained quality of the music which is diametrically opposed to Dionysian extremes, and yet this gravity is enveloped by a lightness of touch, as if the dancers were clad in veils or enfolded by curving wisps of incense.

Rich in materials, this first prélude is a lexicon of the usages to be developed in its twenty-three successive companions. By fragments modal, then diatonic, then pentatonic, then chromatic, it is yet related by a basic assumption of classical relationship in its tone centers, leading from the tonic to the dominant and related keys, and returning to the tonic. It also contains the basic assumption of all the préludes, a distribution of its materials at several separate and independent levels. A contrapuntal usage, and one in which interpretation must as a corollary demand an independence of interpretation for each level. In this particular instance the three levels are: the sustained-plastic melody in

131

dotted rhythm; the gently detached chords which serve as the light frame of the melody, sometimes below, sometimes above, sometimes in the midst of it, and which also serve as the ornamental frame ending each important phrase; the percussive accents, incisive and metallic, of the major seconds representing the "crotals," small cymbals attached to the fingers and used by the priests of Cybele, the Goddess of Earth and mother of Jupiter, Neptune, and Pluto in Greek mythology. They were also used by maiden dancers, such as Bacchantes or the attendants to deities. Many, indeed, are the varied materials that go into the crucible, from which Debussy conjures this remarkably concise but pungent prélude.

INTERPRETATION. The very nature of the three levels of musical development in this piece gives the basic clue to its interpretation: the melody softly sustained and expressive, capable of rhythmic developments; the frame chords gently detached, impersonal, opposed in effect to the expressive melody, and also the third, incisive interpretation of the metallic crotals, which must carry a resonant tone, ringing with multiple harmonies, vibrating in ever-larger circles around their fundamental tones (measures 8-9 and 16-17). Soft pedal (bars 1-2). To emphasize the melody (B♭, B, C, C♯), we suggest abducting the arm, thus lifting the chord, but keeping the melody note depressed. The pedal will maintain the total effect of the three planes: bass, melody, and harmony. (Difference in dynamism, PP and P for the melody).

Note that the melody obtains a crescendo which follows the pitch ascent in each of the two first measures. While this crescendo continues to the completion of the melody in the fourth measure, the third measure also takes into consideration accents on the longer note values. This interpretation holds good to measure 11, where pitch is given preference over duration, and brings accents on the last sixteenth-note of each beat. In the seventh measure from the end, the accents are on the second and third beats, with the chord on the sixteenth-note continuing the crescendo between these strong beats. The last eighth-note of the measure in the right hand, the chord, is light, but the left hand slurred to the first beat of the next measure receives a contradictory accent.

In the pedaling, one must change pedals sufficiently fast and often to avoid catching the frame-chords, particularly in passages such as that beginning eleven measures from the end, in which the pedal is changed each half-beat. Conversely, the crotal chords must be given full chance along with the melody to ring freely for the full note value, but not beyond, for this would result in a blurring of many sounds!

Voiles (Book I)

NATURE. Ascribed diversely as suggesting "sailing boats anchored to a fixed pedal-point," and "mysterious veils enveloping palpitating feminine forms, hiding eyes which fan desire by their devious glances," this prélude in the memory of the author was given both connotations by Debussy, i.e., veils or sails.

One of the most perfect examples of the use of the whole-toned scale, it maintains a sense of supple harmoniousness without lacking in dynamic design and great clarity of structure.

The very use of the whole-tone scale (except for measure 31 which is chromatic, and a short passage in pentatonic, starting at measure 48) offers a color palette more elusive than that of the diatonic system, for the absence of the half-step and the equality of the whole-steps in succession does not form a spatial pull of gravity among the tones of the series. Dissonance cannot be achieved by minor seconds or major sevenths, but only through the major second. As is later stated, rhythm has to interfere to signalize which tones of this unichrome series the composer may elect to consider centers of rest, or centers of tension and activity.

In this particular case the series includes: G♯-A♭-B♭-C-D-E-F♯. From this tonal scheme two teams have been elected to oppose each other, i.e., one to act as the tonic team, the other as the dominant team. Any member of each team represents the full tonal function or flavor of the entire team. Thus G♯-A♭-C and E are the members of the tonic team and can substitute for each other or be used together to form points of rest. Their neighboring tones, F♯-D-B♭ form the dominant team and points of tension. The interrelation of these two teams is described in greater detail as the various materials of this prélude are considered.

LEVELS. The prélude is built with three independent contrapuntal levels: the pictorial ostinato, the pedal, and the melody.

The first of these to appear is the whole-toned ostinato stated in the opening four measures. Here one has a descriptive musical equivalent for the billows of the sails or veils, a gentle breeze setting into motion this material which at one moment is taut, then relaxed. The ostinato in its own design is a counterpart to this conception. In the first measure and a half it rises obliquely from the rest of its tone-center G♯ (or A♭) to the peak and momentary rest on the dissonant neighboring tones of F♯ and B♭. The next two and a half measures relax the tension by a decreasing pitch line and repose attained on the cadence C, E.

The very sharply defined rhythm of the note durations of this opening figure (1 long, 3 short, 1 long, 1 short, 1 long) further emphasizes the movement of the billow and also lends artificial support to the cadences (artificial since such cadences in the whole-tone scale are elected by the composer and not dictated by the physical relationship spatially of the component series of tones).

The pedal B♭ is the next level introduced and one which links the entire prélude. It is a syncopated throb or pulse at first (measure 5), later a sustained pedal (measure 21), and still later a metric pulse (measure 48). Its nature is that of a dominant pedal, sometimes agreeing with the progression above it, and at other times creating friction.

The third level, which enters in the seventh measure, is the melody, or theme, of the prélude, also whole-toned. Its character is legato and the lower range in which it appears lends it body and lyricism, prevailing in dynamics over the two other materials. This melody, too, partakes of a large classical curve. Hesitant at first, its opening three notes are repeated, and gain strength ascending from the tonal center to the fifth above and dwindling back to a cadence on the tonal center, G♯ (or A♭). This curve of the melody must not be destroyed by the entrance of the ostinato above, and the change to the left hand on D. The ascending three notes of the beginning are frequently used as a development and unifying motif of the prélude.

Besides these three levels there are several passages to which attention must be directed. In the section beginning at measure 22, it will be noted that a second pedal figure is added over the now stationary B♭. Its dotted rhythm and skips automatically place emphasis on the notes D and F♯, i.e., members of the dominant team, thus forming a secondary dominant pedal. Over this, both in measures 23 and 24, points of rest are reached on dominant notes, and this well-established dominant feeling leads to the emphasized appoggiaturas of dominant to tonic at measures 26 and 27.

Chromatic contrary motion used antiphonally in the two upper voices in measure 31 is also noteworthy. Both voices converge toward durational rests on notes which belong to the tonic team, a veritable gem of contrapuntal writing.

In measure 32 a new pedal figure is introduced. It is basically a measured trill on the notes D and E; yet split by the skip of the seventh this commonplace practice takes on freshness and foreshadows the type of scoring and spacing which have since been widely used. Measures 54 and 56 bring in chords which use two notes of one team against one of the other (measure 54: C and G♯ against B♭). Does this not greatly resemble the classical coda effect of tonic restatement over a dominant pedal, demanding the rest of the final cadence, which in this case employs two of the notes of the tonic team?

STRUCTURE. It is interesting to note for a clear realization of the delineation of this prélude the classical plan of its development. Observe this strong sense in the opening four measures, a counterpart to the classical phrasing which leads to a first cadence on the dominant and a second one on the tonic. From this small fragment one observes the overall plan which responds readily to the rondo-sonata form, with 22 measures of exposition, followed by 10 measures of development on the opening figure, heightening the sense of excitement. Then at measure 33, a restatement of the main theme at the new dynamic level is immediately followed by further development, including a pentatonic section reaching the classical climax which demands the recapitulation as a dénouement. Note that the motifs used in measures 38-48 are basically related to those in the section beginning at measure 22, which in turn bear derivation from the opening figure of the prélude. At measure 48, the recapitulation is abridged, withholding the opening figure for use later in the coda. Observe that the ornamental glissando-like figures, though reestablishing the whole-tone scale, use each time only five of its notes, a subtle means of transition from the previous pentatonic passage.

PERFORMANCE. In performance note that the quality of touch and pedaling must take into account the three distinct levels upon which the whole is built. These levels, we have seen, have individual personalities and capacities when first stated, and retain these characteristics when superimposed upon each other. In order of relative importance the three levels are: the melody, the ostinato, and the pedals least, since their expressive possibilities are the least developed.

Besides the diversity to be sought in the interpretation of the three levels contrasted to each other, within the first two levels one must also obtain an apt differentiation in dynamics for the points of tension and those of release, and a pedaling which does not mix appoggiaturas with their resolutions.

Le vent dans la plaine (Book I)

Nature. "Wind in the plain." The amazing descriptivism of this prélude needs little explanation. The untrammeled expanse of the plain, the growing momentum of the dry wind, zephyr-like at first ("aussi légèrement que possible"), it whirls and grows, suddenly pauses in its course, there is a deceitful calm, but its strands multiply, rally in squalls, a wicked gust lashes at the landscape, is reiterated, and the rumble spends itself, lost in a last murmured breath.

It will be noted that this prélude is a companion piece of the preceding one, "Voiles." It forms a mid-point between the gentleness of "Voiles" and the tempestuous nature of "Ce qu'a vu le vent d'ouest," a triptych study in wind phenomena, paralleled by a threefold study of the alternate usage of whole-tone and pentatonic scales. Opening and closing in a pentatonic scale, "Wind in the plain" contains a middle section in whole tones, the reverse process of "Voiles," of which the major portion is whole-toned with a brief pentatonic middle portion.

Harmony and Tonality. It is well to remember in this instance that pentatonic is not *a* scale, but a family name for a series of scales built on five tones to the octave. As was noted in the preface, admitting of semitonal pentatonism (containing half-steps, as well as whole steps, and steps and a half) makes possible the conception of an incredible number of such scales within any octave, and a nearly endless variety of these, when transposed to other octaves.

In this particular instance, the pentatonic series elected at the open-

136

ing is B♭-C♭-D♭-E♭-G♭, with B♭ as the main tonal center, viz., the pedal-points, trill with upper neighbor (spaced with intervals of sevenths), and cadences. B♭ acts as the tonic coupled frequently with D♭ as a secondary member of the tonic family. C♭, E♭, and G♭ act as the opposition, or dominant family. The introduction of F natural and E double-flat in measures 5 and 6 is ornamental in nature, but being neighboring tones they give these ornaments the tension of dissonance which enriches the resolution to tonic (B♭-D♭). Observe at measures 9-12 that the series of chords forms, horizontally as well as vertically, series of sevenths composed of the notes E♭-G♭-B♭-D♭-C natural-E♭-G♭-B♭. In view of the preceding page it will be understood that these chords are in the nature of tonic superimposed upon dominant, with the tension at the end of measures 10 and 12 with the movement in the bass, the passage resolving in measures 13 and 14 with the tonic pedal re-established as in the beginning. In the following section, measures 15-21, the introduction of the B double-flat forms a new pentatonic series which paves the way for the ensuing section in whole tones. Measure 22 in turn establishes G and D♭ as tonal centers, and measures 23-25 are in the whole-toned series: G-A-B-D♭-E♭-F, with these tonal centers prominent in the thematic material of the bass. Measures 26-28 modulate to the whole-toned series A♭-B♭-C-D-E-G♭, with A♭ as tonal center. The effect is somewhat similar to the classical repeat of the theme in the dominant. The outburst (measure 29) seems to bring us the clear color of G♭ major, but the melodic pattern is still whole-toned. An attempted modulation to G double-flat (end of measure 31) falls back to G♭ (measures 32-33), but the ensuing three outbursts fulfill definite changes of level from G♭ to G♯ via G-B-D to B-D♯-F♯, to G♯-B♯-D♯. Measures 35-38 resume the pentatonic color with G♯ as tonal center (series G♯-A-B-C♯-E). The chromatic slide (measures 39-40) drops the level to E as tonal center, and a further chromatic descent (measures 43-44) returns us to the original tonic of B♭ with its pentatonic series. It is most interesting to note the use of the temporary contrast of chromaticism, used in "Voiles" and more widely in this prélude with the dual purpose of sliding in level (form of modulation) and of breaking down the large intervals of both pentatonic and whole-toned series. It is used again as a cadential approach (measures 55-60): C♭-B♭-G♭ to

C-E-*G* to D♭-F-*A*♭, to *B*♭; a most telling progression married to the tonic pedal-trill!

STRUCTURE.

Bars 1-8. First material.

Bars 9-12. Transition material foreshadowing the second material in the bass.

Bars 13-22. Development of first material, harmonic preparation for the second material.

Bars 23-25. Second material.

Bars 26-28. Second material repeated at different level.

Bars 29-35. Second material developed with added motif (outbursts).

Bars 35-44. Development of first material, with modulations.

Bars 45-48. Recapitulation of 3-6, first material (condensed recapitulation).

Bars 49-50. Substitute for measure 22.

Bars 51-54. Recapitulation of measures 9-12.

Bars 55-60. Coda on opening trill and cadential progression.

PERFORMANCE. Do not melt together the sounds of the opening trill, of which various forms are used nearly throughout the prélude. These figures must be very light but with each note distinct. A very superficial forte pedal may be used or none at all. This is particularly true of the first and fourth lines of the opening page. The B♮ pedal should be prepared with the sustaining pedal. The rest in the third measure must be observed, and the 32nd-notes must not become 16ths. Gently detach the chords (measures 9-12, and in recapitulation later); in this passage the pedal should be changed according to the movement in the bass. The outbursts must receive the full impact of the forte marked for them, but the immediate resumption of piano and pianissimo must not be missed. No pedal under the chromatic passages (measures 39-40, 43-44). Do not fail to hold the chords forming the chromatic cadential progression (measures 55-60), for the voice-leading from chord to chord is of utmost importance to the final effect of the last B♮.

NATURE. "Sounds and perfumes swirl in the evening air." A hauntingly soft and melancholy melody forms the counterpart to the poem by Baudelaire, from which it is inspired: "Fleurs du Mal" by Charles Baudelaire:

HARMONIE DU SOIR

Voici venir les temps où vibrant sur sa tige
Chaque fleur s'évapore ainsi qu'un encensoir;
Les sons et les parfums tournent dans l'air du soir;
Valse mélancolique et langoureux vertige!

Chaque fleur s'évapore ainsi qu'un encensoir;
Le violon frémit comme un coeur qu'on afflige;
Valse mélancolique et langoureux vertige!
Le ciel est triste et beau comme un grand reposoir.

Le violon frémit comme un coeur qu'on afflige
Un coeur tendre, qui hait le néant vaste et noir!
Le ciel est triste et beau comme un grand reposoir;
Le soleil s'est noyé dans son sang qui se fige.

Un coeur tendre, qui hait le néant vaste et noir,
Du passé lumineux recueille tout vestige!
Le soleil s'est noyé dans son sang qui se fige . . .
Ton souvenir en moi luit comme un ostensoir .

The end of the day, but its overtones are carried in the evening air; nostalgic and poignant are the reminiscences of which the senses can still apprehend snatches in the air's caress; melancholy waltz and vertiginous languor enfold the regrets on the threshold of the black void of night, of the despised vacuum which repels the tender heart.

HARMONY. Opening and closing under the gentle authority of A major as tonal center, this prélude contains in the intervening body of the work an incredible richness of harmony and of subtly capricious harmonic meanders, defying the pleasurable but in this case perhaps unnecessary button-holing of analysis. As Oscar Thompson brings out in his biography, there are fragments "that could arbitrarily be regarded as based on a twelve-tone scale." They can also be conceived as the natural heritage of the fluency of modulation of Fauré, brought here to a degree of virtuosity which no longer necessitates the completion of the modulation but admits only of constantly evolving "melos" which lightly caresses now this tonality, now that, capriciously evading each, forsaking it for the next, until the final return to the sedate home key is effected. In the process, a near chromatic line may be built and the dissonances are richly felt not only in the vertical aggregates but also in the horizontal voice progression at each level. This is not an atonal conception even if its sum total of tones covers the twelve-tone gamut. It is rather in a rapidly evolving (or revolving) diatonic palette that one seeks the secret of such richness.

The superimposition upon this rich harmony of whole-toned and pentatonic fragments (measures 9-23, and other similar fragments later) in eighth-notes, is in the nature of counter-subject, of an added contrapuntal level, a further plurality of the evening messages, a further abundance of the harmonic fluency.

What then holds this prélude from beginning to end in such close cohesion, in perfect integration of such capricious sonorities? The answer is twofold: the melodic line and the structure.

MELODY. The melodic line in which several voices participate has the sweep of a Lied and the close coordination of chamber-music writing. Its opening two measures, expressively curved in contour, form the motif from which much of the later sections are derived. This is immediately continued by a second melodic notion, much more tenuous, formed by four middle voices and which carries through without interruption, despite appearances, from measures 3 to 23. For the remainder of the prélude to within four measures of the end, the two melodic materials alternate and are superimposed upon each other.

STRUCTURE. The consideration of the melodic line in this prélude very naturally brings one to notice the structure; it will be observed that measures 1-23 serve as an exposition of the two principal melodic materials and of their counter-materials or accompaniments. Measures 24-27, in restating the opening material, herald a long development section based on both of the exposed materials but with particular emphasis on the highly expressive two first measures of the prélude. The development section takes over the dual functions of working out and partial restatement, and a condensed recapitulation, four measures from the end. A short new material "like a distant horn call" forms the coda and cadence of the prélude, reaffirming the home key of A major, and bringing a dying finality to reminiscences.

PERFORMANCE. One of the first notions which must permeate this prélude is that its interpretation must not seek after obvious effect, or more precisely, that its accents, crescendi, decrescendi must fit within the opening admonition of "harmonious and supple" and will not allow angular or baroque dynamic effects. Yet a considerable richness of rhythm of the superimposed levels must be respected. For instance, observe that the A pedal, in the first few measures, displaces itself from the first beat to the second, third, second, third, etc. Note that in the second and third measures, and in those only, it forms an acute dissonance with the middle voices. Remark that the melodic accents reach a climax on the third beat of the first two measures (in 5/4 time), then on the third beat of measure 3, the second beat of measures 5 and 7. The first beat of measure 9 carries weight in the lower and middle register and in the upper register the third beat is climaxed. In measure 10, the lower register reaches its accent on the second beat and the upper voices on the third. All these differentiations of dynamics and rhythm must be clearly present, despite the subdued level of the entire piece, of which the majority is PP, and which never reaches beyond a MF, and this only for short periods.

Another important point is keeping the continuity of the middle voice in the twenty-three opening measures and in succeeding fragments. For instance, the E natural in measure 8 (dotted half-note) must lead to the E♯ of the following measure in the same voice level. Another instance: the chord at the beginning of measure 13 leads to that in measure 14, and to that in measure 15, and also to those in measure 18, a feat for which the pedal will have to be largely responsible.

The three "rubato" passages in the second page of the prélude are to be considered as hesitating on the first two notes (long values), and precipitating the arpeggio which succeeds them. A more crystalline touch must be reserved for these outbursts, and also (but softly) for the horn call at the end.

Les collines d'Anacapri (Book I)

NATURE. Anacapri is one of two small cities on the island of Capri. It hangs 1600 feet up on one of the many abrupt hills of this movemented island, and can be approached by a stairway of 552 steps or small coiled roads. The five-and-a-half square miles of the island of Capri are located in the Bay of Naples and command from the many cliffs and hills a view of a remarkably blue sea with only the distant plumet of smoke of the Vesuvius to remind its inhabitants that not all shores share their freedom from worry. The name of Anacapri or Capri (the other small city) comes from the goats (capri), the first inhabitants of the island, yet the history of human life on the island reaches far into antiquity. Founded as a Greek colony about 400 B.C., it has successively passed into the hands of Romans, Lombards, Normans, Austrians, Spaniards, French, English, Italians . . . and the American Air Force, and has remained thoroughly "impractical": devoid of water, crime, stock markets, worry, rush, politics, and other signs of harassed "adulthood." A garden of song, pastel houses, vivid flowers, pungent scents, blatant sun, sky, sea, and hills, it is famous throughout the world for its beauty and joyous spirit. A joy so well expressed in the Neapolitan songs and in their national dance, the tarantella, which was adopted by the inhabitants of Napoli. Danced in groups, with the women carrying tambourines, its 6/8 rhythm takes on a special flavor from both the percussion of the tambourines and the very fast, gay, sensual character of the dance itself, which is supposed to have originated as a cure for the bite of tarantulas.

Debussy matches such a subject matter with one of his gayest, most brightly fashioned palettes of color. The appeal is direct, the musical sky vivid (dazzling). In the distance, bells and snatches of the tarantella are wafted lightly on the breezes. The dancers come closer and the full melody is now heard with its contrasting minor episode. A popular

142

tune (p.18) is punctuated by the pulse of the dance. A further popular melody, amorous and perhaps a little vulgar, portavoce, seems to fit the portly tenor, hero of Italian opera. The tarantella is temporarily forgotten in this more languid melody, but bells sound and herald a headlong flight into the gay folly of this dance in which the bells, tambourines, and popular melody join in a rich and voluptuous fanfare to the azure sea and triumphant optimism.

STRUCTURE.

Introduction, A-B-C, Introduction, A-B-coda.

Bars 1-2. Bells form a motif of great importance from unifying standpoint, nearly an ostinato or pedal figure.

Bars 3-4. Snatches of first theme, tarantella.

Bars 5-6. Bells.

Bars 7-11. Snatches of first theme leading into first theme.

Bars 12-24. First theme, tarantella.

Bars 24-31. Second part of first theme, minor coloring, contrast within the mood of the first subject group, serves as transition.

Bars 31-39. Second theme, popular melody, lower register.

Bars 39-43. Second theme, upper register (note bell ostinato, measure 43).

Bars 43-48. Second theme, middle register.

Bars 49-65. Third theme, love song (Neapolitan).

Bars 63, 65. Note the bell ostinato, paving the way for the recapitulation.

Bars 66-67. Bell motif in diminution, continues mood of recapitulation of the introduction.

Bars 68-72. First theme.

Bars 73-74. Bell motif in diminution which now will form part of the accompaniment of the first theme and a pervading, insistent background.

Bars 74-80. First theme.

Bars 80-86. Second theme superimposed on part of the first theme, and with bell motif (measures 83 and 84).

Bars 86-93. Bell motif in diminution and snatches of the first theme.

Bars 94-96. Final cadence on arpeggi and ornamented added sixth chord of B major tonic.

HARMONY. The introduction presents in its two materials two main chordal formations: the bells, an aggregate amounting to an eleventh on the supertonic, or a superimposition of the tonic and supertonic chords, and the snatches of the first theme, which build around a chord of the ninth on the leading tone. The first theme, oddly enough, for all its gaiety, evades somewhat the major-diatonic color to which it belongs and by the third measure of its presentation is quite consistently pentatonic, not an uncommon medium for folksongs. It further brushes modality (measures 21-24), a transposed Mixolydian. The minor section is fairly well settled on G minor with considerable interest in the diminished seventh. The second theme is in B major, but brings a tantalizing emphasis on G♯, the sixth degree, foreshadowing the final cadence on the added sixth chord. The third material is the most completely diatonic of the four (including the bell motif), i.e., the most straightforward in its harmonic conception.

PERFORMANCE. In the introduction a resonant tone, not harsh or loud but long in its vibrations, must be used for the bell tones,* held by the pedal. In contrast, though still light, the motifs from the tarantella can already be sharper, gaining dynamically the second time. The tarantella must be light and fleet, the lower voice should not be burdened by metric accents. In the minor passage, note that this material is much more expressive and must be phrased very carefully, particularly from the end of measure 26 to 28. Note the dynamic markings and phrasing by three notes. Observe that a certain amount of freedom is allowed in the performance of the second theme ("Cédez"). This popular material is nostalgic, romantic, but it is easy to overdo! The slight lengthening is best felt at the end of the questioning first phrase, to which the answer (second phrase) must reaffirm strict timing. In the third material (measures 49-65) the quarter-notes must be held by the fingers in order to carry their resonance, for the pedal will be changed with the evolving melodic line. The grace notes should not be clipped, but played with the left-hand chord and resolved at ease, so as to melt into the languid nature of the middle-voiced melody. Note that the A natural (measures 63 and 65) must be heard somewhat above the bell motif and linked to the softer resolution on B. Do not shy away from the unparalleled bril-

* See description of slap, above, page 39.

liancy of the last few measures to the prélude: FFF; it is the natural crowning of the joyous exuberance of the dance, of the landscape, of the glaring, blatant sun.

DES PAS SUR LA NEIGE (BOOK I)

NATURE. "Footprints in the snow" is a stark prélude, not at all dedicated to child-like glee in a winter scene evoking snowballs, sleds, or the Christmas season. In Debussy's own words, its basic rhythm "should have the aural value of a melancholy, snowbound landscape." The stumbling rhythm, persistent and immutable, is the counterpart of the faltering steps, placed first on the crusty surface, then sinking deep into the snow of this desolate, pale-gray expanse. The sighing melody, replete with supplications, doubts, regrets, weariness, brings us a vision of the solitude of a tender heart, of a deep sense of loss and distress, to which the footfalls add the obsession of finality beyond recall.

It is immediately important to note that this prélude is conceived at three contrapuntal levels: the footfalls, forming an ostinato, a psychological and pictorial canvas; the melody, expressing emotional fluctuations; the pedal-points, steadily coloring the two other levels by their progressions forming dissonances, passages in bleak open fifths, or bringing points of melancholy rest to the harmonic color.

Remark that the footfall ostinato remains nearly throughout on the same notes, at the same pitch level, and always in close association to pedals. In the opening measure, the ostinato is marked by Debussy with an increase in dynamics paralleling the pitch ascent and durational value of the second note (a sob?—a sigh?). But, from the second measure on, its true interpretation is that of an appoggiatura, with the accent on the first note, and release on the second note.

This character of appoggiatura is particularly well illustrated in the last few measures of the préludes, i.e., the fifth and fourth measures from the end, which contain identically: in the first half of the measure the D of the ostinato is an appoggiatura to the E, which is the third of the diminished-seventh chord of D minor, continued in the staccato notes; in the second half of the measure, the E is an appoggiatura to the F, which is the seventh of the subdominant-seventh chord of D minor. The whole superimposed on a D pedal (tonic), forms a rich harmonic relationship of the parts, which, however, retain their independence even in these last receding measures.

The melodic elements are twofold, and wind their way through the various voice levels. In the seven opening measures the melody is in the upper part, and modal in character (Aeolian transposed or D natural minor) with D as tonal center. In contrast, the second melodic material (bars 8-15) is in the lower voices and diatonic-chromatic in conformation, and goes from the F♯-C♯ axis to the D♭-A♭ axis and back, in the short period of its evolution.

At measure 16, the return of the first material is effected through the use of the three opening notes of this melody, G-A♭-B♭, as a secondary ostinato in the bass with a varied restatement and development of the melody in the soprano, to within five measures of the end. The melodic line, delicately woven as it is, still bears the burden of the emotional message of this piece, and sensitive attention must be given its note-values and pitch line to render truthfully its despairing loneliness. Note that the two important emotional climaxes are at measures 23 and 30, and are built by ascending whole-toned series, receding in descending minor thirds, effectively slurred by two's, in the sob-sigh of renunciation. Yet even these climaxes (particularly A♭ in measure 23, and C♭ in measure 30) are played P, and should not be overreached dynamically. They are the apexes of the piece which starts with PP and ends with PPP. The entire palette of dynamics must be contained within the restrained gamut from P to PPP, with the classical design of the curve reaching its greatest intensity through two-thirds of the piece, and receding again. From measure 29 on, "Comme un tendre et triste regret" ("Like a tender and sad regret"), observe the long ascent of three lower voices in parallel 6/4 position, reaching its climax on the last beat of measure 31, after crossing over the decreasing upper melodic line. Do not interrupt either of these crossing lines, since they are continuous as to interpretation, and independent as to dynamics. It must be noted that this independence of dynamics is of the very nature of this piece, conceived at several independent levels, and in which the melody is marked repeatedly by Debussy, as being a shade louder than the ostinato.

146

The pedaling must be extremely careful so that overlapping of sounds does not break the bleak purity of this small landscape. Change the pedal immediately at the resolution of the appoggiatura in the ostinato. A soft pedal should be kept throughout this piece.

Properly interpreted within its sober frame and desolate accents, this piece conjures within the memory of each a wider connotation than even the limitless horizons of a snowbound landscape, reaching into an equally gray sky. It is an appeal to the basic loneliness of all human beings, oft-forgotten perhaps, but, like the ostinato, forming a basic undercurrent of our history.

CE QU'A VU LE VENT D'OUEST (BOOK I)

This prélude is indeed an illustration of the very relative nature of direction, for to a Frenchman a west wind is the very opposite from what it would be to a New Yorker! Indeed, the west wind is to Debussy that fearsome, tragically destructive, magnificently powerful element gathering force over the expanse of the Atlantic, lashing the coasts, battering cliffs, destroying houses, schooners, and liners, sweeping icebergs and mountainous waves before it, playing havoc with human lives, subjugating each to a state of exalted terror. Here Debussy is no longer the poet of tenderness, the painter of the exquisite; he embodies another aspect of his romantic heritage. This prélude is full of the nightmarish quality of Walpurgisnacht, the Erlkönig, the Faustian destruction, the "Sturm und Drang" of romantic literature. It exhibits a passionate fascination for evil, and a parallel palette of colors, dynamics ranging from PP to FF and SFF with crescendo and indications of "animé et tumultueux" ("animated and tumultuous"), "plaintif et lointain" (plaintive and in the distance"), "strident," "en dehors et angoissé" ("outside and anxiously"), "furieux et rapide" ("fast and furious"), and so forth.

The third in the triptych of préludes based on the alternate use of pentatonic and whole-toned series with chromatic transitional passages, this one is the most complex harmonically. Based, in the overall design, on two separate and opposed pentatonic series (see fragments of A and B below), and a resultant whole-toned series (fragment C below), F♯ (G♭)

serves as the axis and tonal center for most of this prélude, and can be considered in the nature of its tonic.

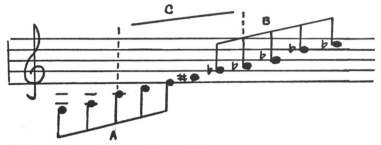

Observe a few of the workings of these patterns:

Bars 1-2. Pattern "A" with F♯ as tonic pedal.

Bars 3-4. Same, with the addition of the melodic line above in pattern B.

Bars 5-6. Horizontal alternation of A and B.

Bars 7-14. Alternation of chordal blocks of A and B, leading to a blend, or resultant whole-toned pattern C.

Bars 15-18. Chromatic successions, PP to MF.

Bars 19-22. Again a blend of patterns A and B.

Bars 23-24. Whole-toned pattern C.

Bars 25-29. Pattern C with the addition of the appoggiaturas A natural (27) and B natural (29). These can also be considered as belonging to pattern A, whereas the B♭ and F♯ of the melody belong to pattern B. The pedal trill (C and D) belongs to pattern A.

Bar 30. End of measure, chromatic slide up in level.

Bars 31-32. Continuation of measures 25-29 at new level.

Bars 33-34. Chromatic ascent.

Bars 35-37. Whole-toned (F-G-A-B-C♯-D♯), transposed pattern C continued, after brief D♯ coloring, in measures 39-41.

Bars 42-45. D♯ natural minor.

Bar 46. Chromatic ascent.

Bars 47-53. D♯ remains the tonal center, chromatics intervene and the texture returns to whole-tone. Note the whole-toned clusters (51-53).

Bars 54-56. Return of F♯ as tonal center.

Bars 57-58. Alternation of patterns A and B, landing on C chord (59), and continued by chords alternating A and B patterns (60-62).

148

Bars 63-71. Whole-toned (C-D-E-F♯-G♯), but the final chord is a pentatonic cluster (D-F♯-A-B♯-C♯).

STRUCTURE. This prélude exposes first a series of motifs making up the first-subject group and giving it a first development (measures 1-22). A short contrasting material (measures 23-34) can be considered to form the second-subject group, followed by development of the first materials (measures 35-53).

A very abridged recapitulation of materials from the first subject group (54-62) leads to a coda of nine measures.

PERFORMANCE. Note the extremes of dynamics used in this composition. They must not be underrated in performance. As a general principle the heavily scored chords are dynamically more important than the atmospheric arabesques in single notes (usually of shorter durations than the chords); when the two co-exist, which is frequently the case, plan a different dynamic terrace for each. Note also the persistent markings of Debussy indicating crescendi and decrescendi respectively on ascending and descending pitch levels. This insistence, which can be said to be a general trait of Debussy's markings and an even more general trait of the interpretation of all music, is here of spectacular effect in view of the nature of the work. At the beginning of the piece, the F♯ pedal is to be prepared with the sustaining pedal in advance, i.e., depressed silently and caught with the pedal in advance, so that its resonance may be kept as desired and yet leave the forte pedal free to do justice to the other voices. In the passage beginning measure 15, the short durations in the bass are to be percussive. In the passage beginning at measure 25, keep the melodic fragments at different levels from the trill, not blurred into it.

LA FILLE AUX CHEVEUX DE LIN (BOOK I)

NATURE. "The Girl with the Flaxen Hair." This calmly lyrical and short prélude is in diametric contrast to the preceding turmoil of the western wind. Frequently heard, it remains fresh and young, for these two qualities are of its very essence. More Nordic than Latin in its mood, the prélude is inspired by the poem of the same name by Leconte de Lisle in the collection *Poèmes Antiques: Chansons Ecossaises,* which we quote below:

LA FILLE AUX CHEVEUX DE LIN

Sur la luzerne en fleurs assise
Qui chante dès le frais matin?
C'est la fille aux cheveux de lin,
La belle aux lèvres de cerise.

L'amour, au clair soleil d'été
Avec l'alouette a chanté.

Ta bouche a des couleurs divines,
Ma chère—et tente le baiser!
Sur l'herbe en fleur veux-tu causer,
Fille aux cils longs, aux boucles fines?

L'amour au clair soleil d'été
Avec l'alouette a chanté.

Ne dis pas non, fille cruelle!!
Ne dis pas oui!!! J'entendrai mieux
Le long regard de tes grands yeux
Et ta lèvre rose, O ma belle!!

L'amour au clair soleil d'été
Avec l'alouette a chanté.

Adieu les daims, adieu les lièvres
Et les rouges perdrix!! Je veux
Baiser le lin de tes cheveux,
Presser la pourpre de tes lèvres!!!

L' amour au clair soleil d'été
Avec l'alouette a chanté.

To those familiar with the works of Debussy, the mood of the opening of the prélude will be reminiscent of the Pre-Raphaelite "Blessed Damozel," but soon a subtle difference in the texture reminds us that the young girl with the flaxen hair, unlike the blessed damozel, is not in heaven, but in a world of—oh, so alive, gay laughter. Hers is not a mystic world, but a young one, like that early morning in which she sings, simple, warm—full of candor and of the daydreams of young womanhood.

Another memory is kindled by the pervading opening motif; despite the transmutation, is there not a faint echo of the spinning wheel and of the famed Gretchen tradition of the romantic period? The psychological association would be an easy one to make, for since Schubert's genial characterization of the innocent blond girl whose fate is one of the pervading motifs of romantic literature and music, her musical counterpart reappears constantly. It is nearly a cliché of the musical language, albeit a most felicitous one.

STRUCTURE. The structure is a very simple one, consisting of an opening section (measures 1-19) based on the material of the first three measures and continuation phrases, then a short middle portion (measures 19-23), more animated, somewhat in contrast to the first section, a gay laughter, and measures 24-39, the return of parts of the first section in augmentation, then in their tranquil rhythm, and the final cadence.

HARMONY. From the standpoint of harmony one has an interesting duality; melodically pentatonic and vertically diatonic (but with a strong leaning toward modal cadences), the prélude's texture has an archaic flavor. We are again reminded of the theory, widely accepted, which brings to our attention that pentatonism is not merely an oriental trait, though it is well developed there, but rather a stage in the evolution of all folk materials, the presence of which to a certain extent insures the authenticity and age of a folksong. For in this prélude, despite its fairly steady use, pentatonism gives us no sense of exotic lands. The remoteness, if any, is one of time, not in geography.

The opening section is based on the pentatonic series Gb-Ab-Bb-Db-Eb with Gb as the tonal center both melodically and harmonically. In the three opening measures, the alternation of outlining of the tonic, submediant, subdominant, tonic chords, are typical of the type of progression which in many fragments of this prélude bring us near to modal usage and remind us of the predominant strength of the fourth and sixth degrees, a sensitivity which they have never quite lost. Measures 12-16 are in C♮ and include a noteworthy measure (14), with expressive suspensions. A transition of two measures, containing a series of appoggiaturas and resolutions in the upper voice, bring the middle portion (measures 19-23) melodically on the pentatonic series E♭-F-G-B♭-C, with E♭ as tonal center of both this series and the diatonic harmonies. The return of the first material brings us back to the tonal center of G♭. Notice the subdominant pedal (measures 28-30), the submediant to tonic cadence (measures 31-32), and the final cadence on tonic approached by the supertonic chord.

PERFORMANCE. It will be noticed that the dynamic strong points are throughout placed at the apex of the melodic line and are often coincident with harmonic stresses (suspensions or appoggiaturas) and with durational weight, i.e., long values. This brings a rather simple scheme of accents but one which forms the entire basis of the interpretation of this piece, and therefore must be given close and steady attention. In the 16th measure, anticipate the grace note somewhat, so that there will be no break in reaching the right-hand apex on the first beat. In measures 22 and 23, observe the accents both times on the fourth eighth-note of the measure, a very charming syncopation in the otherwise fairly metric scheme of this prélude.

LA SÉRÉNADE INTERROMPUE (BOOK I)

NATURE. "The Interrupted Serenade." Debussy leaves us in no doubt that we are here again on the soil of Spain, the scene of several of his very fertile and felicitous musical explorations. Serenading time, most probably a nocturnal scene, an étude on a plaintive Moorish melody, a fragment of Iberia—those are our materials for this ironic, mocking short story of the frustrated serenader. Our hero is persistent and is loath to forego his serenade despite the multiple interruptions that beset him and test his temper. Having tuned his guitar and preluded on it, he begins his serenade. In the second page a violent interruption (A window slams shut? Water is thrown on the nocturnal visitor?). The serenade is resumed but the end of the third page sees another interruption (a night watchman with a wooden leg—or a group of revelers), and our hero's temper flares ragingly, the first time to no avail, but finally the second time brings results, though it takes a few seconds for the serenader to resume his serenading mood. But perhaps by now his heart is no longer in it, for the serenade recedes more and more and is finally lost in the distance, but not before a jarring SFZ enters (a last sarcasm of the heroine—or a final gesture of despair).

It is interesting to remember in connection with this prélude that the guitar, brought to Europe by the Moors of Spain, has a long and important heritage in the history of the music of Spain, both as the ancient "vihuela" and as the modern guitar. Both instruments have two techniques of playing, one for melodic or contrapuntal passages (punteado) and the other for strumming chords (rasgueado), both of which are paralleled in the texture of this piano counterpart. Further, guitars, like early keyboard instruments, have little sustaining power and resort frequently, therefore, to repeated notes to lengthen the resonance of the sounds. Note the use of this effect also in this prélude.

STRUCTURE. The structure, in rondo-sonata form, is very closely knit, despite the capricious nature of the interruptions by the pervading influence of the first material (measures 1-24), and particularly of the last few measures of this material which recurs many times and also serves as the accompaniment to the last statement of the second material. Measures 19 and 20 of the opening section are particularly noteworthy in their insistence, and amount nearly to an ostinato.

Bars 1-24. First subject group containing two elements: the preluding repeated note scale passages (A-1), and the thematic ostinato theme of measures 19-24 (A-2).

Bars 25-40. Second subject, introduced by seven measures of rasgueado chords before the melody enters, incomplete for the present.

Bars 41-49. Return of A-2.

Bars 50-53. Return of A-1.

Bars 54-72. Second subject, now more completely stated.

Bars 73-79. Return of A-2, ending in a short rhapsodic cadenza.

Bars 80-89. Third subject, which serves as central episode, in lieu of development, a short but tense axis upon which the denouement of the form hinges. Measures 85-86 bring A-2 again, measures 87-89 continuing a second attempt at the third subject.

Bars 90-97. A-2 opens the recapitulation and serves as the con-

153

densed introduction to the second subject, to which the second measure of A-2 will serve as accompaniment, temporarily.

Bars 98-124. Second subject.

Bars 125-128. Return of A-2.

Bar 129 to the end. Contains fragments of A-1.

HARMONY. From the standpoint of harmony it will be observed that in the opening section and in the greater part of the piece F is the tonal center. The complete absence of the note A in the opening scale passages and its dual use later as both A and A♭, brings not only interesting cross-relations but a play on the major-minor tonic triad. It further leads us to an interesting duality melodically; with the A♭ and C natural our melodic scheme could be Phrygian, but with the appearance of A natural it brings us the succession F-G♭-A-B♭-C♭ or C natural, D♭-E♭, a close parallel to the Moorish or Arabic scale already described in "Soirée dans Grenade" ("Estampes"). In fact, this scheme sets the pervading color of the prélude, a normal procedure in evoking the Spanish scene. Note, in the passage beginning measure 25, that the overall effect is akin to a strumming over six open strings, and the detailed effect is that of a tonic pedal (F-C), alternately ornamented by the upper double appoggiatura (G♭-D♭) and the lower double appoggiatura (E♭-B♭). The second theme, in its fuller statement (54-72), opens with F as tonal center and the Moorish theme mentioned above, but evolves in its second phrase a diatonic flavor which brings us closer to B♭ minor. The third material is clearly in D major, with the interpolations of the first material still based on F as tonal center. The return of the second subject follows the same tonal scheme as in the original statement, Moorish to B♭ minor. In the last few measures the struggle between the two important centers of harmonic evolution (F and B♭), is finally won in the final cadence by B♭, but not without an insecure qualm as to whether this final B♭ chord is a subdominant or tonic.

PERFORMANCE. Observe that much of the mocking charm of this prélude comes from the abrupt nature of the interruptions and that clear levels of differences in the interpretation and dynamics must parallel the differentiated musical textures. The dryness and brittleness of the guitar effects are destroyed by the use of the pedal. Its use should be extremely limited nearly throughout the prélude, with only fragments of the second material pedaled, still sparingly. Further, the opening section demands a rapid and light staccato touch, with active, articulated fingers, which must be contrasted in the second theme by a lyric, legato, singing tone.

Note that the underlying rhythm of the third material (pedal chord) is light on the first beat and accented on the second, a limping or inebriated gait, which is all too often ignored by performers. Soft as the ending is, the staccato quality must still be preserved in the last few lines, and at the cadence, subdued but exact.

LA CATHÉDRALE ENGLOUTIE (BOOK I)

NATURE. "The Engulfed Cathedral." This prélude is one of the most mystic of Debussy's piano works. Based on a legend of Brittany, it describes the Cathedral of Ys, engulfed in the fourth or fifth century "because of the impiety of the inhabitants," but allowed to rise again and to be seen (as an example to others) at sunrise. Strongly believed in, this legend has long been the center of religious, poetic, and scientific observation. It reminds us of the tenuous mysticism of the Celtic heritage of France, a geographically limited heritage, but culturally widespread and strong in its interaction upon the Latin or Mediterranean strain of the nation.

In Debussy a third element must be added, his pagan rite of the sea, equally esoteric, equally strong. It adds its power to the prélude's fervor, but one wonders if this is the association of two religious concepts or a struggle between them? None would dare answer the question, but the main materials of the prélude characterize both forces, juxtaposed in contrapuntal independence; plainsong treated in medieval organum, motifs of the calm sea and later of a stronger tide.

The tricks that psychological associations play will never cease to arouse wonder, nor the marvel of unity which Debussy's crucible can produce, even out of historically heterogeneous materials, for here a legend of the fifth or sixth century, in association with organum of the ninth or tenth century, and in association with church arches, evolved from Roman to Gothic forms over some six centuries, and bells calling the congregation to worship, yet produces a closely integrated mood to which each element has contributed immeasurably, by its strong psychological association.

You may be wondering what the church arches have to do with this prélude. Look at the score from a slight distance and you will see that few are the measures which do not contribute to graphic representation of one form of arch or another.

(Designs of series of typical arches)

It is indeed a fascinating study to compare the plates in an architectural book with the varied forms found on the score, yet one must not let such a notion carry too far. It is of interest in so far as it is a further link in a long and entertaining lineage of graphic realization of texts or events in more or less subtle forms through the history of music, and a comment on the dual nature of the composer-painter.

A close resemblance is to be found in the various materials used in the prélude, characterized in their melodic flow by conjunct motion, broken by skips of fourths or fifths, their avoidance of certain degrees of the scale, which partakes of both the modal and pentatonic usage, jointly characteristic of archaic plainsong. The opening "gutted" chords, organum in parallel fourths and octaves, seem to evoke in Debussy structures of the past, not presently visible. (Note similar skeleton chords in the "Images": "Et la lune descend sur le temple qui fut.") The first six measures establish a Phrygian modality with the ornamented bass pedals leading slowly from G to F to the tonic E, whereas the individual voices of the quarter-note chords are subdivided; three of the five voices progress to tonic D to E, B, to D to E, and two others to the fourth degree G to A, E to G to A, a plagal counterpart. The C♯ minor tonality of the ensuing section (7-12) is a strong contrast, for though it is the relative minor of our former keynote the jump from Phrygian is greater than from E major. A temporary return to Phrygian (13-15) paves the way for a series of changes of levels (B major, 16-18, C minor bitonally over E♭ major, 19-21, a temporary use of Dorian, which acts as dominant to the next passage in C major, 22-27).

At measure 28 the sonorous color of C major heralds the apparition into full view of the Cathedral, and warm parallel triads are substituted for the gutted chords of the opening. (This parallel use of triads would be remindful of fauxbourdon or gymel rather than organum.) The apparition of the B♮ (33-37) may be interpreted as a modal reference (the B♮ being an early allowed alteration, to avoid the tritone) or as a passage in F, but with C still the prominent tonal center, which it remains to measure 41. The passage, 42-46, reaffirms our concept of the Debussyan use of superimposed major seconds in the depiction of resonant metallic sounds, bells in this case (viz. the crotals in "Danseuses de Delphes," the gongs in "Pagodes," etc.). It also affords us an enharmonic bridging, a slow change of level via the A♭ to G♯ to C♯ minor (measure 47), a return genially devised as from a great distance. It is interesting to note that measures 55-56 and ensuing motifs are the inversion of measures 48-49. The return to C major (with the aforementioned B♮) concludes the prélude. The cadence on a C chord is approached by a series of chords similar to those at the opening with the additional richness of the seconds, the result of superimposition of dominant and tonic elements, also a most significant use within each chord of the typical melodic intervals of the prélude; seconds, fourths, fifths. An element we have not mentioned much yet is the pedal-points, which form a lexicon of usage in their abundant variety, used in the bass, middle voices, top voices; held, ornamented, or moving (waves), forming dissonance-resolution sequences or giving depth to existent harmonies, or aiding in modulations, they are everywhere as a further illustration of the great importance granted their presence by Debussy in his works.

STRUCTURE.

Bars 1-7. A-1, the first subject in its motif form, not yet fully evolved.

Bars 7-13. B, the second subject, accompanied by bell tones.

Bars 13-27. A return of A-1, its development and the gradual emergence of its more developed form, moving pedals, waves.

Bars 28-41. A-2, the fully stated first subject. (Note the bell motif, measures 40 and 41.)

Bars 42-46. Bells, transition.

Bars 46-71. B, return and development of the second subject.

Bars 72-82. A-2, recapitulated over moving pedal, slowly engulfing waves.

Bars 83-84. A-1, leading to the cadence, measures 85-88.

The performance of this prélude must immediately take into consideration the differentiation of levels and touch to be applied to the bells (resonant, slap touch); to the melodies a series of legato arches of which all the voices must be closely integrated as to dynamics and timing (no single voice standing out, or effects of broken chords by dint of an unequal depression of the entire chord), and which must, except in measures 14 and 15, have a singing quality following their melodic line to the moving pedals, the least dynamic material, subdued but constant. One must also envisage the necessity in pedaling, touch and length of motions, weight, of minute variations of these, from the misty calm of the opening, through the gradual emergence of the Cathedral, to the sonorous apex of its victory over the sea, and the receding, engulfing process of the last sections. A further study of pedaling (of the sustaining pedal) is necessitated by the frequent pedal-points mentioned earlier.

La danse de Puck (Book I)

NATURE. A charming caricature of a favorite mischief-maker, impish but not really bad, and whose lightness of touch and fleetness in this prélude is one moment a little serious, and then again capriciously teasing. The "joyous nomad of the night," whom Shakespeare immortalized, has a long heritage of both good deeds and whimsical mishaps to his credit in the Danish and Swedish legends of his mercurial invasion of Dominican monasteries. His titillating role as page to Oberon, and tormenting meddler in the fairy kingdom of the forests, is perhaps better known with the incredible adventure resulting from Puck's mistake (or mischief) in administering the love elixir and the resultant mixup among all the characters in "A Midsummer Night's Dream."

It would be easy in treating this subject to be influenced by the precedent of Mendelssohn's "Midsummer Night's Dream," but though the texture of Debussy's prélude is scherzando, there ends the resemblance, for this prélude is both deeper in meaning and lighter in touch than its romantic counterpart.

Tripping lightly, sliding, vanishing, reappearing, our nimble elf has a mocking laugh. Is he suddenly taken with remorse or made to account for his deeds? A moment later he is defying the gods, and relishing again his mercurial independence.

STRUCTURE. The structure is again closely aligned with the sonata plan; an exposition containing three subjects and one motif (poking fun at Wagner?), a development of the two opening materials and the motif, a condensed recapitulation containing the first material and the pervading motif, and serving also as a coda.

HARMONY. Rich harmonically, the prélude opens in C minor with a strong emphasis on F as tonal center, which obtains a somewhat Dorian connotation. The motif of measure 6, clearly on the tonal centers of E♭, functions temporarily bitonally. The transition passage (measures 14-17) is chromatic and leads to a section in A♭ over a dominant pedal. Note, in measures 24-27, that the chords on the first half of the beats contain a double appoggiatura that resolves only on the second half of the beat. The third material is treated on the bitonal assumption of D♭ minor and E♭ major, and turns toward C♭ major for the opening of the development (measures 40-41). Noteworthy are the bitonal transitions (measures 55-56, 59-60) and the passage of the cadence which leads by rapid segments of five notes from A♭ major to E major, to A♭ major to E major, and finally to C minor. This rapid horizontal bitonality is only a half-step removed from the superimposed usage of bitonality.

A patent (and perhaps Puckish) mishap occurs nine out of ten times in the interpretation of this prélude. The dotted rhythm of the opening and other large sections of the piece is interpreted as if the thirty-second-note was linked to the succeeding dotted sixteenth-note, whereas Debussy has carefully marked the slur as going from the dotted sixteenth-note to the thirty-second. The effect is very different, and redressing this one aspect of interpretation is of considerable importance. The motif (measure 6 and later) will be found to have the value of a muted brass, i.e., more pungent than the dotted material. Observe, in measures 24-27, that the appoggiaturas are accented, the resolutions lifted. The third material softly legato, a definite contrast to the opening material, must yet be dynamically above the accompaniment in seconds.

MINSTRELS (BOOK I)

This is not the medieval scene with troubadours and their ménestrels, the household entertainers of great feudal lords. This is the American scene and one of its rich Negro heritages, born around 1828 in the plantations, where household servants put on minstrel shows with Bones, Sambo, and Rastus; cake-walks, cornet solos, scratchy banjos and drums, a sentimental song, a few corny jokes, and feline dances were the main features of minstrel groups which started appearing in Europe around 1900 in fairs, or on the boardwalks of the seaside resort at Deauville. One minute fascinated by the precision of the dance steps, then by the supple grace of tumbling figures, the spectator would be rocked by laughter at a cocky gesture of the figures in white tailcoats and top hats, and caught offguard by a sudden glimpse of deep pathos and beauty. It was exotic fare for the Europeans, and set a style (more or less well imitated) for generations of music-hall entertainment. The jazz elements which these shows revealed were soon to be followed by ragtime, trots, blues, the Charleston, and Black Bottom, sources of rhythmic fascination for the European composers, the elements of which were soon incorporated into their works, and heralded a series of American influences on the European musical scene.

Debussy was among the first whose discerning curiosity was captivated by the minstrel groups, and this prélude is a tribute to his keen sense of observation and capture of the mime and humor, the quickly shifting moods and offerings of the show, the catlike precision and suppleness of the rhythmic concept.

Again, despite diversified materials, the structure falls cleanly into place, in rondo-sonata, the details of which are:

Bars 1-8. First material, banjo-cornet-drums, and the beginning of the dance.

Bars 9-34. Second material, of which the opening measures remind one of tap-dancing, with possible pirouettes or somersaults intervening. Note that this second material, which contains a number of characteristic motifs, is yet in continuation of the mood of the opening eight measures. In fact, measures 16-17 and 26-27 echo the opening motif.

Bars 35-44. Third material (a corny joke?).

Bars 45-57. Return of second material, modulated to new levels.

Bars 58-63. A drum interlude, fourth material, heralds the following:

Bars 63-77. A sentimental song, interrupted twice by motifs of the second material.

Bars 78-81. A condensed recapitulation of the first material.

Bars 81-85. Recall of the drum interlude.

Bars 85-89. Final measures condense the second material.

The harmonic palette is largely diatonic. The prélude opens in G major, with blatant and therefore surprising (for Debussy) use of dominant to tonic pedals. The second material opens in G major, with emphasis on the added sixth chord of tonic, turns temporarily toward A minor, makes a pirouette into F♯ major, and lands back in G major at measure 19. The same procedure is repeated but the pirouette this time is in E♭ major and remains there (measures 26-31). The original level of G comes back (32-34), a particular motif which seems to have the constant role of transition between modulations. The third material is chromatic and leads to the return of the second material in F♯ major. The same motif at the original level recurs (49-50), then a flight into A♭ major (51-52), the original level for two measures (53-54), then A major. The drum interlude forms a dominant pedal in G, and the sentimental song, despite its chromatic ascent, is in that key. The final cadence, subdominant to tonic with added sixth, is a jazz classic.

PERFORMANCE. In the performance of this prélude, one notes first that the ornaments of the first section are to be played on the beat and must not mix with, nor detract from, the solid though staccato notes in larger type. Measures 9-10, and similar passages, are marked very detached and should be very strict, whereas the succeeding four measures allow for a certain amount of legato and rubato. Observe that precision and sharpness must reassert themselves from the end of measure 14. Note the slurring in measures 28-31, essential to the syncopated gait. The bad-joke episode, sarcastic in nature, allows for some rubato, to which a quick recovery of precision must succeed at the end of the episode. In the drum episode, note the accents on the seconds. The triplets are light but converge to these accents. Freedom is again in order for the sentimental song, but, at the tempo primo of the last page, strictness must be maintained, and in the acceleration ("plus allant-serrez") of the last few bars, the notes beat a clipped tattoo in rapid succession.

BROUILLARDS (BOOK II)

Debussy's pagan spirit garbs the elements with infinite variety of personality, to which one moment he subjects himself, then in the next moment rejects. Full of the fantasy of a child watching fog through a window, the prélude admires the soft wisps, the great white calm, the sudden luminosity reflected in the evaporating mist. But the imagination of evil spirits, lurking dangers, awesome happenings brings a shiver of Poe-like intensity. What indeed may that grayish web conceal whose damp tendrils reach around our throats, envelop us, obliterate all familiar happy landmarks? We recoil in terror, but we are lost, alone, suspended somewhere between sky and land, and to the moment of terror succeeds the spleen of loneliness. It is like our familiar nightmare; the loved one is near, full of comfort, but we cannot see, cannot move. We reach out, but on all sides there is emptiness, nothing firm can be grasped and held to, and like the prélude we resign ourselves to this calm cocoon, imprisoned and powerless. Yet, even the gossamer appearance of this prélude is deceptive, for its technique is closely integrated, its canvas classically solid.

STRUCTURE.

Bars 1-9. First subject.

Bars 10-17. The first subject serves as the accompaniment over which a new motif acts as transitional material introducing the second-subject group.

Bars 18-24. Second subject, which, nevertheless, retains elements of the first subject, nearly as an ostinato.

Bars 24-37. The first subject returns to open a section of development.

Bars 38-40. A condensed recapitulation gives us first the second subject and its echo, in diminution (41-42).

Bars 43-46. Recapitulation of the first subject.

Bars 47-52. A last recall of the second subject, followed also by an echo of the first subject (48-52) serves as coda to the prélude.

HARMONY. The harmonic materials of this prélude are most interesting, for here a systematic polytonality, already foreshadowed fragmentarily in other works, is given its chance at a fuller interplay, and confirms another aspect of Debussy's incredible richness of materials and techniques. As treated in the préludes, one notes the opposition of sections of harmonic opacity (first subject), the superimposition of evolving progression in bitonality, sections of harmonic semi-opacity (birth of second subject), in which the bitonal accompaniment assumes the form of a pedal-point with the melody notes (half-notes and quarter-notes above) agreeing with half of the accompaniment; sections of harmonic transparency (second subject fully stated) where bitonality is successive instead of superimposed, the second half of the short theme acting as a reverberated deformation of the first half, but clear in its unison scoring. It will be noted that in the first subject the tonal balance is precarious; the successive triads in root position, by their very nature, have more tonal body than the arpeggiated thirty-second pattern, which forms a texture blown apart by the wind.

Specifically the bitonal scheme of the opening material is based on chords in C major, over which are superimposed arpeggi in Eb minor (seventh chords of tonic, dominant, tonic). This level takes on a pentatonic scheme in the fourth measure in which the struggle becomes one of white keys versus black keys. The chord level of this material will remain throughout the prélude on all white keys. Its more capricious partner evolves from Eb minor to pentatonic, enharmonically to D♯ minor (measure 10) but with a strong sense of F♯ as tonal center. In the second subject, one opens with the assumption of a possible D minor, but a pirouette quickly turns the melody to C♯ minor, a melody contour it retains throughout the prélude. Many are the combinations, successive and simultaneous, of this plurality of keys, in constant friction, never resolved—like fog, the harmonic texture is in constant evolution, but recognizes no beginning and no ending.

PERFORMANCE. In the performance of this work, it is particularly necessary to remember again that impressionism is not an apology for sloppy performance, inaccurate pedaling, and an indiscriminate fusion of sounds into an inarticulate mass lacking in any design, or reason for existence. It is worth repeating that such works as "Brouillards," which is typical of a small group of more evanescent sketches, have brought a completely erroneous notion of their nature and of impressionism in general by their model harmonic textures, the nature of their subject matters, and by a convenient inertia on the part of the performers, an inertia which at times has extended itself to the interpretation of the entire works of Debussy. How much easier to lump everything under one heading, particularly if that heading demands no effort, allows all licenses, and eventually sounds the death knell of an important heritage.

The balance of the multiple keys, of the superimposed materials, demands, to the contrary, an even greater abnegation of the performer for the successful projection of such a prélude as this. A careful gauging of the relationship of the opening section, with the chords only slightly more in evidence than the opposing sonorities of the arpeggi, and the attention to the minute changes of dynamics for the more dissonant meetings of the contrasted levels are two of the main concerns of the performer in this work. They are best effected with a minimum of pedaling or else with a pedal frequently changed and depressed only to half-depth. Despite the relative rapidity of the thirty-second-notes, the technique used on them must be light but not crisp; the condition of the fingers then must not be vertical or forcibly flexed. The chords, also light, but allowing for somewhat more tone, may be slightly more prehended. At measures 29-30, note the dynamic apex built rapidly over the ascending arpeggi: the G natural in the right hand forms a dissonant element which helps to build the dynamic tension of the passage.

FEUILLES MORTES (BOOK II)

NATURE. It would be a great mistake to try to find here a realistic description of "Dead Leaves," be it on a windy day or a quiet one! Debussy's sentence (*M. Croche*, p. 17)* is the key to this prélude: "From the fall of the golden leaves that invest the splendid obsequies of the trees." This is the Rite of Autumn, in which the falling leaves are a signal of the suspension of life, creating a static expectancy, a mood of

---

* Dover edition, p. 8.

intense regrets of a past now so far gone, of great sadness and the poignant melancholy of fall. The music, sustained, slow, soft, yet seems to touch a deep wound, bleeding, incurable. As in "Canope," one seeks in vain for an answer to the fragility and beauty of life, to the finality of their disappearance, but the questioning suspense spends itself offering no solution but submission to this tenuous cycle, stretching farther back than man's memory, reaching beyond his comprehension into the future.

HARMONY. The harmony fluctuates rapidly in its coloring and in its choice of tone centers; a state of constant suspense, of avoidance of a defined status, is created. In the three opening measures one finds that the use of D natural and A♯ consistently, obviates C♯ minor and F♯ minor or major as possible tonalities, despite the prominence of these tones as centers of attention. Are they the centers of an, as yet, unnamed series? The closest tonality one can come to in the series of tones present is B minor (allowing for the exchange between G natural and G♯ as harmonic and melodic forms of the scale), yet nowhere is this tonal center in evidence—a series of unresolved dominant-family chords? A few chromatic series, and we barely touch on a Phrygian color, with E as tonal center, when the opening measures return. A middle section opens with a melodic whole-toned series, succeeded by a melody in the middle voice in E natural minor, but at "Plus lent" a rapid alternation of chords in conflicting tonalities approaches bitonality in the rapid exchange. Such are the diversified materials of which the rich sonorities remain suspended beyond the beautiful last cadence, a Phrygian progression from A♯ to E♯ over a pedal of C♯. Does one hear a major tonic on C♯, or a sixth degree chord of the Phrygian mode?

STRUCTURE. Notice that the structure brings us a division into three large sections (A-B-A) and smaller divisions of materials within the large sections. The section A, for instance, extending from measures 1-18, is itself subdivided into three sections, of which the last (15-18) is a concentrated repetition of the first (1-5). The irregular alternation of ternary and binary meters in the first section and its later repetitions, is a further element of unsettling in subtly woven work, as are the syncopations (measures 6-8, for instance), in contrast to more squarely rhythmic portions, such as the opening measures.

PERFORMANCE. The interpretation must seek a sustained legato in the opening section, with dynamics following the lines of the melodic curve. The tempo is frequently taken too fast in the softly melancholic opening, and therefore the middle section ("un peu plus allant—a little faster") loses its gravity in overreaching the first section. Less soft, the middle section affords a drier color for its opening bass, and its frame chords (measures 25-30); not to the point of staccato, but light within the subdued dynamic level of these accompaniment figures which must leave a clear field to the melodic elements for fuller expression. A still clearer color can be used for the ensuing section in which the rhythm, harmony, and Debussy's markings achieve the climax of the prélude's tension. Yet this climax is only MF, and it must not break the structure by too loud a conception. A minimum of pedal, if any, is recommended for this section, which in contrast to the first is no longer soft and legato but sharp in its alternation of chords; therefore resonances must not blend.

LA PUERTA DEL VINO (BOOK II)

It is generally agreed (Vallas, Boucher, Carleton Sprague Smith, Virgil Thomson) that this prélude was written upon receipt of a post-card from De Falla, representing El Puerta del Vino, a gateway of the Alhambra Palace in Granada. It will be remembered that the Alhambra was built around 1231-1273, and occupied by the Moorish princes after the invasion of Spain by these Arabic tribes. A surrounding wall contains numerous gates, built at different periods: Puerta de las Granadas (Gate of the Pomegranates), Puerto de la Justicia (Gate of Justice), the latter being used as an informal court of justice. Yet in no way should one try to find the stimulus of this prélude in the door of the Alhambra, but rather in the turbulent life of the piazza in front of it, where daily are celebrated the joys of wine and song, flamenco singing, drunken roistering, the call of mule drivers, and the unifying pervading rhythm of the habanera, feline in its capacity for nervous accents one moment and languid grace the next. It is a scene of violent contrasts between passionate softness and extreme brutality, of un-diluted primary colors. It forms, with "Soirée dans Grenade" and "La sérénade interrompue," a felicitous Spanish triptych for the piano, by this man who never visited Spain and yet was recognized by the greatest master of its music, De Falla, as having written its truest art music. One wonders at the imaginative intuition of the French, who produced Debussy and the Douanier Rousseau, to name but two!

This prélude is built on three independent levels contrapuntally: the habanera rhythm, forcefully enunciated in the opening measures, and held throughout as an ostinato bass; melodies evolving harmonically but based primarily on the assumption of the alternation of rhythmic figures of three and two (♫♪ ♫); and on a variety of middle-voiced pedal-points. There is a fixity of melodic color and rhythm, to which the tenacious ostinato lends an overall aspect of stubborn adherence, a basic canvas for the violent dynamic oppositions.

STRUCTURE. The structure is again clearly ternary.

Bars 1-4. Introduction, setting the habanera rhythm, first subject.

Bars 5-24. Second subject with its middle-voiced pedals.

Bars 25-30. Second subject echoed.

Bars 31-34. A counter-subject for the second material, ironic and roisterous in character, is given in the middle voice.

Bars 33-41. A development of the second subject enters over this material and soon takes over the entire stage.

Bars 42-44. A return of the first subject, the introduction motif.

Bars 44-49. Further development of the second subject.

Bars 50-65. Development section in which figures, ♩ ♫ | ♩ ♫, of the first subject alternate with the triple-duplet figure of the second subject.

Bars 66-90. Recapitulation of the second subject and its echoed phrase and cadence.

HARMONY. The harmonic color is varied, rich in its single elements, and even richer in superimposition. The independence of these various elements as to key brings us again to the consideration of polytonality. The basic habanera rhythm does not vary in the first half of the prélude, and again in the recapitulation, from its position as a tonic pedal of D♭. Yet already in the introduction the upper voice is clearly in opposition, outlining the key of D natural. A second conflict to the pedal is brought by the second subject in Moorish or Arabic scale (built on the succession B-C-D-E-F-A♭-B, with B and D acting as tonal centers, and E as dominant or appoggiatura tone, until a chromatic succession (16-18) brings all voices to temporary agreement, in the key of D♭ major. The following section, partially whole-toned and pentatonic, resumes its opposition to the pedal, with the added richness of superimposed chords of its own (27-30). In measures 33-41, chromatic sequences bridge the gap between the thematic material and the pedal, to again come to a common denominator, D♭, measure 41. The return of the introduction brings again the struggle of D♭ and D natural, succeeded by six measures in which the pedal rests on B♭ assumption and the upper voices in G minor, a not too distant arrangement, but for the cross-relations of F natural and F♯. Chromaticism pervades the ensuing section of development, a coloring Debussy often associates with mockery, but the recapitulation brings back the Moorish scale, and the ostinato on D♭. The final cadence is a resolution of both materials; it includes the E♭ tone center of the transposed echo and the D♭ triad belonging to the ostinato.

PERFORMANCE. Note first that the prélude is marked as "Mouvement de habanera" ("In the motion of the habanera"), not in the *tempo* of habanera. Like "Soirée dans Grenade" this prélude is frequently played too fast, and too rigidly. All dances are characterized more by their rhythm than by their tempo. A waltz may be slow or fast and still remain a waltz. Similarly the habanera can vary in tempo, and within that tempo retain suppleness of line. Observe next that Debussy heads this prélude with "avec de brusques oppositions d'extrême violence et de passionnée douceur" ("with sudden oppositions of extreme violence and passionate softness"). This injunction is usually only half realized, the entire prélude being either uniformly languid or uniformly violent. One should then note the successive markings: F, P, PP, F, FF, MF, P, PP, etc., and further note that Debussy marks the wanted distinction between the various levels; for instance, in the fifth measure, where the bass is marked PP, and the upper part is marked P "très expressif." At the marking "ironique," it is suggested that the upper notes be held for their durations by the fingers, whereas the pedal catches only fleetingly the bass notes. Further, the note on the second beat can be slightly

anticipated, and the last melodic note of the measure may be slightly
lengthened.

Les Fées sont d'exquises danseuses (Book II)

This prélude, "Fairies are exquisite dancers," dedicated to the
ephemeral charm of mythological characters, reminds us of the delightful illustrations of some editions of fairy tales. For these tales are split
into two diverging heritages, going far back to the dual role of good and
evil, which fairies have always enjoyed in Egyptian, Greek, Scandinavian, and Celtic lore. In more recent times one branch of this rich
lore eventually underlined the grotesque, evil, humped, bad-tempered,
jeering forms of bad spirits, an association with witchcraft and medieval superstition, scenes of obscene revelry and ghoulish delights. Another branch endowed this lore with an ever more exquisitely refined
beauty, ethereal, and nearly mystic in their powers. Fairies became associated with the purest aspirations of knighthood and even later were
invoked as helping Muses, or guardian angels to the geniuses of Cer-
vantes, Shakespeare, Tasso; immortalized as the poetic counterpart to
the Eternal Feminine, shy, capricious but tender, diminutive and fleet
in their motions, enchanting in their capacity for beauty and grace of
motion, rewarding, scolding, inspiring from their gossamer pedestal,
they live in a rarefied atmosphere, free from the ugliness of worldly ills
and squalor.

This last is indeed the romantic heritage of the Debussy prélude,
which does not contain one heavy-footed note in its eight pages. Debussy's sylphs dance a round in the air, sing tender melodies, dance
again, dream awhile, resume their harmonious course, their wings
tinted by opalescent reflections. Debussy witnesses them, entranced, restrained for fear of breaking the spell, but, at the cadence, those last
three notes are like a dancer frozen in the midst of a motion. Has one
of the sylphs spied the human intruder, horrified at the alarming secrets
of her pastime, which he now shares?

Structure. A rondo unified by the recurrence of the opening "flying" theme, the prélude alternates in its episodes between fleet dance

measures and more lyric passages, in a richly capricious form, yet classically treated.

Bars 1-10. A, flying theme.

Bars 11-14. B, a small echo of its later lyric statement.

Bars 15-23. A returns briefly.

Bars 24-31, 32-45. B, fully stated, in two contrasting phrases.

Bars 45-65. C, a fleet cadenza related to the texture of A.

Bars 66-71. D, tender, lyric, a family member of the B episode.

Bars 72-86, 88-89. B, a recall of the opening of the second phrase of the B episode under a trill, with the addition of a nostalgic call—"un peu en dehors."

Bar 87. A brief recall of A.

Bars 100-115. A, flying theme, recapitulated and extended.

Bars 116-119. D, recalled but in a slim scoring.

The prélude ends with a last recall of A, and the aforementioned three first notes of the D♭ scale.

HARMONY. The harmonic texture of this prélude is basically modal, and except for transitions, chromatic or modulatory, based on the Dorian mode transposed at different levels, with E♭ as tonic in the A section, then D♭ as tonic in the first B section, to C♯ for the second phrase of this B section, and so forth. Further, the flying theme is not bitonal but contains, within its arabesque, both a series of triads and appoggiaturas to these triads. For instance, the opening two measures contain the progression IV, III, I/ IV, VII, I/. The E natural on the first beat is in both cases an appoggiatura to the A♭-C-E♭ chord. The C and A natural of the second beat in the first measure are appoggiaturas to a G♭-B♭-D♭ chord. The B natural and G natural of the third beat of the first measure are appoggiaturas to the E♭-G♭-B♭ chord, etc. Yet in the rapid lightness of this passage no dynamic recognition is to be given these successive dissonances, which, however, give a certain unreality to the otherwise clear harmonic progressions.

PERFORMANCE. The performance demands a very rapid and light finger action for the opening section. A more singing tone, lyric, rubato, is afforded for the contrasting sections (rubato, sans rigueur, caressant) in which dissonances and curves of the melodic line can be given minute attention in giving full expression to these sections. These sections can also afford the coloring of the pedal which is quite out of keeping in the opening section. The many forms of trills, some incorporated into the texture and others indicated by symbol, should be fluent and unmetric in their pulses.

BRUYÈRES (BOOK II)

A quaint and calm pastoral scene, with a touch of loneliness, is evoked by this prélude. Be it in the moors of the Scottish highlands, or in Ireland, or on the severe coast of Brittany wherein the lavender-rose bushes thrive, their dainty blossoms stir a childlike delight, a nostalgic sentimentality. One is suddenly reminded of the Paris exhibits of the years 1900 to 1914, with the annual reappearance of the works of a painter who specialized in hilly landscapes at sunset, with blond wheat in the foreground, the lavender heather above it, and the reddish-purple sun setting in a seashore horizon. It is much more than a remote possibility that Debussy, an assiduous exhibit visitor, would have seen some of these works and been captivated both by the singleness of their subject matter and by the Mauve Decade charm of their conception. This would account for both the rustic and the nostalgic quality of loneliness of this prélude.

Though the melodic line of the opening section and other portions of the prélude elects a pentatonic series in contrast to portions in which the scalewise passages shun none of the eight possible tones of the scale, this melodic subtlety, evoking a folk quality, is underlined nearly throughout by a straightforward diatonic framework. The greater proportion of the sections are in A♭ major, with a middle section in B♭ major.

A structure similar to that found in a majority of the préludes is here again in evidence, and brings us a very charming contrast of tender, introspective improvisations with livelier cadenza-like passages, both so reminiscent of the timbre of the flute heard in the clarity and quiet of the early evening air, that the pianist is hard put to realize this tonal conception of his instrument. One observes first that dryness and staccato effects are herein nearly non-existent. Even the shortest note-values, performed exactly as to timing, are yet given a legato singing quality. Curves, and not angles, are of the nature of this composition, which means in effect that dynamic jerks or sudden outbursts are also to be eliminated. The use of the soft pedal will give the very desirable feeling of a faraway scene. Yet the abuse of an anemic or over-romantic boudoir lushness would fall in the other no less pernicious extreme, for the simplicity of this charming scene does not condone perverse effects. A plastic but naive grace, capable in turn of joy, tenderness, nostalgia, yet subdues these emotions within the great calm of the whole.

General Lavine—eccentric (Book II)

This charmingly humorous and biographical prélude brings us once more to the American scene, for its hero, Edward Lavine, typifies the Anglo-Saxon dexterity of clowning, and Debussy in his choice of musical materials makes clear Lavine's American birthright. It was only recently that a most touching letter from Mrs. Lavine brought us the sad news that "General Lavine" was no more.

It is all too tempting, in considering this prélude, to quote at least sections from Alfred Frankenstein, in his detailed and very documented article in "This World" section of the *San Francisco Chronicle*, of March 11, 1945, a little more than a year before the passing of Mr. Lavine, on March 25, 1946. We quote:

"Whenever you look at a campaign ribbon on a soldier's chest you are, in all probability, inspecting the handiwork of the only human being, living or dead, of whom Claude Debussy composed a musical portrait. Today Edward Lavine lives in the desert town of Twenty-nine Palms, Calif., hard by the Joshua Tree National Monument, and calmly manufactures most of the 'service bars' that are used in the Army, but when Debussy wrote about him he was one of the most celebrated figures in international vaudeville. He was a comic juggler, half tramp and half warrior, but more tramp than warrior, and he was billed as 'General Ed Lavine, the Man Who Has Soldiered All His Life.' . . . He made his first appearance in Paris at the Marigny Theatre on the Champs-Elysees in August, 1910, and he returned to that establishment two years later. . . . Lavine is a tall man, and his 'uniform' was calculated to make him look taller—one of the New York reviewers said he seemed to be at least nine feet high."

172

Mr. Frankenstein then describes in detail the prodigiously amusing act, its many props, the costume, the imaginary fight, and the juggling. Apparently Debussy was eventually approached by the manager of the Marigny Theatre in view of music for a show built around General Lavine, a project which never bore fruit. It is a question if the prélude can have incorporated some early sketches for the revue, or is a reaction, a souvenir of Debussy's repeated attendances at the Marigny. We quote:

"But whether it be an impression pure and simple or an impression concocted from music originally conceived as accompaniment to the General's antics, the prelude certainly does convey an atmosphere of jerky movement and fantastic comedy. The little burlesque trumpet-call of the opening, the preparatory bars 'dans le style et le mouvement d'un cake-walk,' and above all the marking 'spirituel et discret' at the point where the actual cake-walk begins, are Debussyan humor at its best. I find the 'puppet limp' hard to discover, but there are strong suggestions of jugglery all the way through, not the least of them being the abrupt chromatic passage in 16th notes first heard in the 29th and 30th bars."

In the mood, the harmonic and melodic language, the opposition of strident rhythms with sentimental moments, one cannot escape the comparison to "Minstrels"; indeed, these excursions into American humor share even motifs in common, but there the logic of composition ends, and the infinite psychological subtlety of Debussy contrives sufficient difference to mark his degree of observation. Lavine is more discreet, more refined in his humor, albeit perhaps less direct. His is not a folk expression, but a highly sophisticated satire. The effects are more studied, polished, further from the feline pulse of the minstrel cake-walker, and also of his bawdy jokes.

The rondo-sonata structure takes us through a fascinating alternation of the two main materials (A and B) of this prélude, each of which can in turn be subdivided into characteristic motifs. The details of the form:

Bars 1-10, First subject, containing an ornamented pedal-point (A) and a motif in triads (A-2).

Bars 11-17. Second subject, containing a first motif in eighth- and sixteenth-notes (B-1) and a second one in dotted rhythm (B-2).

Bars 17-18. A-1 forms a small bridge to a fuller statement of the second subject materials.

Bars 19-34. Second subject, B-1, but a syncopated and chromatic second phrase substitutes for B-2, and gives a capricious development to this section.

Bars 35-42. B-1 and B-2, second subject returns as in original statement.

Bars 43-45. A-1 serves as bridge again.

Bars 45-69. First subject, A-2 alternates with a drum motif derived from A-1.

Bars 70-76. Second subject, B-1 and B-2.

Bars 76-78. A-1 serves as bridge.

Bars 78-94. Recapitulation of measures 19-34 (varied second subject).

Bars 94-100. B-1 stated twice.

Bars 100-102. A-2, last statement.

Bars 103-109. Final measures, based on A-1.

The harmonic material is varied and capricious, though limited by diatonic assumptions, inclusive of chromatic successions. The first motif (A-1) which pervades the prélude as a sort of pedal-ostinato opens with a strongly diatonic movement of dominant to tonic in C major (the dominant key). In later usages it alternates between this position and that on tonic, i.e., F major. The second motif (A-2) has a bitonal flavor in its alternation between chords in flats and chords on white keys, its overall effect being that of a brass instrument badly out of tune. Its structure in thirds, both horizontally and vertically, belies its serious intent at dissonance. The second subject is in F major; its seeming pentatonism (C-D-F-G-A) is found to be the outline of the tonic added sixth chord, plus the G as passing tone, a chord which accompanies the dotted rhythm B-2, with its clashes of tonic and dominant harmony. At measures 23-25, a series of felicitous suspensions opens the gate for a chromatic passage, tensing the dynamic canvas to a molto crescendo. In the immediately ensuing section, B-2 in F major, is now superimposed upon an A♭ pedal and harmonies, a passing bitonalism, continued measure 45-69 by the rapid alternance of chords on various tone centers, a successive polytonality born of the essence of A-2.

In the performance observe first that the thirty-second-notes of motif A-1 must be rapid and very sharp (strident), whereas the A-2 motif,

174

though dry, is more at ease, phlegmatic in its trend, with the exception of the SFF measure 7. The second subject is good-humored, discreet, easy-going, but is frequently jolted by the motif A-1, or by chromatic sequences. This alternation of dry, staccato, loud accents, with softly laconic passages is of utmost importance to the humor of this clown, full of tricks, surprises, sudden turnabouts from a poker face to exaggerated expressions of surprise, pain, laughter. It is baroque music, enjoying fully these extreme oppositions of dynamism, and the performance must not underrate their effects.

LA TERRASSE DES AUDIENCES DU CLAIR DE LUNE (BOOK II)

"Moonlit Terrace" is the common but incorrect translation. "The Terrace for Moonlight Audiences"? The exact origin of the poetic, esoteric, and charmingly tortuous title of this prélude seems to have been the subject of some controversy. It is variously ascribed as originating in Pierre Loti's *L'Inde Sous les Anglais,* in which he describes the terraces to hold counsel at moonlight, ("terrasses pour tenir conseil au clair de lune"), and to René Puaux, French author, in a letter written to the newspaper, *Le Temps.* In *Le Beau Voyage,* René Puaux, while describing the Durbar ceremonies for the coronation of King George V, as Emperor of India, speaks of "the hall of victory, the hall of pleasure, the garden of the sultanesses, the terrace for moonlight audiences. . . ."

Both origins would suggest a Hindu scene, of which there is not the slightest counterpart in the music of this prélude. Is it not likely that this charming phrase captivated Debussy's sensitive imagination, and that from this initial stimulus a series of chain-reactions, of associations brought about the mood of this deeply thoughtful and moving composition? A daydream which has meandered far from its inception in reality invests the moonlit scene with innumerable sentiments: tenderness, cold loneliness, passionate unrest, delight and sensuous languor, but all permeated by an evanescence, a sense of unreality with which moonlight endows all that it touches. That sense of sleep-walking, a strange uneasiness (caused perhaps by the opening motif so often reiterated in its strange harmonies or by the ethereal chromatic arabesque over it), stirs in us the question as to who are those under this moonlight. They are wrapped in secrecy and remoteness. Is it because we are dreaming that we cannot reach them? Or is it that they are intangible because they are lost in time, or in space, far away, or long ago? Is it by association of texts, or by similarities in musical texture or mood, that one is in this prélude reminded of some of Debussy's songs? A little of the eerie pathos of the ghostly lovers of "Colloque sentimental" (Verlaine); a few bars (59-65) of "Fantoches" (*Fêtes galantes*—Verlaine) resembling measures 12-14 of the prélude; and the poem of "Clair de lune" (*Fêtes galantes*—Verlaine), with its disenchanted masks and sadly beautiful moonlight. One wonders if Debussy in this less morbid prélude still might have been under the influence of a similar stimulus? There is, at least, little doubt of the far-off waltz rhythm, of the sentimental, hyper-romantic accents of this turn-of-the-century poem.

In its large lines the prélude forms into a ternary form. The first section (measures 1-12) acts as a prelude to the prélude; it sets a lonely, uneasy mood in its two opening measures, which many consider to be based on a deformed opening motif of the folksong "Au clair de la lune," a very remote resemblance. The salient aspect of these two measures is the bitonal effect they achieve, the hollowness of the motif of the second measure, B-F-G-B, the moonlight shafts of the soft chromatic arabesques, the compactness of these materials which deal out such a psychological punch here and in their later recalls. In contrast, the next measures (3-4) foreshadow the passionate middle section, the waltz rhythm which will permeate the contrasting moods of the prélude. Measures 5-8 return to the first materials to which a sudden reaction, as if a will not to be engulfed by this one pervading thought, brings a transition material (measures 9-12) leading into the second main portion of the prélude.

The second portion of the prélude (measures 13-36) is a development on the stylized waltz of which the barest accents were set forth in measures 3-4, and which now become explicit in two motifs (measures 13-15, and measures 16-18). Both are chromatic in texture and in evolution, epitomizing late nineteenth-century romanticism in harmony, melody, and mood (a temptation which reminds us of Ravel's "Valses"). There are moments of great surging, then of loneliness and pleading, unrest, and a jagged dynamic line leads to the emotional apex of measures 29-32; a very subdued return of the two materials of this portion concludes the section, and from a structural standpoint could be said to start a condensed recapitulation in which the second-subject group would appear first.

The third section opens in measure 36, with the return of the motif of the second measure of the prélude, followed in due course by the materials of the first measure. The cadence, which by fragments of voice-leading could be considered whole-toned, seems better explained as an admission of the bitonal nature of the first and last sections, i.e., as bitonal in C major and F♯ major, with this last tonality winning out in the final chord.

Note in the performance that the two levels of action at the opening are marked by Debussy in such a way as to give dynamic preference to the lower level, and subduing the upper arabesque which, at PPP, should be a bare whisper. The notation "un peu en dehors" (somewhat brought out) is certainly in view of preserving this important motif from becoming mere accompaniment to the arabesque. As to tempo, observe that, at the opening of the large middle section, one returns to "au Mouvt."; the return is obviously to the slow tempo of the opening, since the only change since has been for slightly more animated, three bars before the middle section. This middle portion is frequently performed too fast, due to an erroneous assumption that "au Mouvt." means to assume that the music has now "gotten under way"! There are, though, two fragments which are accelerando in this section, i.e., measures 20-24 and 28-31. The remainder is in the tempo of the beginning. In the last section, the seven measures of the end are slower than the opening tempo. It will be noticed that the measures of six counts are not metrically identical; they fluctuate readily between measures of two plus two plus two, or measures of three plus three, or measures of six equalized beats. One of the interesting and challenging effects is given in the third measure and in many later portions, i.e., the Viennese waltz, which divides the measure in two bars of three beats with a strong first beat, a swell to the third beat which is somewhat elongated or suspended in the air. The swell indicated by Debussy is an orchestral effect difficult even to approximate at the piano. The low pedal

177

(C♯ in this measure) can be of some help in heightening the dynamics in transit to the third beat. In measure 30 the lower accent to the second beat of the measure realizes even better this effect of swelling, or fast crescendo. It should be obvious that the romantic character of the middle portion would demand an expressive, singing tone, an interpretation lavish in its observance of the curves of the melodic line and the rich dissonances, appoggiaturas, and sensitive harmonies, yet keeping the proportions within the scope of this thoughtful sketch, which never quite forgets its opening mood, and which in synthetizing the turn of the century has retained the control born of perspective.

ONDINE (BOOK II)

Debussy's interest in supernatural beings, and his pagan yet mystic love of nature and its elements (sea, wind, forests), an interest which he shares with the romantic movement, again furnishes us with subject matter for a prélude. From the impish Puck, to the elegant elves and Fées, and now to the equally graceful Ondines, one finds the romantic expression in Debussy has undergone an idealistic transformation. All gross connotations, or obvious effects, have been refined out of the substance he uses to achieve the liberation of these delightful spirits from the mortal fetters of heavy handling—a most welcome restoration of their evanescence and mystery.

Ondines belong to the mythological lore of Scandinavian and Germanic countries. They are water nymphs, whose crystal palaces are in deep pools of river beds or lakes; singing, dancing, flitting through the waters, they lure unwary fishermen and voyagers, and transport them to their deep palaces where days pass in oblivious bliss, surrounded by beauty, and timeless forgetfulness—a legend to which we owe Die Lorelei, and the Rhine Maidens, and innumerable other nineteenth-century musical counterparts.

The allusions to water, to ripples, to flitting figures darting capriciously, splashing gracefully, pervades much of the prélude in its melodic materials and accompaniment figures. It is contrasted by two materials which are more metric, less fluid in delineation, perhaps dancing, and in the middle section, a satiric, subtly ominous material over an augmented fifth pedal, reminds us of the hollow jeering quality of the song, "Le faune."

HARMONY. It is interesting to note that the very elusive deformation effected upon an image by rippling water finds its very natural counterpart in successive polytonality (measures 4-6-7) applied to a small motif. This polytonality in larger sweeps, and applied to a variety of motifs, conveys the fluidity, the escape from tone-centers, of the sections descriptive of the aquatic play of the water nymphs. The antique minor is used to give a nostalgic twist to the round-tune of the second main section, interspersed yet with balneal motifs (measure 16 on). The third material, chromatic in the faunish theme is bitonally superimposed upon the assumption of a whole-toned series (Eb-F-G-A-B-Db-Eb); the tone centers, Eb and B natural (augmented fifth), are shared by both levels. The final cadence, born of the polytonal first section, hesitated between F♯ major and D major, and elects this last as final tonic chord.

STRUCTURE. The structure is clearly conceived in three successive sections with the return of part of the first at the end, i.e., A-B-C-A. The central portion, C, is the axis of the entire work; it receives the most development and its coloring exerts particular fascination.

Bars 1-15. A, varied motifs, water music.

Bars 16-27. B, a round, scherzando dance-steps with allusions to A.

Bars 28-31. Transition, a backward look to motifs of A and a forward look to the pervading melody of C.

Bars 32-61. C, treated as a set of variations, in successive presentations of its theme, with a recall of B (38-39), and of A (40-41). After its full statement, the C section could be considered as the development section of this sonata-rondo.

Bars 62-74. A, condensed in its recapitulation serving as coda.

PERFORMANCE. In the performance of the opening section, and the last also, one must be aware that the many motifs fall into two types; one evoking the opalescence of underwater, and the others the scintillating surface effects. The dynamics will be softer for the first group, sharper for the second, and will also determine the touch, which will alternate between a singing tone, born of flexible, relaxed fingers, and a crisper tone, born of curved finger action, but not heavy in dynamism.

179

Measures 11-13 are excellent illustrations of the rapid interplay of these two types of material, the notes in small type demanding the crisp rapidity, whereas those in heavy type are more singing, softer. The second section brings the performer the problem of the minute slurs by two, of the melody, which, however, must not detract from the scherzando lightness of the passage. Observe in the C section the staccato bass, the long legato middle pedals, and the melody, part staccato, part legato. These oppositions are very important. In a number of sections the bass pedal tones should be sensitized by the sustaining pedal. Note the climaxes on the apexes of the melodic lines: a swelling wave motion of the opening section, expressive and suggestive in its orchestral colors, so apt to such effects.

HOMMAGE A S. PICKWICK ESQ. P.P.M.P.C. (Book II)

NATURE. A Dickensian tribute, which worthily matches its good humored wit with that of the famed author of *The Pickwick Papers*, gives us a rapid glance into the activities and moods of Samuel Pickwick, Esq., general chairman of the Pickwick Club, immodestly named after him, and dedicated to "the purpose of investigating the source of the Hampstead ponds." Our hero serves as guardian and adviser to three members of the club, with whom he travels about, meeting laughable adventures. Elderly but most verdant, Sam Pickwick is a benevolent soul, but has his moments. Starting off with a pompous complacency, wittily scored by the sonorous use of "God Save the King" in the bass, our hero soon recovers his genial good nature, absent-minded at times, diffident, gay, engrossed in his own superiority. One visualizes his house: "here and there souvenirs of Zululand, views of Christiania, terrible rifles (which, happily, do not shoot anymore), family portraits, a peaceful garden." *

The prélude is rich with sudden and comic contrasts, from the sweeping line of the opening measures in its full contrapuntal use, large range, dynamic force, albeit tongue-in-cheek, to the minute little dotted melody, light, animated and soft, in the middle register, which works up a temper to crashing chords, in two opposite sequences, in a comic

* Debussy, *Lettres à son éditeur,* p. 182.

deformation; but again the dotted rhythm brings us benevolence and good nature, but—what ho!—a crescendo molto, two bitter phrases, our hero controls himself just in time; no crashing chords, but instead a most disarmingly diffident phrase found already in the sequel of the first page. A distant unaccompanied popular jig-tune (whistled?), the dotted figure in augmentation slows down the movement, but do we detect a last trace of pompousness in our hero's farewell?

HARMONY. The harmonic colors are very straightforward, diatonic. The key of F major is predominant, but shares the spotlight with numerous allusions to D minor in the opening 19 measures. A section in C major, an alternation of C major and B♭ major, lands us in this last key for a brief section (measures 30-31) then to E♭. A chromatic passage (35-36) brings four measures of G minor. The whistled tune in D major, but pentatonic (D-E-F♯-A-B) brings us back to the home key of F major, with a completion of our rondo form.

PERFORMANCE. It is obvious that the best performance of this piece depends on the amount of humor one sees in it! A letter-correct performance, but not imbued with the spirit of fun could be well-nigh deadly. All those violent contrasts must be realized, given their proper character; their timing is of the art of good story-telling. A heavy, sluggish accentuation of the dotted rhythm theme robs it of all its character, and takes away the humor of its querulous crescendi. Similarly, a light and charming interpretation of the opening section would be treachery indeed. One must also watch for the more expressive melodies superimposed above or below the dotted rhythms and which must be placed on a different interpretative level. In the third page the thirty-second-note runs must continue without interruption, to land on the longer note value on the upper staff; an effect of "hiccups" in cutting these runs off from their landing place may be humorous, but is not indicated by Debussy. The whistled air, very light, distant, scherzando.

CANOPE (BOOK II)

Canope or Canopus, a city of ancient Egypt on the river Nile not far from the Mediterranean, gave its name to porous, earthen urns, four of which, containing the principal digestive organs of a deceased person, were buried with the mummy. Covered by a lid in the form of the head of Osiris, one of the main Egyptian divinities, these jars played an important part in the funeral observances. By analogy, similar vases used by the Etruscans some six centuries B.C., but covered by a likeness of the deceased, are also called Canopic jars. Very simple in line, these jars bear no ornaments, and the sculptured head that covers them has a nearly stylized classical simplicity of traits.

But again, the object is not what concerns Debussy in this prélude. He is not describing a funeral urn for us, but the mood evoked by the object and his personal reactions to this series of associations. He reaches far back to archaic ceremonials, to the magnificent Canope, of which there remain only the ruins of temples and palaces. As in a dream he evokes antique processionals, stately, calm, permeated by a dignified, gentle, and resigned sadness. There are pleading, questioning accents, often repeated, insistent but not impatient, as, one with the mourners of this ancient ceremonial, Debussy seems to seek the key to this infinitely old mystery of death, of ruin, of the passing of all things, however magnificent, however vital, however tender. There is no revolt in the questioning, for the answer is lost in the infinity, in the strains of the receding processional, and a last, far-off, murmured sob.

In its very simplicity the opening melody of this prélude is perhaps one of the most deeply touching phrases in all the préludes. The parallel chords succeed each other, unhurried, even, and yet so deeply poignant. Modal in treatment, with D as tonic, a temporary modulation at the fourth bar has a most telling effect, not only in contrast to the three opening measures, but in the progression to the tonic cadence of the fifth measure. The partial unison statement of this melody brings us to even greater simplicity. We expect its second phrase, but instead the first of two insistent and plaintive motifs makes its appearance (measures 7-10), the chromatic design (through G minor), the repeated note, the broken rhythm of its short ascent and descent, its recitative character, are all the more tragic after the simple opening. A second motif, more tender, but equally sad, enters (measures 11-12). Its accents indicate the assumption of an appoggiatura resolving upward to B♭, which in turn falls back, slurred to A, as if emotion-spent, a descent which is haltingly continued to D. The ascent is attempted again, but with the same desolate result. The opening melody, and the two motifs are the materials of this prélude, with a central portion of six measures, transitory in character, which returns us to our three materials, but with the opening melody placed between the two motifs instead of before.

The calm legato and the phrasing marked by Debussy seem the two most important factors to recommend to the performer in the opening material. In the ensuing two motifs the minute differentiation, within the "piano" dynamic level, of the notes marked with a dash, accented and held, while those marked by a dot are lightly detached, and those that are slurred and legato, joined together, are the most important in these short but highly expressive materials. Note that the A at the beginning of measure 7 is the end of the preceding phrase and should not be detached from it. The final chord, a pedal of superimposed fifths (C-G-D), does not assuage our thirst for a final cadence. We are left with a choice of three tonal centers, and yet none. Our question, too, remains unanswered, lost in infinity!

LES TIERCES ALTERNÉES (BOOK II)

Our problem in this prélude is no longer the subtle, stark, tender, or forceful depiction of a scene, a legend, an imaginative portrait with literary connotations. So close to terminating the series of "Préludes," we are already anticipating the series of "Études," and our imagination, which so far has been stimulated by such an engrossing array of materials, must now readjust to this study in abstraction, with its purely musical significance, its singleness of problem—thirds! What indeed are the resources of the field Debussy has now elected? With what materials will he weave this exciting prélude so purely dedicated to the keyboard, that it reminds one of Debussy's rich inheritance from the French clavecinistes? Major, minor, augmented, diminished thirds—Debussy leads us through rapid alternations of these, of distant thirds that can evoke clusters of thirds piled high into an infinite chord, thirds that belong to one key against thirds from another, friction of chord against chord, stationary thirds which form pedal-points, melodic thirds which outline a melody, middle-voiced thirds that suggest the harmony (often outlining intervals of thirds in succession as well as vertically), chromatic thirds which tense the texture. They are all there, and we suddenly realize that what had seemed a somewhat limited field, has become under Debussy's guidance a rapid exploration of innumerable horizons; now tense and whirring like turbines, and later lyric and soft, gracefully playful, and again lightly tattooing their pattern on the ears, these Debussy thirds are capable of limitless expression.

From the slower introduction which sets the basic premise of the entire prélude's alternation of thirds (sometimes closely related, and sometimes distantly linked) through the large first section, a soft contrasting middle portion, and the return of the condensed first section, one realizes that Debussy has not lost sight of his classical structural assumptions in this clear A-B-A structure, reminiscent of the dance form with its contrasting trio.

In the alternation of the thirds Debussy elects, in a number of large sections of the prélude, to keep one team of thirds moving and the other in a more static pedal-point role, yet these pedals are far from being inactive, not only in their consonance-dissonance roles to the moving thirds, but in that they have a pattern of ascendence and descendence, which is fruitful in the dynamic increases and decreases of the main phrases. For instance, in measures 11 and 12, the pedal on B-D moves in the next two measures up by a skip of thirds to D-F. These measures are repeated, then the pedal moves again by thirds from D-F to F-A, to A-C. It is at this level that the first climax is reached, clinched by a change of tonal color. Another change in tonal color, also climactic though a half-step lower, brings a second climax from which the line descends, but stepwise this time. Brief transition passages (and the middle section) make use of all the thirds as moving voices. For instance, measures 34-39, in which the two teams of thirds parallel each other's motion in transition to a developmental section in which the pedal is now in the lower voice. This switching of materials from the right hand to the left hand, and vice versa, as well as the frequent passages calling for hands crossing over each other, are two more, though superficial, earmarks of this prélude's lineage from the clavecinistes.

The very materials described cannot but form a varied harmonic color. We have already mentioned the interplay of the two teams of alternating thirds, one moving and one nearly static, which can, in some passages, agree, and in others, disagree, somewhat or violently, as to harmony. And this harmony may be diatonic with straightforward inferred progressions, or, in investigating the superimposition of distant thirds, it may lead to far-reaching alterations of the diatonic pattern, to chromatic progressions, or, in other passages, to aggregates better analyzed as bitonal or polytonal, a door which Debussy has more than once opened, and which in view of the evolution of this principle since his time, we should acknowledge with interest in the texture of Debussy's music wherever it applies.

Note that besides the evolving pedal-points, and the evolving harmony, we have a further material to investigate in the great portion of this prélude: the melody formed within the framework of the alternating thirds and signalized by Debussy by a dash under its component notes. "Les notes marquées du signe − doucement timbrées" ("The notes marked with the sign − softly ringing"). These notes, so frequently lost in the maze of thirds, form a true melody, curving down, then up, evolving in its design. Observe that in some measures the dash designating the melodic notes occurs on the first beat, in others on the second beat, or not at all, and later on the half-beats as well, or still on both beats. In this manner the melody is not only endowed with a varied pitch line, but that pitch line is given rhythmic significance as well.

For the dynamics of the performance then, one is concerned with several elements: the large dynamic levels of the phrases, of which the evolution of the pedal-points is a good barometer, the harmonic rhythm of the progressions, and the melodic contour as to pitch and rhythm of the melodic notes. As to tempo, moderately animated at the beginning and a little more animated after the introduction, which does not mean a sudden headlong rush, full of acceleration and ritardando. The tempo remains even, the dynamics fluctuate. The middle portion by its note values makes a welcome contrast, but there is no reason to assume a slower basic tempo except at the word "retenu," and slight holding back, after which the original tempo is reinstated at "au Mouvt.," with no lapse to the end. No rubato is permissible in this prélude, and one of the greatest charms is the exactness of rhythm and tempo which follows through to its last soft notes.

Even a cursory glance at the texture of the prélude should warn the performer that pedaling should be used only as a restrained coloring. In the introduction and the middle section, the texture is more adaptable to normal pedaling. The evolution of the materials in slower motion will be equally so, and in the other sections a better effect will be obtained through very reduced pedaling, and only in the crescendi marked by Debussy.

It is suggested that the hand concerned with the moving thirds be placed over the hand playing the pedal-like thirds. It gives a slightly greater prominence to the moving material, and a greater clearance for motion to the hand which is under, which should have a lowered metacarpal bridge. Despite this slight dynamic advantage granted the moving voice, it must be remembered that both hands are limited by the markings of Debussy, "lightly detached but *without* dryness" (italics author's). A crisp, crackling touch is not welcomed in this prélude. The motions of lift must be gentle and the fingers pliable in their muscular condition. This absorbency of the fingers becomes even more marked in the softly legato middle section.

FEUX D'ARTIFICE (BOOK II)

There is a well-established custom which prescribes that the last display shot off in a fireworks exhibit (le bouquet) should be the richest, most varied, most powerful one of the evening, a vertiginous climax to which the children (old and young) look forward with eager anticipation. It is the embodiment of a general aesthetic principle, and, deeper yet, of a philosophy of life which aspires to ever greater achievements and expects a final crowning achievement.

Such is indeed the role, both aesthetically and poetically, of this last of the twenty-four préludes. In its predecessors one has run the gamut of emotions from youth to death, candor to furor to melancholy. An exacting pianistic technique has been developed to match the rich effects of a multiplicity of rhythms, melodies, harmonies, the like of which responds to our wildest dreams of treasure chests in Baghdad. How can a composer finish such a series of compositions? Debussy, the magician, has still one further trick up his sleeve, for this performance, and an endless resource for a lifetime of such surprises. Nearly out of his own backyard he plucks the enchantment of the evening of Bastille Day celebration, with its myriads of jewels exploding in the blue velvet sky, and reflected in the silvery river below. For few are the connoisseurs who do not find a place on one of the many bridges over the Seine River on the evening of the 14th of July to witness sky and earth joined in this fiery interplay of pyrotechnics and reflections, brilliant colors, kaleidoscopic in patterns, flashing in speed: red fire, pinwheels, rockets, Roman candles, Bengal lights, multicolored stars, entire scenes or landscapes vibrating momentarily in the sky and showering sparks in the July air, already charged with electricity. It has been a long day of military display, popular dancing on street corners, picnics in the woods and parks, loitering in cafés; and when this booming, crackling, spinning dream-world of the evening subsides, Debussy, the subtle humanist, uses an echo of the theme of this rowdy day, the "Marseillaise," as a nostalgic "au revoir" to this turbulently gregarious holiday, but with the promise of many more returns of the popular festival.

STRUCTURE. The general structure of the piece is based on the classical assumption of a long ascent, reaching a climax from which a shorter, more rapid line descends nearly vertically. The dynamics of this design are formed from a calm early material, to which complexity of melody, of rhythm, of harmony bring increasing richness and vigor to a boiling point, or apex, when the denouement of the emotional tension and the resolution of the musical complexity are so imminently needed as to dictate a nearly immediate ebb, a drop in level so rapid that, although it furnishes a solution, a conclusion, it leaves one still vibrating from the reverberations of the apex. This does not mean that in the ascending line one carries through a steadily measured crescendo of dynamics and of complexity; Debussy breaks his ascending line several times, but these periods of relative quiet still remain active. There is no finality in their texture, but rather an ominous restlessness which forebodes with assurance the explosions to come, and contributes to the long tense line.

The thematic materials center on one pervading subject in its many developments. In its most complete form this material includes (measures 27-31) a skip up of a fifth (C-G), then the same skip with the intervening upper appoggiatura (C-A-G). A second phrase restates this last motif, only a half-step higher (C♯-A♯-G♯), and leads directly into a complementary motif, closing the curve (B natural, A natural, D natural), before returning to the opening skip of a fifth up. One is in the presence of successive polytonality within this one short theme, opening wide horizons for experimentation through the prélude, in which this material is taken through an infinite variety of keys, rhythms, fragmentations, differences in scorings and levels. Companions to this explosive main subject are numerous arabesques, at times fluid, at times angular, adaptable to the pictorial exigencies of this scintillating display.

The harmonic dexterity of this prélude is not among the least of its many "tours de force." From the beginning the palette is rich; a bitonal arabesque which can be interpreted as a superimposition of F major, ascending, and G♭ major descending, or, better still, as the interplay of opposing fragments of the two whole-toned scales (F-G-A-B-C♯-D♯) and (G♭-A♭-B♭-C-D-E) sets the mood of the sixteen first measures. The octaves above, which, it will be noted, already have a family resemblance to the main theme to come, belong to the last of the two series mentioned. At measure 17, a pentatonic glissando on all black keys breaks the texture. Its dying echo (measures 18-19) brings the whole-toned C♭-D♭.

In the next passage (measures 20-24), alternating clusters formed of the notes B-C-D♭ and C-D♭-E♭, bring the C natural in close friction to its neighboring tones, and the tension mounts with the support of heightened pitch levels, a transition to the central, main portion of the work. At measure 25 the harmonic premise is built around the pentatonic scale on G-B♭-C-D-E, with C and G elected by the main theme as temporary tonal centers, with the aforementioned polytonal progression at measure 30, for which the arabesques change to fragments of the two whole-toned scales, (one series ascending, and the other descending).

A return to the harmonic material of measure 25 leads to a transition, and at measure 35 the arabesques and main theme elect a pentatonic scale built from five tones of whole-toned series (C♭-D♭-E♭-F-G-A) with the omission of the A. Measures 39-40, transitional in character, are built on alternation of whole-toned and pentatonic elements. Measures 41-43 seem to me best explained as a superimposition of the theme in E♭ over arabesques in D♭. It is granted, however, that the theme violates the D♭ tonality only in its choice of E♭ as tone center, and could be reconciled to the large dominant chord of D♭.

The ensuing section (measures 44-52) borders on atonality in its complex mechanism based on the bitonal character of the last phrase of the main theme. The first note of each triplet figure seems to act as an appoggiatura to the ensuing chord to which it is slurred. One hears in the rapid progressions of this passage a series of chromatic successions, but also a struggle of fragments of the two whole-toned series. Measures 53-56 are whole-toned.

Note at measures 61-62, the C major, all white keys, contrasted at the end of each measure by quickly evolving polytonal successions. A similar process (measures 63-64) has as background the pentatonic series on all black keys. Pentatonism wins out at measure 65, and bitonalism F-A-C, over C-E♭-G♭, makes up the harmonic material of the cadenza.

Observe, a few measures later, the rapid interplay of tonalities in the development of the last phrase of the theme. In several segments one borders on atonalism again. The end of the piece returns to the opening bitonal arabesques, and the bitonal statement of the segment of the "Marseillaise" in C major over a D♭-A♭ pedal, and the main theme, which in its capriciously dual harmonic nature at first abides by the C major notion and then resolves to agree with the pedal.

PERFORMANCE. In the performance of this work one is faced with a most taxing technical feat, for if this work concludes the series of "Préludes," it also foreshadows, along with "Les tierces alternées," the series of "Études" in its demands upon the performer. A new phase of piano virtuosity is entered upon, and although its patterns and difficulties have been led up to through all the previous works, yet they do not "fall under the hand" in the accustomed nineteenth-century virtuoso style. Their harmonic basis already demands of the performer a ready adaptability to rapid changes of level between patterns on black keys and on white keys, which in their interpretation must of necessity command an equal touch and kinesiological condition of the fingers and arm technique employed but transposed rapidly in levels. Further, observe that the rapid changes of dynamics over the long ascending line of this most exciting piece require control. So many performances of this work become a headlong, overfast dash for the finish, in which the piece becomes a jumble of sounds. All effects of sudden, strident accents contrasted to whirring crescendo softness are lost. The clear outlines of the main theme are lost in the various designs, which themselves take on the aspect of heavily amalgamated chords. Note that the tempo is marked "modérément animé," "moderately animated." Within this tempo the clarity of texture will actually give a greater sense of speed than will a performance of the work at presto tempo, in which nothing can be heard. A judicious use of pedal is also of importance. For instance, in the opening passage no pedal, or a very shallow one, is best, as it is also in the transitional passage in clusters, bottom of third page. In the sections dealing with the theme, pedal may be used to good effect, but must not slur together its succeeding tonalities. Observe that election of dynamic levels must take into account the marked differences Debussy entrusts to the theme ("très en dehors") F, etc., and to the arabesques which follow the thematic coloring but always a shade under in dynamics. It is another illustration that the care with which Debussy selects his materials and fits them together, allows for no romantic nonsense, if the performer is to obtain the utmost effect. By and large this is true of the interpretation of all works by really good performers. The less the performer places his idiosyncrasies to the fore and the more he lets the composer speak his message, the surer the results, but the leeway for "personal" performances of Debussy is even smaller, and it has been abused to such a point as to necessitate constant rectification—with which, it is hoped, the reader will be patient and in sympathy.

5.

Piano Works 1915

When one views in perspective the long range of "études," whether they are called by this name, or functioning as such in the problems they propose, one can signalize only a handful of the truly great contributions to this form out of a sea of meaningless materials, meaningless in that their adequacy as study pieces is not matched by a musical importance, meaningless in that they do not contribute to the evolution of music, but repeat again and again the already well-defined, oft-trodden tracks. How many "Well-Tempered Clavichords," Chopin, Szymanowsky and Debussy "Études" are there in the history of music? Few indeed, for these are the mature works of musical giants, intimately imbued with the *à-propos* of the instrument, multiply endowed in the technique of composition, and, above all, using both these second-nature requisites to the service of an intense imaginative power, and an unremitting search of the musical future which they project lavishly, within strict disciplines of varying aesthetics. They are landmarks which indefinitely feed succeeding generations, opening horizons unknown to the performer and to the composer alike.

These "Études," the last works for piano solo written by Debussy, are a gift of his life-blood, and were to him a sublimation and escape from intense physical and mental suffering. In these last years Debussy had become further removed from the social and professional world. His long and incurable illness was to continue to his premature death at fifty-six, and cause untold sufferings. He was also acutely aware of the war's ravages, of the unwarranted, aimless destruction of all values, of the many artist colleagues, his friends, killed and maimed by stupid shells—his hopes in mankind's intelligence were deeply shattered. A strong discipline, the religion of creation, came to his aid and called forth the tremendous surge necessary to obliterate the outside world and inner pangs, to meet the challenge of proving himself one last time, in that instrument with which he always had such an intimate affinity . . . and beyond that, to show the world that balancing force which builds from within destruction, that power of still creating when all is falling in ruins, which is the heroic cry of "We are not defeated yet!"

To the technical problems which he set for himself, he brought the directness and conciseness which is everywhere apparent in his music, and that realism and strength which denote certainty of the goal to be attained . . . "strength held in leash," as Maggie Teyte so aptly puts it. That he should have chosen "Études" for this crowning work is easily understandable in complement of his series of "Préludes," in view of his wartime absorption in the French edition of the complete works of Chopin, which he undertook and completed, and in the ever-renewed problems such a series would propose musically and technically, and which Debussy was stimulated to solve.

It is interesting to note that until August 19, 1915, Debussy was still hesitating as to the dedication to Chopin or to Couperin, both of whom he held in high esteem and toward whom he felt respectful gratitude; he eventually decided on Chopin, though this series owes as much (or as little) to both composers in its point of departure, which rapidly evolves in fearless innovations which the musical world is barely starting now to understand some thirty-five years after their epoch-making publication.

Their scope is musically most varied from fierce to tender, very fast to slow, soft to strident, modal through diatonic and bitonal to near atonal, and a matching array of technical problems of performance; for, to the more frequently treated double-thirds, double-sixths, octaves, which he completely revaluates, Debussy has added studies in the problems of such fascinating equations as ornaments, opposed sonorities, double-fourths, and repeated notes, and embodies the expansion of the instrumental capacities of the piano, and research into the differentiated timbres and tone colors it is capable of, simultaneously or singly.

In view of the attention which has been given in preceding works to general interpretative concern for levels, Debussy's markings, harmonic color, structure, these aspects will be dealt with more summarily in these works, to permit the addition of certain aspects of piano technique in keeping with the problems presented by each étude, and in view of the lengthy research which led to the publication of *The Capture of Inspiration*,* to which a number of references will be made. These are noted merely as an indication of fields which may be investigated by those who wish to do so, and preserving the spirit of Debussy, who in prefacing the twelve "Études," and explaining the absence of fingerings, writes, in part:

> "To impose a fingering cannot logically meet the different conformations of hands. . . . Our old Masters—I mean 'our' admirable clavecinistes—never indicated fingerings, relying, probably, on the ingenuosity of their contemporaries. To doubt that of the modern virtuosi would be ill-mannered. To conclude: the absence of fingerings is an excellent exercise, suppresses the spirit of contradiction which induces us to choose to ignore the fingerings of the composer, and proves those eternal words: 'One is never better served than by oneself.' Let us seek our fingerings!"

Now, we may view the twelve "Études," bearing in mind their musical as well as their technical problems and import, and remembering the love and faith that Debussy had placed in them, as a challenge to the matching understanding and capacities which he expected in us.

Pour les "cinq doigts" (Étude I)

In this first "Étude" we find Debussy describing the progressive transformation of a five-finger exercise into a fanciful gigue, bringing us the humorous picture of a bored student becoming unruly and imaginative. The "Étude" is dedicated to Czerny, one of the most prolific, if not musical, writers of piano exercises and studies. Debussy's dedication, then, takes on somewhat of a tongue-in-cheek gesture, and has the artistic impudence which we have found already in "Doctor Gradus ad Parnassum," to which it shows a resemblance by more than just the mood.

Five-finger exercises! Why start there in a series of twelve "Études,"

---

* E. Robert Schmitz. A treatise on piano technique, 1936, published by Carl Fischer, New York.

you may ask? Because these five-finger exercises are the basis of all passage work; they are the matrix from which, by extension, many other important forms are derived. They are then, in their simplicity, the first technical proving grounds for the beginning student, the first base from which, with the addition of the passage of the thumb, one derives scales, or from which, with additional spacing between the fingers, one derives arpeggio passages, and from these, in turn, the conception of chordal playing.

The first problem one will assess in the five-finger exercises, is that of even tonal production,* the mastery of which is essential to passage work, not as an end in itself, but as a training principle assuring the control necessary, so that the will or musical intent of the student will be the deciding control, not accidents of tonal production which maliciously accent this note, leave out that note. Once the even tonal production of a series of notes is assured, one will find that their willful musical differentiation (crescendo, decrescendo, accents if desired) can also be assured.

This evenness of tone depends upon several factors. One is the even point of contact upon each key, i.e., even leverage. Another is the even degree of relaxation or contraction of the fingers in depressing these consecutive keys, i.e., even muscular condition.

For the first consideration, that of leverage, it will be found from experimentation and from laws of physics, that a point near the front edge of the key is the most efficient point of contact.

For the even muscular condition of the fingers, it will be found that the first immediate difficulty to overcome is the variance in length of fingers and of keys. We have short and long fingers, short and long keys, and this difference must not be made up by extension of some fingers and flexion of others, for then the difference in muscular condition of the fingers will result in a difference in tone. For instance, the solution of performing a passage on white keys is not obtained by curving the long fingers and extending the short fingers, in order to equalize their length, in view of even key contact, for throughout the passage the tone production of the two sets of fingers will be heard as two sets of tonal color. Further, this assumes an energy-wasting stiffness, and a

* *The Capture of Inspiration*, p. 23.

194

disruption of the bridge of the hand (through a flattening of its two side pillars, 1 and 5), making even weight distribution very difficult.

In the scales of B major, F♯ major, and C♯ major, an ideal combination is offered in which the unevenness of keys and fingers neutralizes each other. A minimum of difficulty is then encountered in obtaining even tonal production, maintaining the bridge of the hand, and avoiding stiffness.

But, in other patterns, those in which not all short fingers fit on long keys, nor long fingers on short keys, there is technique which comes into play. To lengthen the thumb and fifth finger, a slight motion of the arm toward the keyboard; to shorten the second, third, and fourth fingers, a similar motion of the arm away or out from the keyboard. This assures then that the problem of long and short fingers and keys be solved without differences in muscular condition within the fingers.

It was most interesting to find in Warsaw in 1930, a manuscript of Chopin, which Mr. Binental was using in his book * and in which Chopin, in sending advice to his niece, recommended the use of the B-major scale as the first one to experiment with. The fingering which he put on this manuscript is 1-2-3-1-2-3-4-1, naturally, but the implications are clear enough.

Debussy, who was molded in his early years in the music of Chopin, may have been conscious of this idea, or have deduced it, as we did, long before the finding of this Chopin correspondence, as in this first "Étude" he alternates or juxtaposes such neutralized scales as F♯ major, C♭ major, D♭ major, to the C-major scale, one of the most difficult, and with intervening degrees of difficulty in such scales as E♭ major, A♭ major, F major, etc. The fascination for the alternation of black-key scales with all white-key scales is obvious here, and much in evidence in the "Étude pour les huit doigts," which basically is dedicated to the same problem, in its extension.

The harmonic mood of the first "Étude" is diatonic but with a very rapid and constant friction of successive polytonality, or of superimposed bitonality. C major is the canvas (as in "Doctor Gradus ad Parnassum") upon which the various harmonic colors are embroidered in

---

* *Chopin—On the 120th Anniversary of His Birth—Documents and Recollections* by Binental. Warsaw; Lazarski.

baroque contrasts. We may briefly enumerate some of these tonal changes:

Bars 1-6. "Sagement," the prim C major five-finger exercise is soon contradicted by A♭, in a rapid bitonal reference.

Bars 7-10. Consecutive diminished sevenths, with the second note of each measure an appoggiatura to the chord, eventuate to the dominant seventh of C major.

Bars 11-14. Alternation of C major and F♯ major (most typical of bitonal writing).

Bar 17. Consecutive diminished sevenths, with insistence on that of C minor, and a number of enharmonic spellings.

Bars 28-34. New pattern begins in C major but is soon in conflict with E♭ major.

Bars 35-40. The left-hand harmony revolves around a pedal-point of C, soon colored toward dominant harmony of F major. The pedal descends to D, and prepares the tonality of G major.

Bars 41-47. G major, interrupted at measures 44 and 47 by D♭ major.

Bar 48. The section opens with the key signature of C♭ and the melody that enters in the third measure responds to this signature, but the tenor ostinato is strongly attached to G♭ as tonal center; the effect is then of tonic over dominant tonality, or yet of C♭ over Mixolydian.

Bar 74. Note the consecutive polytonality of the right-hand part over the D♭-E♭ pedal trill.

Bar 90. From this measure in F major, one plunges into a cadenza in which scale fragments bring successive polytonality in four fragments (G♭, G natural, D♭, D minor), which are sequenced in succeeding measures.

Bar 96. C major returns with the contradiction of E♭ major (97 and 101.)

Bar 110. The cadence is approached by the D♭ major scale landing, without further ado, on the C major final tonic chords.

It will be noticed that the texture is contrapuntally rich in its uses of pedal-points, ostinato figures, melodic patterns, à la Bach, diminution, inversion, contrary motion, oblique motion, appoggiaturas, and so forth. We would particularly recommend the close inspection of the pattern which begins at measure 28, in view of singling out those notes within it which act as chordal notes, those which are passing notes, and those which act as appoggiaturas.

The form in its large sections is quite complete and proportioned, built on three main materials and their combinations.

Measures 1-27, A; measures 28-47, B; measures 48-74, C; measures 75-89, development of fragments of A and C; measures 90-95, cadenza; measures 96-115, coda (recalling fragments of A and B) and cadence.

In the performance one will be concerned with the notion of the five-finger exercise in its various forms and into extensions, bringing non-conjunct motion, and the question of the most apt fingerings for these patterns.

The second problem of performance to be observed, in this rapidly fluctuating work, is that of tempo, if it is not to sound fragmented. The relationship of these tempo changes must be very exactly calculated in their relationships to each other and must neither be anticipated nor continued into sections where they no longer apply. This is particularly true of the several passages in which short fragments are marked "rubato," or "rit.," followed soon after by the marking "Mouvement" or "Tempo" in which the normal tempo is resumed after the exceptional deviation of the fragment. Note also the dynamic range from PPP to FF and SFF.

Pour les Tierces (Étude II)

In this "Étude" Debussy gives us an exhaustive presentation of the problem of double-thirds, complementary in its interpretation to that of "Les tierces alternées" of the "Préludes." To the whirring, mechanical lightness and precision of the latter, he now opposes a more Chopinesque study in thirds, in which the legato and sostenuto phrasing sets into undulating relief the melodious movement, ever present.

This expression of life offers an excellent opportunity for study in pitch line crescendi and decrescendi. The frequent modulations and short chromatic passages bring natural variations in tone color and stresses. As in the Chopin étude in double-thirds, a more incisive middle portion is found, as well as a most interesting contrast of materials and contrapuntal independence of the left-hand material.

In the Debussy "Étude" this contrast is subtly interwoven with sections in which parallelism, or contrary motion in a third voice, minutely reproduces and then tenses the movement of the two voices in thirds, over stabilizing pedal-points.

It will be noted that the harmonic color, unlike that of the stringent tonal contrasts of the first or sixth "Études," enjoys the ambiguity of half-shades. For instance, in the opening section, the tonal scheme is analyzable both in D♭ major with considerable emphasis on the sixth degree, or in B♭ natural minor (Aeolian) with emphasis on the third degree. In the eighth measure the considerable interest in the fourth degree of C major will bring ambiguity between this tonality and Lydian. Intervening chromatic passages dissonantly tense the texture, but do not resolve its deceptive subtlety.

In the general technical aspects of the performance of double-thirds, it will be found that the verticalization of finger work, and the maintenance of a supple but high bridge, intimately webbed with arm action, will bring the clarity of even weight distribution on the two component notes in succession. It will be found that the task of fingering is rendered much easier by the basic assumption of five black keys in a majority of sections, and the oft-repeated possibility of neutralized fingerings, i.e., bringing long fingers on short keys and short fingers on long keys. Since the general aim is smoothness in tonal legato, when the fingering does not permit this exclusively through finger legato, an adequate use of the pedal can supplement the finger work in achieving the desired interpretation. For those who may wish a closer inspection of these ideas I would refer them to the fingerings of double-thirds (diatonic and chromatic) and to the consideration of motor fingers used on pivot notes in the playing of all forms of double intervals.*

It will be further found that in the use of motor fingers and pivot notes, one or the other of the two component voices can achieve a complete finger legato whereas the other voice is lightly detached. This effect can be applied in interpretation in a number of ways:

* *The Capture of Inspiration*, pp. 108-109.

198

(1) The distribution of weight on the lifted voice may be so equalized with that employing pivots as to give both voices an even dynamic importance.

(2) One may elect, if the texture warrants it, to emphasize one voice and lighten the other throughout.

(3) One may vary, again in direct relation to analysis of the musical import, the relative dynamic effect of the two voices in relation to each other in successive sections.

Observe that the sustaining pedal will have to hold the pedal-points in order to liberate the use of the forte pedal in its minute subservience to the musical demands of the moving voices.

Note again in this "Étude," that rapid fluctuations in rubato, accelerando, ritardando, are marked by Debussy for the exact segment in which he desires their effect, and that precision in their approach and immediate recovery in interpreting passages that succeed these indications, will project their musical significance. Observe also that the dynamic and interpretative palette is wide-ranged again, from PP "murmurando" through FF "con fuoco."

Pour les Quartes (Étude III)

In his emancipation from harmonic taboos of the eighteenth and nineteenth centuries, Debussy does not hesitate to dedicate an étude to the double fourth, and to liberate it most completely from the many forbidding rules of harmonic treatises. Here it returns to its contrapuntal aspect of organum, but of a form of organum already assimilating the later contrapuntal independence in direction, for we find that the set of two voices in the right hand, and those in the left hand, have a delightfully complementary as well as cooperative relationship.

Their curves may coincide or come in imitation, or again in partial inversion, or the activity in the one hand may be suspended to the staticism of a pedal-point or rhythmic figure. This interaction of the parts in contrapuntal designs and the modal pentatonic harmonic color, with the pure sonority of the fourths, is a most felicitous and fresh palette, which the strong contrast in sections of tender whimsical quality to sonorously hammered stretti, further sets into sharp perspective. We recommend attention to the cadential idiom, exceptionally rich and diversified. The interesting harmonic turn and staggered effects of such cadences as measures 8-9 or 11-12 remind us of the "Sarabande" ("Suite pour le piano"). The insistent and near-ostinato cadence of measure 18 has the ornate formality of baroque cadences and the querulous sonority which is one of the alternate qualities of parallel fourths.

That Debussy had a rightful pride in this particular "Étude" is quite understandable, for it further pioneers the role of the fourth in musical literature. In mentioning it to his publishers, Debussy said, "In it you will find some novel sonorities, although your ears are acclimatized to many an oddity."

The technical notions which we have discussed in the preceding Étude, "Pour les tierces," will apply to all double-note passages, with the differentiation of fingering necessitated by the wider or less wide intervals encompassed.

The principles of motor-fingers, of humeral rotations, and of supple arm action will therefore be applicable in obtaining even weight distribution and the fluid legato of the opening and of successive passages.

In the stretto passages, as well as in the descending runs in double fourths (measures 54, 56, 57 and so forth), the arm weight must be over-distributed forward for maintenance and support of a higher bridge of the hand and very verticalized finger strokes. A flat hand or flat bridge, or flat fingers with weight of arm at the elbow, would render impossible the clarity and "hammered sonority" requested by Debussy, in the stretti, and which when lightened will apply to the runs which form the basis for a crescendo and accelerando. It is important to note that this building of dynamics and tempo is gradual and steady without even the slightest amount of rubato. One will also observe the separate levels of interpretation in this passage: (1) the sustained longer note-values in the inner voices, (2) the detached bass notes, and (3) the top level in fourths with maximum clarity and gradual dynamic reinforcement, climaxing measure 61.

The last section (from measure 65) returns to the softly sustained quality of the opening of the "Étude" and loses itself in a far-off, nostalgic calm, to which the quasi-ostinato cadential figure mentioned earlier brings a distant echo of its former belligerence.

Pour les Sixtes (Étude IV)

In a letter of August 28, 1915, to his publishers, Debussy writes:

"For a very long time, the continuous use of sixths reminded me of pretentious Misses, sitting in a drawing room, sulking over their embroidery, while envying the scandalous laughter of the mad ninths, (des folles neuvièmes). . . . Yet, here I am writing this étude, in which attention to the sixth goes so far as to organize its harmonies solely with the aggregates of this interval, and—it is not ugly! (Mea culpa . . .)." *

Indeed Debussy's sixths are not ugly! We can fully agree with him that their charm and tenderness, their passionate qualms and unrest, their sensitive abandon, have nothing of the envious spinster, and need fear nothing of the more raucous ninths. It would have been so easy in dealing with sixths to have fallen into the trite, the easy, the superficially joyous—in Italian opera tradition. But by now, we well know Debussy will not travel the rutted road; in facing any musical problem he will bring it ever-renewed freshness of his curiosity and taste for the rare and exquisite. From the opening phrase, the designs of the right hand alone and the entrance of the left hand bring an expressive pitch line, which is simple and yet deeply felt. In the "mezza voce, dolce sostenuto" timbre, their value is given a far-off antique grace, which slowly awakens and unfolds, like a butterfly from its cocoon, in the more tightly woven colors of succeeding passages to the restless middle section—to recede again in the last section.

What an opposition in texture to the Chopin étude in sixths (Opus 25, No. 8) and its turbulent "moto perpetuo"! One would nearly think that Debussy had planned this étude as a complementary treatment of the interval.

From a general technical viewpoint, one may say that the performance of double-sixths is often conducive to stiffness and fatigue, unless the arm technique is adequate in distributing the fingers. The attempt to insure absolute legato simultaneously at both voices of the same hand, by the fingers, is superfluous on the modern piano, and, moreover, tends to create strain. One of the two voices can be maintained by the fingers, through the use of motor-fingers and pivot notes, and the other voice may be gently detached. The application of this principle

* Debussy, *Lettres à son éditeur*, p. 147.

to the upper or lower voice will be alternated; the analysis of the musical phrase will be the mode of determination, which can then be embodied in the proper fingerings to allow the pivot action to occur in the fifth finger, or in the thumb side of the hand.

Lateral displacements of the arm will insure equal distribution of the fingers in equalizing their lengths on the successive sixths.

Again the use of the sustaining pedal, for held pedal-points, will liberate the forte pedal for a very precise creation of resonance and tides of tone in the moving parts.

Observe in the central portion (beginning measure 21) the intervals which are slurred together in appoggiatura-resolution fashion in opposition to those notes marked by a dot and lightly detached.

POUR LES OCTAVES (ÉTUDE V)

The restrained and melodious studies in thirds, fourths, and sixths give way now to a veritable burst of joyous outpouring, freely sonorous, in primary colors. A stylized waltz, the "Étude" brings both rhythmic and harmonic zest to the staid octave interval. Syncopated accents, rests on the first beat, swelling upward surges, work out an infectiously gay romanticism in the opening and closing sections, to which a square cut, near military precision, in the middle section brings stark contrast.

Let us examine at close range some of the interesting points of interpretation in the first section, also applicable to its terminal restatement. One finds that the first four measures furnish us with the germs from which nearly the entire section is built and from which its interpretation is therefore derived. In the first measure, note that the first beat culminates in the second beat, which receives a very strong accent (SFF), then the entrance of the right hand in turn is lifted on the first note, with a drop on the second note of its pattern (i.e., third beat) slurred to the third note, which is lifted. This pattern will be found again in measures 11-21 quite steadily in the upper voices; further it generates the interpretation also of its derivative pattern in measures 5-8 (right hand), in which the first note is again lifted to drop on the second note and continue through the pattern legato. In the second measure an answering pattern to that of the first measure is found, with the main accent on the second beat and lift on the third beat, silence on the first.

The interpretation of this measure in turn is found to apply again at measures 9-10, and 22. The third measure is preceded by a four-note run, anacrusis to the strong first-beat cadence on the tonic; this cadential turn appears again at measure 23, to E♭ major instead of E natural major, then in the restatement and at the final cadence. It has the bright and affirmed countenance of clearly diatonic intent, which serves as pillar in the rapidly evolving polytonal frictions and varied harmonic schemes of the work.

The third and fourth measures expose another and very important pattern which, instead of syncopated stresses, brings us a rapid surge to the top of its pitch ascent, an orchestral effect of swelling, within which a subtle slurring by twos will set into value the successive fifths. This third pattern will be found again (measures 23-28, 33-37) with the addition of a strongly accented appoggiatura and resolution on the first beat of alternate measures. Further, it is this pattern which generates the entire central portion, beginning at measure 49.

Voice leading must also be closely watched, particularly in middle parts; many interpretations of this work fail to project the birth of the melody in the tenor (measure 11), and its continuity, despite rests, in four-measure phrases (measures 11-14, 15-18) and its conclusion reached only when the G♯ of measure 20 has resolved to the F♯ of the second beat of measure 21.

Note the interesting cooperation of chromatic and whole-toned series, measures 29-32, and the bitonal transition beginning at measure 43.

In the middle section, the "very equally rhythmed" admonishment by Debussy precludes rubati, but should also limit abuses of the grouping of the passages by threes. This intimate linking, in which a slur is presupposed over the two first notes of each beat and a lift on the third note (single note), is legitimate only as an intimately felt pulsation of the pattern, not as an obvious alternation of a metric character. Rapidly evolving tonalities take up this pattern, first given in D♭, with the lowered second (E double flat) as a passing tone, in the ornamental cadence leading to the tonic at the beginning of measure 50. The delineations of the pattern are rather interesting: two consecutive open fifths followed by this staggered cadence on the degrees 3-2-4-3-2-1. The overall tonal character is aurally aligned with pentatonism.

The last page of the "Étude" is a field-day of harmonic color and motion, contrary, parallel, oblique—pentatonic, chromatic, bitonal, successive polytonal, all intimately linked on the last exuberance of the waltz patterns, and unified by the crashing E-major cadence.

For technical principles in octave work, one may refer to the training of arm shifts, and arm release and retraction, the first principle applying to legato octaves, and the second to lifted, staccato, or dropped chords and octaves. Various performing minimizations and specialized techniques for octave passages will be found in Compounds Nos. 5-11, 21, 33, 34, 38, 41.*

Pour les huit doigts (Étude VI)

This "Étude" is in truth an extension of the range and design of the first "Étude," "Pour les cinq doigts." It is both complementary and supplementary in its harmonic considerations and in its technical general requirements. Poetically enough, it opens with the nearly identical notes of the first étude, now transposed a semitone down, but soon the realm of discovery enlarges and the five-finger concept is transmuted to an eight-finger range.

The musical patterns are, very largely, graphically divided into four plus four, in complementary directions, i.e., four notes ascending and four descending. Harmonically, however, the tonal frictions occur by groups of eight notes, later by fours, and even by twos.

On the first page there is a footnote by the composer: "In this étude, the changing position of the hands makes the use of the thumbs awkward and acrobatic in performance."

Without undue presumption, I believe one can conceive that in the development of a supple but precise arm technique this objection could be remedied, in favor of the great advantages to be gained by the use of the thumb. The first of these advantages is the maintenance of a hand bridge which requires the use of its two extreme pillars (thumb and fifth finger) for structural strength, for symmetry of weight distribution,

* *The Capture of Inspiration.*

and for the arch of the palm created by the crosswise pull of the thenar and hypothenar eminences.

Further, the absence of the thumb for passing (always preferable on a long white key after a long finger on a short black key) will limit the performer to the succession of fingers 5-4-3-2 and will render difficult the fingering of this work with a view to equal leverage and equal muscular condition of the fingers on successive keys. As a result the performance may be marred by sudden accents or sudden unheard notes, not at all in relation to the crescendi and decrescendi or accents marked and intended by Debussy.

Perhaps an illustration can best serve to clarify this point. I would suggest an unprejudiced trial of the opening measure without thumbs. Then, the same measure with the following fingering:

Left hand, 5-3-2-1; right hand, 4-1-3-2; left hand, 3-1-3-2; right hand, 4-3-2-1; left hand, 4-1-3-2; right hand, 4-1-3-2.

With a slight angle of the arms away from the body, and with a rapid retraction or escape of the hand from the keyboard as soon as it has completed its four-note pattern, it will be found that this fingering will both satisfy the demands of leverage and bridge to the maximum possible and with the aid of the arm will avoid the coming together and mutual hampering of the two hands. For further details on the use of arm angles, for which we do not have space here, I would refer the reader to the chapter on "Humeral Rotations" in *The Capture of Inspiration*.

We have already noted the interesting interaction of the four-note patterns in complementary directions; one should also observe their use in cooperation of one direction, their pedal-like staticism in the middle portion in which many patterns take on the aspect of chord outlining, or turning notes, and their superimposition at the two hands in contrary motion (measures 40 and 60). Further, it will be noted that dashes or added stems indicate in a number of passages a slightly exteriorized melodic progression born of the patterns.

Again the harmonic color is diatonic, with rapid frictions of successive polytonality or juxtaposed bitonality. As opposed to the first étude the canvas elected (Gb major) has a majority of black keys, whereas in the first étude it was on all white keys. This is only a difference of departure in both these rapidly fluctuating études. There is a decided fascination again for the superimposition or alternation of all-white-key patterns and all-black patterns (or patterns containing a majority of black keys); these strong extremes bring a play of harmonic shade and light, brought in stringent relief by the neat and precise line of the arabesques. The middle section (beginning at measure 17) brings a less extreme, though not less varied, alternation of tonal colors, tensened again from measure 27, to bring the rapid alternations of measures 31-32. These alternations are, in fact, so rapid as to give the effect of double appoggiaturas (first and second notes) resolving to the next two notes, and so forth. The tension is further built by the pentatonic black-key glissandi, alternated with white-key segments and glissandi. Note the bitonal superimposition (measures 40-41), which ushers in the recapitulation of the first section; a similar treatment is found from measure 60 on, until measure 67, in which the pattern brings out the sensitive degrees of G♭ in a most remarkable fashion, using the degrees 2-1-4-5 to end on the lone tonic.

Observe the free changes in meter of the opening section and its return, and the subtle differentiation of phrasing, accents, and of nuances which endow this uni-rhythmic and precise pattern with a live sensitiveness.

The initial practice of this étude will require a slow key-bedded appraisal of the rapidly fluctuating tonal patterns, but in performance the general character of the interpretation must be imbued with the opening admonition of legato but with great lightness, a lightness which Debussy does not abandon even in the more dramatic sections, or in the F passage of the last page.

Pour les degrés chromatiques (Étude VII)

A new era in the presentation of the worn-out chromatic succession is heralded with this freshly stimulating étude, for continuous whir, or the chromatic successions punctuated by minute pulses and accents, is now the basic level to which contrapuntal juxtaposition of diatonic melodic lines brings a bitonal friction at totally independent levels. In other words, the present contrast in diatonic versus chromatic does not rely on the ornamental value of chromaticism over a basically dia-tonic assumption to which it will resolve, to resume its subservient or-namentation in a later fragment, and so forth. We have here a clearly moto-perpetuo level written in the chromatic scale to which is added, contrapuntally by fragments, a diatonic melody, each following its evolution without apparent concern for the other, or subservience to the other. Other passages oppose fragments of the chromatic scale to other fragments of this scale in contrary or in parallel motion.

We shall, then, examine the two levels separately, and our first con-sideration will be for the minute pulsations of the interpretation of the chromatic line. In the opening measures we find it in association with an E pedal, from which it departs, to which it converges, but to the staccato of which it opposes its own legato, and a minute accent of pitch on the first note of each group of four. In measure 7, against the sharp accents of the bass which culminate on the second sixteenth-note, the chromatic succession opposes minute accents on the F's beginning the first and third groups, since this is the main note which E♭ and G♭ ornament, and converge to. In measure 11, the chromatic pattern is frequently performed with many holes in it, occasioned by undue em-phasis on the first note of each group of four, to the detriment of the three succeeding notes. Though this passage is extremely light, and a minute emphasis is permissible on the first notes of groups, the other notes must be heard clearly in their succession. In measure 19, the left hand converges to a strong accent on the second beat, which influences the right hand to a cooperative (anti-pitch line) crescendo in sympathy with the left-hand accent. In measure 23, the partially contrary and partially parallel motion of the two hands results in an alternation of the accents; beginning of the first group (right hand), of the second group (left hand), and so forth. In measures 36-37, the chromatic passage again cooperates with the lower level in building a crescendo to the dissonance achieved on the first beat of measure 37. From meas-ure 47, the chromatic level gradually asserts a greater sonority toward the sharp accents of measures 53 and 55, and to the acute stridency of dissonance and spacing of measures 57 and 58. Observe that the chro-matic counterpoint from measure 59 is now at three voices. From meas-ure 63, the chromatic level is phrased by two groups of eight notes each, of which the first four set the pattern and the second four echo it at the lower octave and therefore at a softer dynamic level. From measure 71, note the dotted seconds which bring swift accents to the whirring chromatics.

Now for the melodic level, which, born in the eleventh measure, recurs and develops to the very last measure of the étude. The first consideration is that by its very character and rhythmic content, and later its chordal scoring, it enjoys a more sonorous life than that of the rapidly evolving chromatic level; in fact, this more marked dynamic level is essential to insure the hearing of its continuity under the other level. Observe that in its statement beginning at measure 25, the mid-measure portamento notes must in no way detract from the linkage of the chord of measure 25, to that of measure 26, to those of measures 27, 28, 29, and 30. Further, in measure 27 the true character of the accentuation of the sixteenth-notes and succeeding eighth-note in the middle of the measure becomes apparent and holds in subsequent statements. The two chords are slurred, the first thereby receives an accent, but so does the second in virtue of the crescendo mark indicated by Debussy. Yet the second one takes the accent briefly, before its staccato retraction. The same will apply in measures 32, 45, 48, 52, 65, 80, i.e., at each restatement of this theme, which must also be checked for continuity and expressiveness, despite preoccupation with the interpretative and technical demands of the chromatic level. In this instance, it is suggested that the last statement of this theme be given to the left hand from measure 78 through measure 82. This will insure its legato and flow, and will make it possible for only one of the hands to jump in distant location, i.e., the right hand, which will undertake the chromatic level (over the less arched left hand in measures 78, 80, and 82, and independently in measures 79, 81). At measure 83 and to the end, the right hand can undertake the chromatic level with the A-E pedal-point, and the left hand will be free to move over the staccato seconds, and single notes.

In all the passages in which the melody is present the forte-pedal usage will be predicated by the evolution of the melody, i.e., changed for it. In other sections its use will be sparing and shallow, adding a rapid resonance to the intimate points of accent or pulsations of the chromatic level, some of which have been signalized earlier in this discussion.

For the technical principles involved in the chromatic levels, it will be found that, starting on C natural ascending for the right hand, the fingering 1-3-1-3-1-2-3-1-3-1-3, etc., not only permits even leverage, points of contact, and weight distribution, but also the use of forearm and upper-arm rotations. This mechanism in alternation with linear motions will obviate cramped stiffness and, further, will give excellent opportunity for the calculation of its mechanism to the minute accents of the chromatic level.

Pour les agréments (Étude VIII)

Though this étude now stands as number eight, it was composed last, and is mentioned by Debussy: "It borrows the form of a barcarolle on a somewhat Italian sea."

Translated into English, the word "agréments" is either ornaments or embellishments, and in studying these with a view to determining Debussy's sources and inspirations, we find that his tendencies relate more closely to the school of French ornamentation than to either the German, Italian, or English usages.

It will be remembered that ornamentation is not the property of just one period of the history of music, but is a general aesthetic concept found equally in the music of aborigines, in folk materials, and in various periods of the history of music. The form that these embellishments take, however, evolves, changes, is added to or subtracted from, and it is in these aspects that one can determine their style. For instance, the trill, which existed as a vocal ornament as early as the third century, and probably even before, has been treated in many various ways since. Embellishments are found in the Gregorian chant, in the measured music of the medieval period, in the enriched vocalizations of the Renaissance, and eventually in the keyboard style of the clavecinistes, among whom Couperin gave particular attention to the codifying of such of these accumulated ornaments as were employed in the French style (coulé, port de voix, chute, tremolo, fermatas, scale passages, arpeggi, diminutions, as well as the more universal uses of appoggiaturas, changing and turning notes, mordents).

The function of embellishments, which one may find most aptly described in the book by C. P. E. Bach on the art of playing keyboard instruments, is to impart stress and accents to tones, to connect them, and to give certain notes a differentiated life in either its melodic or harmonic importance; but this function remains strictly subservient to the effect of a piece, i.e., to the emotion or mood of the piece, for, and this is a capital point, Bach's premise is undeniably that music is capable of being more than a mere pattern of sounds, but expresses many passions and cannot be interpreted by a merely technically correct performance. The effect, or mood, be it sad or joyous, slow or fast, playful or solemn, will not only determine the interpretation of the main lines, but also of the ornaments embellishing those lines.

It will follow from this that the fluctuating moods of the barcarolle, which Debussy has set forth as the basic principle of this étude, will be closely observed with a view to matching the interpretation of the ornaments to that of the various sections; light or more marked, faster or slower, crisp or languid, legato or staccato, these ornaments can blend into each section, and contribute in their fittingness to the overall mood.

What are some of the forms of ornamentation one finds in the étude? Arpeggiation terminating in a mordent (measures 1-2, etc.); also in the less ornate and more openly spaced form of measures 3-4, converging straight to the note without mordent; fermatas (measures 1, 42, and, by duration, in measures 5-6 and others); upper and lower changing notes around a chord (measure 1, in section starting at measure 35; measure 42), and around notes (accompaniment starting at measure 11 in various forms); cadenza passage work in mixed conjunct and disjunct motion over fairly large compass (measures 7-8, 31, 48-50); appoggiaturas (end of measure 3, within patterns of measures 9-10, and innumerable other instances); grace notes (measures 11-12; double in measure 15; triple and varied as to spacing in measure 30; chordal, end of measures 31, 32-33, etc.); broken chords (measures 17, 27-29); runs and turning notes in triads (section beginning measure 35); and an infinite variety of passing, upper, and lower auxiliaries.

210

And this is only a brief survey of the more obvious forms of ornaments used in the étude, the closer inspection and cataloguing of which would be a most worthwhile and rewarding project in a survey that would then relate these forms to their ancestral evolution.

This richness of ornamentation must not, though, blind the interpreter to the basic levels to which these ornaments are applied and to the contrapuntal independence of these levels which are everywhere to be found and respected, but which are perhaps most salient in such sections as measures 9-10, 17-23, 33-41. At measure 33, for instance, it is essential that the notion of the interpretation be clearly felt at three levels: the melody on top, the pedal-point bass, and the embellishment pattern with its harmonic portent in the middle. In the succeeding passage the chordal aspect should not blind the performer to the contrapuntal independence which again obtains strict levels of action and further brings the problem of binary and ternary juxtapositions.

It derives, from the consideration of these multiple ornaments, and the necessity of their closely following the affect of the notes upon which they are placed, a texture which is itself contrapuntally complex; thus, the interpretation of this étude will depend on thorough musicianship and good taste, rather than on virtuosity per se. This is everywhere true in Debussy, but this is a particular case in point. The use of the sustaining pedal will again facilitate the resonance of long pedal-points; for instance, in measures 1-3. As for the forte pedal of this étude on embellishments, it demands a light foot!

Technically, the variety of problems prohibits a detailed survey of each in this book, but a few general principles may be given. Lateral motion of the arm (rapid location) will distribute the weight, helping the hand in the various forms of arpeggi, cadenzas, and runs. Linear motions of the arm (in and out from the keyboard) will supplement the lateral action in detailed patterns by equalizing finger points of contact. Rotary motions (upper-arm and forearm rotations) will bring an alternation with linear motions for trills and mordents.

A final point should be mentioned in the performance in regard to rhythm; the minute differentiation in note durations from half-notes to sixty-fourth-notes, with triplets, sextuplets intervening, must retain their exactitude of timing in relation to each other and to the general tempo.

For instance, a sixty-fourth-note is not just an "awfully fast" note; it is a duration exactly twice as fast as a thirty-second-note, four times as fast as a sixteenth-note, and eight times as fast as an eighth-note.

By the period of the "Études," Debussy had developed a veritable grammar of musical signs. If the task of interpretation seems a staggering responsibility from the account we have just given of this musically taxing work, remember that the dots, slurs, dashes, accents, verbal indications, and their combinations are there as a minutely detailed indication of Debussy's conception and as a constant help to those who really wish to encompass its intent and translate it in their performance.

POUR LES NOTES RÉPÉTÉES (ÉTUDE IX)

The ninth étude is a brilliant toccata very much imbued by the precision, clarity, and sobriety of claveciniste virtuosity, light, dry, and dynamically movemented. The repeated note technique is given a thorough appraisal in the alternate use of both hands, or one hand in playing repetitions which can be either slurred, staccato, portamento, lifted or dropped, accented in groups of two, four, or gradually over a phrase.

This scherzando research into the sonorities of rapid repetition and the technical pitfalls they present is further enhanced by a bitonal use of chromaticism and whole-toned series, which eventuates into a near twelve-tone overall harmonic color despite the G-major signature and final cadence. This does not mean that this work is atonal in the narrow sense of the word as defined in twentieth-century specialization, for the étude does not adhere to the predetermined tonal order, or to the non-repetition laws of early atonality. We may give an interesting instance of the working of the étude's system. Beginning at the end of the second measure and continuing to the end of the fourth measure, we will find the succession F natural-E♭-F-G-A-B-C♯ in whole tones to which the next three notes (D-C natural-F♯) answer bitonally from the opposite whole-toned series with a break of a half-step between the two fragments. In another fragment (page 12, second line) it will be found that the horizontal progress of the levels is chromatic, but each chord is within one of the two whole-toned series. In the second subject (bottom of page 12) the melodic outline is partially diatonic and partially chromatic, the harmonic pedal is whole-toned and the resolution is to the C-major triad. These are only passing examples of the mischievous harmonic nature of this work.

The opening measure of the étude and the second subject mentioned above are the main materials, very opposed in character, which are developed in alternations until the last page in which a last statement of the first material, now grotesquely changed rhythmically, leads to a passage of whole-toned suspension and a rapidly soft run to the final chords.

Now it is obvious that the mainstay of the performance of this work will be a capacity for the playing of rapidly repeated notes, clear and precise within varying dynamics and with varying accents, slurs, groupings. This capacity depends on three principal technical notions: (1) that of fingering of repeated notes; (2) that of linear motion to which the arm gives rapid precision; and (3) that of minimized lifts and drops derived from the principle of arm release and retraction. A typical mechanism, that of the first measure, may be taken as an example:

The fingering of the single notes played by the left hand in the first measure will be 3-2-4-1, with the arm assuming an angle away from the body and thereby facilitating its motions of rapid retraction, to clear the way for the right hand. Its action will be that of rapid drops, quickly retracted, but which, even in the minimized form permissible in this tempo, will yet be initiated by the upper arm (not as a mere wrist, forearm, or finger action). The right hand will finger each repeated group of three notes with 3-2-1, and will play them with a linear motion forward, with a repartition of the arm weight drop over the three notes, followed, after the third, by a retraction.

In the performance of this étude, we will again advocate a most restrained use of the pedal; mere dabs of shallow pedaling may enliven certain effects, but many segments require none at all. The second theme is more compatible to pedaling, but of a precise nature. Again do not hesitate to give the full dynamic scope of this work as required by Debussy, from "più PP" to SFF, "strident."

In this "Étude," Debussy makes it plain that his conception of the ultimate in pianistic art and in the requisites of a performer, is not limited to a thoroughgoing musicianship and a well-developed classical technique. These, we find, form only two of the three requirements he expects of the virtuoso performer, the third being an acknowledgment and research of the infinite varieties of timbres which can be produced by the piano, by the 88 keys, ten fingers, and three pedals in their multiple relationships. There are only a few pianists who have realized this extension of the instrument's properties from mere piano playing to the transmutation of the subtlest orchestral effects to its expressive range, and who have given lifelong attention to this aspect. Paderewski was one of these.

In an instrumentation-conscious era, which had produced the orchestration of Berlioz, Strauss, Rimsky-Korsakoff, and then Debussy and Ravel, and innumerable individual palettes since, the piano was bound to be reassessed in its capacities, as was each and every other instrument in common usage. The search for coloring has been steadily toward the more differentiated: the violins, trombones, percussion section, wood winds, all have been explored and innumerable new possibilties in their effects have been discovered—the same now applies to the piano.

The keyboard was late in coming of age as a solo instrument, but its starring role was quickly determined by the romantic composers, who enlarged its scope in all directions of musical expression (dynamics, range, technical virtuosity) save one: its "registrations," and orchestral potentialities, which were still in infancy at the turn of the century.

That great composers frequently write beyond the presently accepted scope of the instruments they are dealing with is a well-known historical experience. Certainly Bach was in no way hampered in his musical conceptions by the technical deficiencies or performing idiosyncrasies attached to the organs and keyboards of his day. He clearly wrote beyond and above them, creating the demand for better instruments and new conceptions of their handling by his works.

In the same way Debussy transcends the piano of his day, *and* the pianism of his day, to bring us this étude, the purpose of which is the differentiation and simultaneous usages of timbres in relation to differentiated coloring intents expressed in scoring, harmony, and so forth. That this conception applies to all his piano works is true; the étude is only a *concentrated* study of the phenomenon, the various aspects of which are applicable here, or there, depending on effect and texture.

What are some of the oppositions of sonority brought to bear? We will point some of them out as an indication of the direction in which to search, which is that of the timbre to be accorded to continuous contrapuntal levels which are superimposed in close or open scoring, and which contain wide oppositions as to effect and rhythmic, melodic, dynamic life.

It will be noted first that those notes which are held (linked) are to be held for the entire duration, not replayed, but either taken by the sustaining pedal, wherever possible, or held by the fingers so that their sonority will not be lost despite the other materials which may be evolving and which will require changes of the forte pedal, or its absence.

In the three first measures the timbres must be so calculated as to put in relief the plucked A, for a dotted-quarter-note duration and marked with a dash, against a long-sustained but limpid G♯, and the light and short bass G♯. In the succeeding three measures the G♯ pedal is moved two octaves down and is restruck at the beginning of each bar. In close opposition the alto and mezzo-soprano enter, and the far-off bass proposes a fourth level. From measure 7, the close quarters in which the contrapuntal levels operate make absolutely necessary the horizontal recognition of their evolution by differentiated timbre; note that the melodic voice (which starts with a hold C at the beginning of measure 7) evolves without break, clear through measure 14, and its voice leading must not be interrupted, or mixed into other levels. For instance, the A♭ accented octave in measures 7-11, the mid-measure octave motif, measures 12-13, the bass superimposed pedal-points—none of these must be confused with the aforementioned melodic line which terminates only measure 14 by a single A♭ resonance.

Beginning measure 15, the opposition in levels is that of legato chords forming a six-voiced chorale to the staccato chromatic passages in their midst. Note that the set of three voices played by the right hand in the bass is given timbre and dynamic preference over the voices in the left hand an octave above, which, though legato, are lightened by the dots marked on each. It is, then, three levels of differentiation one must seek.

In the section beginning measure 31, the levels vary in number. In measure 31, two levels: a bass pedal to be held by the finger since the use of the sustaining pedal would also hold the E, and a joyous theme. Measure 32 brings in a third voice, to be played by the right hand with its theme, rhythmically and melodically independent, and measure 33 brings in the fourth part. It will be observed that the two upper parts of measure 33 lead on through measures 34, 35, 36.

Measures 38-40 bring three successive expressions to the chords; all within the shading of piano, these must be soft in measure 38, marked in measure 39, and expressive and penetrating in measure 40, where a long melodic line is born from the A♯ of the first-beat chord. The preservation of the continuity of this melody through the long passage that follows, allowing nothing to break its tendrils and linkages, is a study in itself; while still building a sustained accelerando and a very strong crescendo to FF, it presupposes, then, a comprehension of the pedal-points, chordal inner-voice progression, and melody, as independently colored but unbroken lines.

A PP subito brings us back to the opening of this theme which is continued in the calmato section. Note that the pedal chords can be taken by the sustaining pedal.

These are only a few instances to illustrate the direction—mainly horizontal—in which research of levels will bring to light their design out of apparently conflicting graphics, and will then be projected clearly in performance, not only by variety of dynamics, accents, legato-staccato, but by an orchestration of touches to produce individual timbres for each superimposed entity.

Pour les Arpèges composés (Étude XI)

This étude for compounded or combined arpeggi is an imaginative and modernized tribute to the Liszt conception of transcendental études, and one in which a certain amount of humor enters into play, particularly in the central section.

The compounded arpeggi, i.e., arpeggi extending beyond the range of an octave, serve in the opening portion as the softly fluid canvas and ornamental aura of sonority for a slowly unfolding theme of broad lines, which is born in the second measure of the étude and evolves nearly uninterrupted for two and a half pages. Its nature and continuity must then be disengaged from the webbings of the arpeggi and given a slightly more marked dynamic level. Difficulties in the accomplishment of this aim may come in the form of engrossment in the ternary over binary groupings in measures 2 and 5, and more conspicuously in the section beginning measure 7, with the complexly timed ornamental arpeggi. But in this last case a graphic aid is given in the score by the use of bold-face versus small type. It will be immediately noted that the note values in the bold, even when equal to those of the ornaments, have an extra dynamic value and a durational life relative to their level, rather than to that of the ornamentation. For instance, in measures 11 and 12, the sixteenth-notes or thirty-second-notes of the bold-faced melody are not identical in duration or in dynamism to the same note values in small type. One therefore arrives at a form of polyrhythm in which the measure of the ornaments is not identical to that of the melody, but their fitting together is indicated in the printing very accurately by their placement over each other. For the ornaments too have variance in note durations which are certainly not to be ignored. For instance, in measure 7, second beat, the A♭ at the bass, already held by the sustaining pedal, has slightly more duration and dynamism than the arpeggio group. In the same measure, the last-beat arpeggio cannot be calculated on the basis of the bass melody's durations, but rather must be proportioned in relation to the preceding arpeggi. It gives this last-beat arpeggio a sense of lengthened scope which is more dynamic than durational in leading to the C as apex of the line. In measures 8-10, 12-15, and many others, one will find again this differentiation of rhythm in the embellishments, the observation of which is most important to the musical intent.

At "lumineux" (luminous), the middle portion of some twenty-two measures presents strong contrasts within itself and to the opening fluidity. Note, in its third and fourth measures, the elegant romanticism of the opening of the phrases which suddenly turns into a staccato-marcato pompousness at the end of the measures, pirouettes in laughter, and continues in this vein of humorous contrasts and scherzando style, some aspects of which have a slightly Spanish flavor. Note, at the change to four sharps, that the chords are slurred by twos. The return to the first material, in its fluid and thoughtful outlines, is interrupted in the last page by recalls of the middle section, but the final cadence is imbued with a softly vibrant peace.

From the technical standpoint it will be found that development of an arpeggio technique is based on an enlargement of the five-finger exercises in several respects: (1) enlargement of the arm technique in proportion to the greater demand for lateral displacement; (2) enlargement of the arm technique in linear motions, because when the hand tends to be more spread, the difference between long and short fingers is magnified; (3) selection of the most neutralized fingering as in the five-finger equation; (4) with the addition of observance of the passage of the thumb whenever possible on a white key following a long finger placed on a black key; (5) a careful consideration of lateral distances between the consecutive notes of the arpeggi and the relation of these widths with the lateral spread between the various fingers (most particularly that between the thumb and the second finger) because the extent of such distances indicate which fingers to select; the aim is to avoid any unnecessary stretching or bunching of the hand, as this would tend to interfere with the independence of action of the fingers; (6) in specific cases, a consideration of the metric, rhythmic, or harmonic accents desired may legitimize a departure from the basic laws of fingering; and (7) arpeggi in which a regular alternation of black and white keys may render possible the use of alternated thumbs (on white keys), and the third finger (or second) on black keys, and the application to these passages of rotary action.

In the use of the pedals, we have already brought out the use of the sustaining pedal for held basses, such as are found in measure 7, and similar passages. The forte pedal finds its greatest use in the opening section in which, however, it must be changed with great care: at each half-beat in the first measure, at each beat in the second measure, on the first and third beats of the third measure, and so forth. From measure 7, the forte pedal gives only a very brief and shallow resonance to the apexes of the arpeggi, or to the individually pedaled melodic notes. In the central portion its coloring will again be rapid in the scherzando and detached character, and the rapidly evolving patterns and harmonies which must not be blurred together.

Pour les accords (Étude XII)

How can one finish such a series of "Études" as the eleven we have just described, and why did Debussy elect this particular "Étude," which was not the last written, to conclude the series!

The answer can be found in general aesthetic principles of music in various forms and in program making, namely, that an ending (be it of a concert, or of a sonata, or a concerto) generally fulfills a number of psychological demands: its character is decided and buoyant, bringing a final enthusiastic apex to that which has preceded. It is straightforward, and direct in its coloring, bringing a relief from the complexities which have previously been presented, debated, developed, serving then as a form of resolution or answer to the questions of form, melody, harmony, counterpoint, which have made great demands on intellectual processes. It must then, without falling into triteness or vulgarity, bring liveliness which will enroll the physical as well as the mental activity— approaching the dance movement, in its more virile and folk aspects, as an aesthetic. This presupposes, in turn, that the rhythmic life will be bountiful but also striking in its contrasts rather than minutely subtle. In the climactic effect to be obtained this ending also presupposes a wide dynamic range, which, with spacious contrasts of PPP to FFF, will yet bring a brilliant final color; and a corollary to this assumption will be that the orchestration or scoring will seek less a differentiation of individual levels or parts through timbre, but will accept a blocked, unified cooperation of all the voices in presentation of the direct melodic or rhythmic content; the tutti of the concerto grosso!

From this discussion one can readily see the reasons for the adoption of the "Étude" for chords as the terminal work in this series, for it fulfills all these demands. In examining its rhythmic vigor which is very twentieth-century in its elemental force, but without heaviness, we find an assymetric alternation of lifts and drops, of staccato and slur, and it will be immediately noted that the lifts here are not necessarily unaccented, but they are shorter than the drops. In the first phrase we find that the opening chord is lifted, the second one (measure 1, beat 1) is dropped and slurred to the second beat, octaves which are sharp but short. The third beat is again lifted, but this alternation is broken in the third full measure in which the third beat, instead of lifting in anacrusis to another drop and slur, is itself a drop, which is slurred to the first beat of the fourth measure. The second and third beats of this fourth measure are both lifts which lead to the original alternation in measure 5, broken again beginning at measure 7. This alternation of binary and ternary meters can be graphically illustrated, in its lifts and drops, pedaling, accents, as follows:

The harmonic underpinning of this rhythmic alternation is worth a cursory glance. In the voice-leading of the opening chord to the second chord (first beat of measure 1), it will be seen that A♭ at two voices leads to A natural, that C natural at two voices leads to C♯, and that F in two more voices leads to E. These three semitonal motions duplicated at the octave have the linkage of appoggiaturas to resolutions, and can explain that accented character of the third-beat lift. But this is far from the entire picture, for this intimate linkage is contradicted by the contrast in sonorities of the minor triad going to the major triad, an effect parallel to that of the "Tierce de Picardie," and which always results in a swelling resonance on the major chord. This, then, places a great weight and legato on the first beat (of measure 1, for instance) which continues its surge in the slur to the octaves, which are part of the same chordal harmony, but which in thinner scoring and terminating the resonance span of the first beat are short and quickly lifted.

In the section beginning at measure 21, to these considerations will be added that of a bass melodic progression which has an independent pitch line decrescendo and crescendo, over which harmonic pedals evolve by two-measure phrases (measures 21-22, 23-24, etc.). The performance must then take into consideration the harmonic rhythm of the pedals, the pitch line of the bass, the friction of this latter to the harmonic pedals, and the earlier established accentuation of the material from which this section is derived.

In the section of measures 33-38, it will be noted that insistence on masculine cadence G to C is negated by intervening chords; then, at measure 37 and 38, the cadence is forcefully asserted. In these two measures the second-beat chord, which is "marked" but P, is an anticipation and anacrusis to the material beginning in measure 39.

In the section of measure 39, note that the slurs by two are yet differentiated by dots and dashes, in which the two slurred chords are sometimes equal, and sometimes accented on the first. Note the contrary motion of the chords (measure 47) which lead to diminution and E-major cadence before the resumption of the opening material of the étude, with new features of metric modulation.

The middle section brings us an aesthetic contrast in tempo, dynamics, and in texture, from the driving force of the opening (and closing) section. The study here is that of ornaments applied to chordal forms; for their interpretation we refer the reader to the étude "Pour les agréments," and also caution the interpreter on several counts: (1) not to let the ornaments destroy the melodic continuity of the section which, though hidden, is tangibly there, and similarly not to let the enharmonic change (see "a tempo") likewise break the melodic flow; (2) to remember that Debussy nearly always expresses rubato in the actual durations given each note, and that his indication of this section as molto rubato is an indication of general mood of performance, rather than license to revaluate the durational relations.

Note, in the return of the first section, how its rhythm slyly and from a distance, little by little, asserts itself; first in the bass in single notes spaced widely over a sustained right-hand part, then gaining grounds and pervading the entire texture. A similarly exciting effect is obtained in the last twenty-one measures of the étude, in which thinly scored sections, very soft, serve as the basis from which, in short time, a tremendous dynamic ascension is built to ultimate brilliance.

And now, in concluding these twelve "Études," the reader and the author may fully participate in the words of Debussy:

"The six remaining études are finished, it is only a matter of copying. I admit to being happy to have brought to fruition this work, which, without false vanity, will have a particular place. Beyond technic, these 'études' will serve as an apt preparation to pianists in understanding better, that one may not approach music armed solely with fierce hands!! . . .

"Last night, at midnight, I copied the last note of the 'Études'. OUF! . . . The most detailed Japanese print is child's play, compared to the graphism of some of the pages, but I am happy. It is good work."

Appendices

Note: The word "melody" is used in the table for the French word "mélodie," meaning art song.

I. Chronological Table of the Works of Claude A. Debussy

Date:

1876—Nuit d'étoiles (melody, voice and piano)

1878—Beau soir (melody)
       Fleur des blés (melody)

1880—Romance (melody)
       Paysage sentimental (melody)
       La belle au bois dormant (melody)
       Caprice (melody)

1882 ⎱
1883 ⎰ —Fêtes galantes (melodies, voice and piano)

          Pantomime
          En sourdine
          Mandoline
          Clair de lune
          Fantoches
          Pierrot

1884—Apparition (melody)
       Enfant prodigue (cantata, orchestra)

1886—Almanzor (orchestra)
       Le Printemps (orchestra)

1887—La Damoiselle élue (choir and solo)
       La belle au bois dormant (melody)
       Voici que le printemps (melody)
       Paysage sentimental (melody)
       Les Cloches (melody)
       Romance (autre texte) (melody)

1888—C'est l'extase (*from* Ariettes oubliées):
       Il pleure dans mon coeur
       L'ombre des arbres
       Chevaux de bois
       Green
       Spleen

223

1888—Deux Arabesques (piano solo)
1889—Fantaisie (for piano and orchestra)
1890—Suite Bergamasque (piano solo)
        Prélude
        Menuet
        Clair de lune
        Passepied
      Rêverie (piano solo)
      Danse (Tarentelle Styrienne) (piano solo)
      Valse romantique (piano solo)
      Ballade (piano solo)
1890—Mazurka (piano solo)
      Nocturne (piano solo)
1890—Cinq poèmes de Baudelaire (voice and piano)
        Le Balcon
        Harmonie du Soir
        Le jet d'eau
        Recueillement
        La Mort des Amants
      Les Angélus (melody)
      La mer est plus belle . . . (melody)
      L'échelonnement des haies (melody)
      Mandoline (melody)
1891—Marche écossaise (piano, four hands)
      Rodrigue et Chimène (theater, unpublished)
1892—Prélude à l'après-midi d'un faune (orchestra)
1893—Quatuor à cordes (string quartet)
1893—Proses lyriques (voice and piano) :
        De rêve
        De grève
        De fleurs
        De soirs
1898—Trois Chansons de Bilitis (voice and piano)
        La flûte de Pan
        La chevelure
        Le Tombeau des Naïades
1898—Trois Nocturnes (orchestra)
        Nuages
        Fêtes
        Sirènes
1901—Suite pour le piano (piano solo)
        Prélude
        Sarabande
        Toccata
1902—Pelléas et Mélisande (opera)

1903—Estampes (piano solo)
  Pagodes
  Soirée dans Grenade
  Jardins sous la pluie
 D'un cahier d'esquisses (piano solo)
 Dans le jardin (voice and piano)
1904—Masques (piano solo)
 L'Isle joyeuse (piano solo)
1904—Fêtes galantes, II (voice and piano)
  Les Ingénus
  Le Faune
  Colloque sentimental
 Trois Chansons de France (voice and piano)
  Le temps a laissé son manteau
  La grotte
  Pour ce que Plaisance est morte
 Deux danses pour harpe chromatique
  Danse profane
  Danse sacrée
 Le Roi Lear (musique de scène) (orchestra)
1905—La Mer (orchestra)
1905—Images, I (piano solo)
  Reflets dans l'eau
  Hommage à Rameau
  Mouvement
1907—Images, II (piano solo)
  Cloches à travers les feuilles
  Et la lune descend . . .
  Poissons d'or
 Le Jet d'Eau (orchestration)
1908—Trois Chansons de Charles d'Orléans (voice and piano)
  Dieu! qu'il la fait bon regarder
  Quand j'ai ouy le tabourin
  Yver, vous n'estes qu'un villain
 Children's Corner (piano solo)
  Doctor Gradus ad Parnassum
  Jimbo's lullaby
  Serenade for the doll
  Snow is dancing
  The little shepherd
  Golliwog's cake-walk
1908—Printemps (re-orchestration)
 Marche écossaise (orchestration)
1909—Images (orchestra)
  Ibéria

Gigues tristes
Rondes de printemps
Hommage à Haydn (piano solo)
1910—Rhapsodie pour clarinette en si bémol et piano (also orchestrated)
Le promenoir des amants (voice and piano)
Auprès de cette grotte sombre
Crois mon conseil, chère Climène
Je tremble en voyant ton visage
1910—Douze Préludes, I (piano solo)
Danseuses de Delphes
Voiles
Le vent dans la plaine
Les sons et les parfums tournent dans l'air du soir
Les collines d'Anacapri
Des pas sur la neige
Ce qu'a vu le vent d'ouest
La fille aux cheveux de lin
La sérénade interrompue
La Cathédrale engloutie
La danse de Puck
Minstrels
La plus que lente (valse, piano solo)
Trois Ballades de François Villon (voice and piano)
Ballade de Villon à s'amye
Ballade que feit Villon à la requeste de sa mère
Ballets des femmes de Paris
1911—Le Martyre de Saint-Sébastien (theater)
1912—Khamma (ballet)
1913—Jeux (ballet)
Trois Poèmes de Stéphane Mallarmé (voice and piano)
Soupir
Placet futile
Eventail
Boîte à joujoux, ballet enfantin (piano solo)
Douze Préludes, II (piano solo)
Brouillards
Feuilles mortes
La Puerta del Vino
Les Fées sont d'exquises danseuses
Bruyères
General Lavine—eccentric
La terrasse des audiences du clair de lune
Ondine
Hommage à S. Pickwick Esq. P.P.M.P.C.
Canope

Les tierces alternées

Feux d'Artifice

1914—Six Épigraphes antiques (piano, four hands)

Pour invoquer Pan

Pour un tombeau sans nom

Pour que la nuit soit propice

Pour la danseuse aux crotales

Pour l'Egyptienne

Pour remercier la pluie au matin

1915—Berceuse héroïque (piano solo) (also orchestrated)

Douze Études (piano solo)

Pour les "cinq doigts"

Pour les Tierces

Pour les Quartes

Pour les Sixtes

Pour les Octaves

Pour les huit doigts

Pour les degrés chromatiques

Pour les agréments

Pour les notes répétées

Pour les sonorités opposées

Pour les Arpèges composés

Pour les accords

En blanc et noir (two pianos)

Noël des enfants qui n'ont plus de maison (voice and piano)

Sonate (flûte, alto, harpe)

Sonate (violoncelle et piano)

Sonate (violon et piano)

II. Bibliography

Boucher, M., 'Claude Debussy' (Essai pour la connaissance du devenir) (Les Éditions Rieder, Paris, 1930).

Debussy, C., 'Monsieur Croche, The Dilettante Hater' (Lear Publishers, New York, 1938; In *Three Classics in the Aesthetic of Music*, Dover, 1962).

Debussy, C., 'Lettres à son Editeur' (Durand, Paris, 1927).

Dumesnil, M., 'Claude Debussy, Master of Dreams' (Ives Washburn, New York, 1940).

Dunlap, K., 'Elements of Psychology' (C. V. Mosby, St. Louis).

Durand, J., 'Quelques Souvenirs d'un Editeur de Musique' (Durand et Fils, Editeurs, Paris, 1924)

Frankenstein, A., San Francisco Chronicle, March 11, 1945 (This World Section).

Koechlin, C., 'Les Musiciens Célèbres: Debussy' (Henri Laurens, Editeurs, Paris, 1927).

Laloy, L., 'Debussy' (Aux armes de France, Paris, 1944).

Lavauden, T., 'L'Humour dans l'Oeuvre de Debussy' (Article in the Revue Musicale, Paris, 1930).

Lockspeiser, E., 'Debussy' (J. M. Dent & Sons, Ltd., London, 1936).

Manuel, R., La musique des origines à nos jours: 'Claude Debussy' (Librairie Larousse, Paris).

Oleggini, L., 'Au Coeur de Claude Debussy' (René Julliard, Editeur, Paris, 1947).

Pratt, C. C., 'The Meaning of Music' (McGraw-Hill, New York, 1931).

Shera, F. H., 'The Musical Pilgrim': Debussy and Ravel (Oxford University Press, London, 1925).

Thompson, O., 'Debussy, Man and Artist' (Dodd, Mead & Co., New York, 1937).

Vallas, L., 'Claude Debussy, His Life and Works' (Oxford University Press, London, 1933).

Index

A CATALOGUE OF SELECTED DOVER BOOKS
IN ALL FIELDS OF INTEREST

A CATALOGUE OF SELECTED DOVER BOOKS
IN ALL FIELDS OF INTEREST

WHAT IS SCIENCE?, *N. Campbell*
The role of experiment and measurement, the function of mathematics, the nature of scientific laws, the difference between laws and theories, the limitations of science, and many similarly provocative topics are treated clearly and without technicalities by an eminent scientist. "Still an excellent introduction to scientific philosophy," H. Margenau in *Physics Today*. "A first-rate primer . . . deserves a wide audience," *Scientific American*. 192pp. 5⅜ x 8.
Paperbound $1.25

THE NATURE OF LIGHT AND COLOUR IN THE OPEN AIR, *M. Minnaert*
Why are shadows sometimes blue, sometimes green, or other colors depending on the light and surroundings? What causes mirages? Why do multiple suns and moons appear in the sky? Professor Minnaert explains these unusual phenomena and hundreds of others in simple, easy-to-understand terms based on optical laws and the properties of light and color. No mathematics is required but artists, scientists, students, and everyone fascinated by these "tricks" of nature will find thousands of useful and amazing pieces of information. Hundreds of observational experiments are suggested which require no special equipment. 200 illustrations; 42 photos. xvi + 362pp. 5⅜ x 8.
Paperbound $2.00

THE STRANGE STORY OF THE QUANTUM, AN ACCOUNT FOR THE GENERAL READER OF THE GROWTH OF IDEAS UNDERLYING OUR PRESENT ATOMIC KNOWLEDGE, *B. Hoffmann*
Presents lucidly and expertly, with barest amount of mathematics, the problems and theories which led to modern quantum physics. Dr. Hoffmann begins with the closing years of the 19th century, when certain trifling discrepancies were noticed, and with illuminating analogies and examples takes you through the brilliant concepts of Planck, Einstein, Pauli, Broglie, Bohr, Schroedinger, Heisenberg, Dirac, Sommerfeld, Feynman, etc. This edition includes a new, long postscript carrying the story through 1958. "Of the books attempting an account of the history and contents of our modern atomic physics which have come to my attention, this is the best," H. Margenau, Yale University, in *American Journal of Physics*. 32 tables and line illustrations. Index. 275pp. 5⅜ x 8.
Paperbound $1.75

GREAT IDEAS OF MODERN MATHEMATICS: THEIR NATURE AND USE, *Jagjit Singh*
Reader with only high school math will understand main mathematical ideas of modern physics, astronomy, genetics, psychology, evolution, etc. better than many who use them as tools, but comprehend little of their basic structure. Author uses his wide knowledge of non-mathematical fields in brilliant exposition of differential equations, matrices, group theory, logic, statistics, problems of mathematical foundations, imaginary numbers, vectors, etc. Original publication. 2 appendixes. 2 indexes. 65 ills. 322pp. 5⅜ x 8.
Paperbound $2.00

THE MUSIC OF THE SPHERES: THE MATERIAL UNIVERSE — FROM ATOM TO QUASAR, SIMPLY EXPLAINED, *Guy Murchie*
Vast compendium of fact, modern concept and theory, observed and calculated data, historical background guides intelligent layman through the material universe. Brilliant exposition of earth's construction, explanations for moon's craters, atmospheric components of Venus and Mars (with data from recent fly-by's), sun spots, sequences of star birth and death, neighboring galaxies, contributions of Galileo, Tycho Brahe, Kepler, etc.; and (Vol. 2) construction of the atom (describing newly discovered sigma and xi subatomic particles), theories of sound, color and light, space and time, including relativity theory, quantum theory, wave theory, probability theory, work of Newton, Maxwell, Faraday, Einstein, de Broglie, etc. "Best presentation yet offered to the intelligent general reader," *Saturday Review*. Revised (1967). Index. 319 illustrations by the author. Total of xx + 644pp. 5⅜ x 8½.
Vol. 1 Paperbound $2.00, Vol. 2 Paperbound $2.00,
The set $4.00

FOUR LECTURES ON RELATIVITY AND SPACE, *Charles Proteus Steinmetz*
Lecture series, given by great mathematician and electrical engineer, generally considered one of the best popular-level expositions of special and general relativity theories and related questions. Steinmetz translates complex mathematical reasoning into language accessible to laymen through analogy, example and comparison. Among topics covered are relativity of motion, location, time; of mass; acceleration; 4-dimensional time-space; geometry of the gravitational field; curvature and bending of space; non-Euclidean geometry. Index. 40 illustrations. x + 142pp. 5⅜ x 8½.
Paperbound $1.35

HOW TO KNOW THE WILD FLOWERS, *Mrs. William Starr Dana*
Classic nature book that has introduced thousands to wonders of American wild flowers. Color-season principle of organization is easy to use, even by those with no botanical training, and the genial, refreshing discussions of history, folklore, uses of over 1,000 native and escape flowers, foliage plants are informative as well as fun to read. Over 170 full-page plates, collected from several editions, may be colored in to make permanent records of finds. Revised to conform with 1950 edition of Gray's Manual of Botany. xlii + 438pp. 5⅜ x 8½.
Paperbound $2.00

MANUAL OF THE TREES OF NORTH AMERICA, *Charles Sprague Sargent*
Still unsurpassed as most comprehensive, reliable study of North American tree characteristics, precise locations and distribution. By dean of American dendrologists. Every tree native to U.S., Canada, Alaska; 185 genera, 717 species, described in detail—leaves, flowers, fruit, winterbuds, bark, wood, growth habits, etc. plus discussion of varieties and local variants, immaturity variations. Over 100 keys, including unusual 11-page analytical key to genera, aid in identification. 783 clear illustrations of flowers, fruit, leaves. An unmatched permanent reference work for all nature lovers. Second enlarged (1926) edition. Synopsis of families. Analytical key to genera. Glossary of technical terms. Index. 783 illustrations, 1 map. Total of 982pp. 5⅜ x 8.
Vol. 1 Paperbound $2.25, Vol. 2 Paperbound $2.25,
The set $4.50

IT'S FUN TO MAKE THINGS FROM SCRAP MATERIALS,
Evelyn Glantz Hershoff
What use are empty spools, tin cans, bottle tops? What can be made from
rubber bands, clothes pins, paper clips, and buttons? This book provides
simply worded instructions and large diagrams showing you how to make
cookie cutters, toy trucks, paper turkeys, Halloween masks, telephone sets,
aprons, linoleum block- and spatter prints — in all 399 projects! Many are easy
enough for young children to figure out for themselves; some challenging
enough to entertain adults; all are remarkably ingenious ways to make things
from materials that cost pennies or less! Formerly "Scrap Fun for Everyone."
Index. 214 illustrations. 373pp. 5⅜ x 8½.   Paperbound $1.50

SYMBOLIC LOGIC and THE GAME OF LOGIC, *Lewis Carroll*
"Symbolic Logic" is not concerned with modern symbolic logic, but is instead
a collection of over 380 problems posed with charm and imagination, using
the syllogism and a fascinating diagrammatic method of drawing conclusions.
In "The Game of Logic" Carroll's whimsical imagination devises a logical game
played with 2 diagrams and counters (included) to manipulate hundreds of
tricky syllogisms. The final section, "Hit or Miss" is a lagniappe of 101 additional puzzles in the delightful Carroll manner. Until this reprint edition,
both of these books were rarities costing up to $15 each. Symbolic Logic:
Index. xxxi + 199pp. The Game of Logic: 96pp. 2 vols. bound as one. 5⅜ x 8.
                                                            Paperbound $2.00

MATHEMATICAL PUZZLES OF SAM LOYD, PART I
selected and edited by M. Gardner
Choice puzzles by the greatest American puzzle creator and innovator. Selected
from his famous collection, "Cyclopedia of Puzzles," they retain the unique
style and historical flavor of the originals. There are posers based on arithmetic,
algebra, probability, game theory, route tracing, topology, counter and sliding
block, operations research, geometrical dissection. Includes the famous "14-15"
puzzle which was a national craze, and his "Horse of a Different Color" which
sold millions of copies. 117 of his most ingenious puzzles in all. 120 line
drawings and diagrams. Solutions. Selected references. xx + 167pp. 5⅜ x 8.
                                                            Paperbound $1.00

STRING FIGURES AND HOW TO MAKE THEM, *Caroline Furness Jayne*
107 string figures plus variations selected from the best primitive and modern
examples developed by Navajo, Apache, pygmies of Africa, Eskimo, in Europe,
Australia, China, etc. The most readily understandable, easy-to-follow book in
English on perennially popular recreation. Crystal-clear exposition; step-by-
step diagrams. Everyone from kindergarten children to adults looking for
unusual diversion will be endlessly amused. Index. Bibliography. Introduction
by A. C. Haddon. 17 full-page plates, 960 illustrations. xxiii + 401pp. 5⅜ x 8½.
                                                            Paperbound $2.00

PAPER FOLDING FOR BEGINNERS, *W. D. Murray and F. J. Rigney*
A delightful introduction to the varied and entertaining Japanese art of
origami (paper folding), with a full, crystal-clear text that anticipates every
difficulty; over 275 clearly labeled diagrams of all important stages in creation.
You get results at each stage, since complex figures are logically developed
from simpler ones. 43 different pieces are explained: sailboats, frogs, roosters,
etc. 6 photographic plates. 279 diagrams. 95pp. 5⅝ x 8⅜. Paperbound $1.00

PRINCIPLES OF ART HISTORY,
H. Wölfflin
Analyzing such terms as "baroque," "classic," "neoclassic," "primitive," "picturesque," and 164 different works by artists like Botticelli, van Cleve, Dürer, Hobbema, Holbein, Hals, Rembrandt, Titian, Brueghel, Vermeer, and many others, the author establishes the classifications of art history and style on a firm, concrete basis. This classic of art criticism shows what really occurred between the 14th-century primitives and the sophistication of the 18th century in terms of basic attitudes and philosophies. "A remarkable lesson in the art of seeing," *Sat. Rev. of Literature.* Translated from the 7th German edition. 150 illustrations. 254pp. 6⅛ x 9¼.   Paperbound $2.00

PRIMITIVE ART,
Franz Boas
This authoritative and exhaustive work by a great American anthropologist covers the entire gamut of primitive art. Pottery, leatherwork, metal work, stone work, wood, basketry, are treated in detail. Theories of primitive art, historical depth in art history, technical virtuosity, unconscious levels of patterning, symbolism, styles, literature, music, dance, etc. A must book for the interested layman, the anthropologist, artist, handicrafter (hundreds of unusual motifs), and the historian. Over 900 illustrations (50 ceramic vessels, 12 totem poles, etc.). 376pp. 5⅜ x 8.   Paperbound $2.25

THE GENTLEMAN AND CABINET MAKER'S DIRECTOR,
Thomas Chippendale
A reprint of the 1762 catalogue of furniture designs that went on to influence generations of English and Colonial and Early Republic American furniture makers. The 200 plates, most of them full-page sized, show Chippendale's designs for French (Louis XV), Gothic, and Chinese-manner chairs, sofas, canopy and dome beds, cornices, chamber organs, cabinets, shaving tables, commodes, picture frames, frets, candle stands, chimney pieces, decorations, etc. The drawings are all elegant and highly detailed; many include construction diagrams and elevations. A supplement of 24 photographs shows surviving pieces of original and Chippendale-style pieces of furniture. Brief biography of Chippendale by N. I. Bienenstock, editor of *Furniture World.* Reproduced from the 1762 edition. 200 plates, plus 19 photographic plates. vi + 249pp. 9⅛ x 12¼.   Paperbound $3.50

AMERICAN ANTIQUE FURNITURE: A BOOK FOR AMATEURS,
Edgar G. Miller, Jr.
Standard introduction and practical guide to identification of valuable American antique furniture. 2115 illustrations, mostly photographs taken by the author in 148 private homes, are arranged in chronological order in extensive chapters on chairs, sofas, chests, desks, bedsteads, mirrors, tables, clocks, and other articles. Focus is on furniture accessible to the collector, including simpler pieces and a larger than usual coverage of Empire style. Introductory chapters identify structural elements, characteristics of various styles, how to avoid fakes, etc. "We are frequently asked to name some book on American furniture that will meet the requirements of the novice collector, the beginning dealer, and . . . the general public. . . . We believe Mr. Miller's two volumes more completely satisfy this specification than any other work," *Antiques.* Appendix. Index. Total of vi + 1106pp. 7⅞ x 10¾.
Two volume set, paperbound $7.50

THE BAD CHILD'S BOOK OF BEASTS, MORE BEASTS FOR WORSE CHILDREN, and A MORAL ALPHABET, *H. Belloc*
Hardly and anthology of humorous verse has appeared in the last 50 years without at least a couple of these famous nonsense verses. But one must see the entire volumes — with all the delightful original illustrations by Sir Basil Blackwood — to appreciate fully Belloc's charming and witty verses that play so subacidly on the platitudes of life and morals that beset his day — and ours. A great humor classic. Three books in one. Total of 157pp. 5⅜ x 8.
Paperbound $1.00

THE DEVIL'S DICTIONARY, *Ambrose Bierce*
Sardonic and irreverent barbs puncturing the pomposities and absurdities of American politics, business, religion, literature, and arts, by the country's greatest satirist in the classic tradition. Epigrammatic as Shaw, piercing as Swift, American as Mark Twain, Will Rogers, and Fred Allen, Bierce will always remain the favorite of a small coterie of enthusiasts, and of writers and speakers whom he supplies with "some of the most gorgeous witticisms of the English language" (H. L. Mencken). Over 1000 entries in alphabetical order. 144pp. 5⅜ x 8. Paperbound $1.00

THE COMPLETE NONSENSE OF EDWARD LEAR.
This is the only complete edition of this master of gentle madness available at a popular price. *A Book of Nonsense, Nonsense Songs, More Nonsense Songs and Stories* in their entirety with all the old favorites that have delighted children and adults for years. The Dong With A Luminous Nose, The Jumblies, The Owl and the Pussycat, and hundreds of other bits of wonderful nonsense. 214 limericks, 3 sets of Nonsense Botany, 5 Nonsense Alphabets, 546 drawings by Lear himself, and much more. 320pp. 5⅜ x 8. Paperbound $1.00

THE WIT AND HUMOR OF OSCAR WILDE, *ed. by Alvin Redman*
Wilde at his most brilliant, in 1000 epigrams exposing weaknesses and hypocrisies of "civilized" society. Divided into 49 categories—sin, wealth, women, America, etc.—to aid writers, speakers. Includes excerpts from his trials, books, plays, criticism. Formerly "The Epigrams of Oscar Wilde." Introduction by Vyvyan Holland, Wilde's only living son. Introductory essay by editor. 260pp. 5⅜ x 8. Paperbound $1.00

A CHILD'S PRIMER OF NATURAL HISTORY, *Oliver Herford*
Scarcely an anthology of whimsy and humor has appeared in the last 50 years without a contribution from Oliver Herford. Yet the works from which these examples are drawn have been almost impossible to obtain! Here at last are Herford's improbable definitions of a menagerie of familiar and weird animals, each verse illustrated by the author's own drawings. 24 drawings in 2 colors; 24 additional drawings. vii + 95pp. 6½ x 6. Paperbound $1.00

THE BROWNIES: THEIR BOOK, *Palmer Cox*
The book that made the Brownies a household word. Generations of readers have enjoyed the antics, predicaments and adventures of these jovial sprites, who emerge from the forest at night to play or to come to the aid of a deserving human. Delightful illustrations by the author decorate nearly every page. 24 short verse tales with 266 illustrations. 155pp. 6⅝ x 9¼.
Paperbound $1.50

THE PRINCIPLES OF PSYCHOLOGY,
William James
The full long-course, unabridged, of one of the great classics of Western literature and science. Wonderfully lucid descriptions of human mental activity, the stream of thought, consciousness, time perception, memory, imagination, emotions, reason, abnormal phenomena, and similar topics. Original contributions are integrated with the work of such men as Berkeley, Binet, Mills, Darwin, Hume, Kant, Royce, Schopenhauer, Spinoza, Locke, Descartes, Galton, Wundt, Lotze, Herbart, Fechner, and scores of others. All contrasting interpretations of mental phenomena are examined in detail—introspective analysis, philosophical interpretation, and experimental research. "A classic," *Journal of Consulting Psychology.* "The main lines are as valid as ever," *Psychoanalytical Quarterly.* "Standard reading . . . a classic of interpretation," *Psychiatric Quarterly.* 94 illustrations. 1408pp. 5⅜ x 8.

Vol. 1 Paperbound $2.50, Vol. 2 Paperbound $2.50,
The set $5.00

VISUAL ILLUSIONS: THEIR CAUSES, CHARACTERISTICS AND APPLICATIONS,
M. Luckiesh
"Seeing is deceiving," asserts the author of this introduction to virtually every type of optical illusion known. The text both describes and explains the principles involved in color illusions, figure-ground, distance illusions, etc. 100 photographs, drawings and diagrams prove how easy it is to fool the sense: circles that aren't round, parallel lines that seem to bend, stationary figures that seem to move as you stare at them — illustration after illustration strains our credulity at what we see. Fascinating book from many points of view, from applications for artists, in camouflage, etc. to the psychology of vision. New introduction by William Ittleson, Dept. of Psychology, Queens College. Index. Bibliography. xxi + 252pp. 5⅜ x 8½.   Paperbound $1.50

FADS AND FALLACIES IN THE NAME OF SCIENCE,
Martin Gardner
This is the standard account of various cults, quack systems, and delusions which have masqueraded as science: hollow earth fanatics. Reich and orgone sex energy, dianetics, Atlantis, multiple moons, Forteanism, flying saucers, medical fallacies like iridiagnosis, zone therapy, etc. A new chapter has been added on Bridey Murphy, psionics, and other recent manifestations in this field. This is a fair, reasoned appraisal of eccentric theory which provides excellent inoculation against cleverly masked nonsense. "Should be read by everyone, scientist and non-scientist alike," R. T. Birge, Prof. Emeritus of Physics, Univ. of California; Former President, American Physical Society. Index. x + 365pp. 5⅜ x 8.   Paperbound $1.85

ILLUSIONS AND DELUSIONS OF THE SUPERNATURAL AND THE OCCULT,
D. H. Rawcliffe
Holds up to rational examination hundreds of persistent delusions including crystal gazing, automatic writing, table turning, mediumistic trances, mental healing, stigmata, lycanthropy, live burial, the Indian Rope Trick, spiritualism, dowsing, telepathy, clairvoyance, ghosts, ESP, etc. The author explains and exposes the mental and physical deceptions involved, making this not only an exposé of supernatural phenomena, but a valuable exposition of characteristic types of abnormal psychology. Originally titled "The Psychology of the Occult." 14 illustrations. Index. 551pp. 5⅜ x 8.   Paperbound $2.25

FAIRY TALE COLLECTIONS, *edited by Andrew Lang*
Andrew Lang's fairy tale collections make up the richest shelf-full of traditional children's stories anywhere available. Lang supervised the translation of stories from all over the world—familiar European tales collected by Grimm, animal stories from Negro Africa, myths of primitive Australia, stories from Russia, Hungary, Iceland, Japan, and many other countries. Lang's selection of translations are unusually high; many authorities consider that the most familiar tales find their best versions in these volumes. All collections are richly decorated and illustrated by H. J. Ford and other artists.

THE BLUE FAIRY BOOK. 37 stories. 138 illustrations. ix + 390pp. 5⅜ x 8½.
Paperbound $1.50

THE GREEN FAIRY BOOK. 42 stories. 100 illustrations. xiii + 366pp. 5⅜ x 8½.
Paperbound $1.50

THE BROWN FAIRY BOOK. 32 stories. 50 illustrations, 8 in color. xii + 350pp. 5⅜ x 8½.
Paperbound $1.50

THE BEST TALES OF HOFFMANN, *edited by E. F. Bleiler*
10 stories by E. T. A. Hoffmann, one of the greatest of all writers of fantasy. The tales include "The Golden Flower Pot," "Automata," "A New Year's Eve Adventure," "Nutcracker and the King of Mice," "Sand-Man," and others. Vigorous characterizations of highly eccentric personalities, remarkably imaginative situations, and intensely fast pacing has made these tales popular all over the world for 150 years. Editor's introduction. 7 drawings by Hoffmann. xxxiii + 419pp. 5⅜ x 8½.
Paperbound $2.00

GHOST AND HORROR STORIES OF AMBROSE BIERCE, *edited by E. F. Bleiler*
Morbid, eerie, horrifying tales of possessed poets, shabby aristocrats, revived corpses, and haunted malefactors. Widely acknowledged as the best of their kind between Poe and the moderns, reflecting their author's inner torment and bitter view of life. Includes "Damned Thing," "The Middle Toe of the Right Foot," "The Eyes of the Panther," "Visions of the Night," "Moxon's Master," and over a dozen others. Editor's introduction. xxii + 199pp. 5⅜ x 8½.
Paperbound $1.25

THREE GOTHIC NOVELS, *edited by E. F. Bleiler*
Originators of the still popular Gothic novel form, influential in ushering in early 19th-century Romanticism. Horace Walpole's *Castle of Otranto*, William Beckford's *Vathek*, John Polidori's *The Vampyre*, and a *Fragment* by Lord Byron are enjoyable as exciting reading or as documents in the history of English literature. Editor's introduction. xi + 291pp. 5⅜ x 8½.
Paperbound $2.00

BEST GHOST STORIES OF LEFANU, *edited by E. F. Bleiler*
Though admired by such critics as V. S. Pritchett, Charles Dickens and Henry James, ghost stories by the Irish novelist Joseph Sheridan LeFanu have never become as widely known as his detective fiction. About half of the 16 stories in this collection have never before been available in America. Collection includes "Carmilla" (perhaps the best vampire story ever written), "The Haunted Baronet," "The Fortunes of Sir Robert Ardagh," and the classic "Green Tea." Editor's introduction. 7 contemporary illustrations. Portrait of LeFanu. xii + 467pp. 5⅜ x 8.
Paperbound $2.00

EASY-TO-DO ENTERTAINMENTS AND DIVERSIONS WITH COINS, CARDS, STRING, PAPER AND MATCHES, *R. M. Abraham*
Over 300 tricks, games and puzzles will provide young readers with absorbing fun. Sections on card games; paper-folding; tricks with coins, matches and pieces of string; games for the agile; toy-making from common household objects; mathematical recreations; and 50 miscellaneous pastimes. Anyone in charge of groups of youngsters, including hard-pressed parents, and in need of suggestions on how to keep children sensibly amused and quietly content will find this book indispensable. Clear, simple text, copious number of delightful line drawings and illustrative diagrams. Originally titled "Winter Nights' Entertainments." Introduction by Lord Baden Powell. 329 illustrations. v + 186pp. 5⅜ x 8½. Paperbound $1.00

AN INTRODUCTION TO CHESS MOVES AND TACTICS SIMPLY EXPLAINED, *Leonard Barden*
Beginner's introduction to the royal game. Names, possible moves of the pieces, definitions of essential terms, how games are won, etc. explained in 30-odd pages. With this background you'll be able to sit right down and play. Balance of book teaches strategy — openings, middle game, typical endgame play, and suggestions for improving your game. A sample game is fully analyzed. True middle-level introduction, teaching you all the essentials without oversimplifying or losing you in a maze of detail. 58 figures. 102pp. 5⅜ x 8½. Paperbound $1.00

LASKER'S MANUAL OF CHESS, *Dr. Emanuel Lasker*
Probably the greatest chess player of modern times, Dr. Emanuel Lasker held the world championship 28 years, independent of passing schools or fashions. This unmatched study of the game, chiefly for intermediate to skilled players, analyzes basic methods, combinations, position play, the aesthetics of chess, dozens of different openings, etc., with constant reference to great modern games. Contains a brilliant exposition of Steinitz's important theories. Introduction by Fred Reinfeld. Tables of Lasker's tournament record. 3 indices. 308 diagrams. 1 photograph. xxx + 349pp. 5⅜ x 8. Paperbound $2.25

COMBINATIONS: THE HEART OF CHESS, *Irving Chernev*
Step-by-step from simple combinations to complex, this book, by a well-known chess writer, shows you the intricacies of pins, counter-pins, knight forks, and smothered mates. Other chapters show alternate lines of play to those taken in actual championship games; boomerang combinations; classic examples of brilliant combination play by Nimzovich, Rubinstein, Tarrasch, Botvinnik, Alekhine and Capablanca. Index. 356 diagrams. ix + 245pp. 5⅜ x 8½. Paperbound $1.85

HOW TO SOLVE CHESS PROBLEMS, *K. S. Howard*
Full of practical suggestions for the fan or the beginner — who knows only the moves of the chessmen. Contains preliminary section and 58 two-move, 46 three-move, and 8 four-move problems composed by 27 outstanding American problem creators in the last 30 years. Explanation of all terms and exhaustive index. "Just what is wanted for the student," Brian Harley. 112 problems, solutions. vi + 171pp. 5⅜ x 8. Paperbound $1.35

SOCIAL THOUGHT FROM LORE TO SCIENCE,
H. E. Barnes and H. Becker
An immense survey of sociological thought and ways of viewing, studying, planning, and reforming society from earliest times to the present. Includes thought on society of preliterate peoples, ancient non-Western cultures, and every great movement in Europe, America, and modern Japan. Analyzes hundreds of great thinkers: Plato, Augustine, Bodin, Vico, Montesquieu, Herder, Comte, Marx, etc. Weighs the contributions of utopians, sophists, fascists and communists; economists, jurists, philosophers, ecclesiastics, and every 19th and 20th century school of scientific sociology, anthropology, and social psychology throughout the world. Combines topical, chronological, and regional approaches, treating the evolution of social thought as a process rather than as a series of mere topics. "Impressive accuracy, competence, and discrimination . . . easily the best single survey," *Nation*. Thoroughly revised, with new material up to 1960. 2 indexes. Over 2200 bibliographical notes. Three volume set. Total of 1586pp. 5⅜ x 8.
Vol. 1 Paperbound $2.75, Vol. 2 Paperbound $2.75, Vol. 3 Paperbound $2.50
The set $8.00

A HISTORY OF HISTORICAL WRITING, *Harry Elmer Barnes*
Virtually the only adequate survey of the whole course of historical writing in a single volume. Surveys developments from the beginnings of historiography in the ancient Near East and the Classical World, up through the Cold War. Covers major historians in detail, shows interrelationship with cultural background, makes clear individual contributions, evaluates and estimates importance; also enormously rich upon minor authors and thinkers who are usually passed over. Packed with scholarship and learning, clear, easily written. Indispensable to every student of history. Revised and enlarged up to 1961. Index and bibliography. xv + 442pp. 5⅜ x 8½. Paperbound $2.50

JOHANN SEBASTIAN BACH, *Philipp Spitta*
The complete and unabridged text of the definitive study of Bach. Written some 70 years ago, it is still unsurpassed for its coverage of nearly all aspects of Bach's life and work. There could hardly be a finer non-technical introduction to Bach's music than the detailed, lucid analyses which Spitta provides for hundreds of individual pieces. 26 solid pages are devoted to the B minor mass, for example, and 30 pages to the glorious St. Matthew Passion. This monumental set also includes a major analysis of the music of the 18th century: Buxtehude, Pachelbel, etc. "Unchallenged as the last word on one of the supreme geniuses of music," John Barkham, *Saturday Review Syndicate*. Total of 1819pp. Heavy cloth binding. 5⅜ x 8.
Two volume set, clothbound $13.50

BEETHOVEN AND HIS NINE SYMPHONIES, *George Grove*
In this modern middle-level classic of musicology Grove not only analyzes all nine of Beethoven's symphonies very thoroughly in terms of their musical structure, but also discusses the circumstances under which they were written, Beethoven's stylistic development, and much other background material. This is an extremely rich book, yet very easily followed; it is highly recommended to anyone seriously interested in music. Over 250 musical passages. Index. viii + 407pp. 5⅜ x 8. Paperbound $2.00

THREE SCIENCE FICTION NOVELS,
John Taine
Acknowledged by many as the best SF writer of the 1920's, Taine (under the name Eric Temple Bell) was also a Professor of Mathematics of considerable renown. Reprinted here are *The Time Stream*, generally considered Taine's best, *The Greatest Game*, a biological-fiction novel, and *The Purple Sapphire*, involving a supercivilization of the past. Taine's stories tie fantastic narratives to frameworks of original and logical scientific concepts. Speculation is often profound on such questions as the nature of time, concept of entropy, cyclical universes, etc. 4 contemporary illustrations. v + 532pp. 5⅜ x 8⅜.
Paperbound $2.00

SEVEN SCIENCE FICTION NOVELS,
H. G. Wells
Full unabridged texts of 7 science-fiction novels of the master. Ranging from biology, physics, chemistry, astronomy, to sociology and other studies, Mr. Wells extrapolates whole worlds of strange and intriguing character. "One will have to go far to match this for entertainment, excitement, and sheer pleasure . . ."*New York Times*. Contents: The Time Machine, The Island of Dr. Moreau, The First Men in the Moon, The Invisible Man, The War of the Worlds, The Food of the Gods, In The Days of the Comet. 1015pp. 5⅜ x 8.
Clothbound $5.00

28 SCIENCE FICTION STORIES OF H. G. WELLS.
Two full, unabridged novels, *Men Like Gods* and *Star Begotten,* plus 26 short stories by the master science-fiction writer of all time! Stories of space, time, invention, exploration, futuristic adventure. Partial contents: *The Country of the Blind, In the Abyss, The Crystal Egg, The Man Who Could Work Miracles, A Story of Days to Come, The Empire of the Ants, The Magic Shop, The Valley of the Spiders, A Story of the Stone Age, Under the Knife, Sea Raiders,* etc. An indispensable collection for the library of anyone interested in science fiction adventure. 928pp. 5⅜ x 8.
Clothbound $4.50

THREE MARTIAN NOVELS,
Edgar Rice Burroughs
Complete, unabridged reprinting, in one volume, of Thuvia, Maid of Mars; Chessmen of Mars; The Master Mind of Mars. Hours of science-fiction adventure by a modern master storyteller. Reset in large clear type for easy reading. 16 illustrations by J. Allen St. John. vi + 490pp. 5⅜ x 8½.
Paperbound $1.85

AN INTELLECTUAL AND CULTURAL HISTORY OF THE WESTERN WORLD,
Harry Elmer Barnes
Monumental 3-volume survey of intellectual development of Europe from primitive cultures to the present day. Every significant product of human intellect traced through history: art, literature, mathematics, physical sciences, medicine, music, technology, social sciences, religions, jurisprudence, education, etc. Presentation is lucid and specific, analyzing in detail specific discoveries, theories, literary works, and so on. Revised (1965) by recognized scholars in specialized fields under the direction of Prof. Barnes. Revised bibliography. Indexes. 24 illustrations. Total of xxix + 1318pp.
Vol. 1 Paperbound $2.00, Vol. 2 Paperbound $2.00, Vol. 3 Paperbound $2.00,
The set $6.00

HEAR ME TALKIN' TO YA, *edited by Nat Shapiro and Nat Hentoff*
In their own words, Louis Armstrong, King Oliver, Fletcher Henderson, Bunk Johnson, Bix Beiderbecke, Billy Holiday, Fats Waller, Jelly Roll Morton, Duke Ellington, and many others comment on the origins of jazz in New Orleans and its growth in Chicago's South Side, Kansas City's jam sessions, Depression Harlem, and the modernism of the West Coast schools. Taken from taped conversations, letters, magazine articles, other first-hand sources. Editors' introduction. xvi + 429pp. 5⅜ x 8½.   Paperbound $2.00

THE JOURNAL OF HENRY D. THOREAU
A 25-year record by the great American observer and critic, as complete a record of a great man's inner life as is anywhere available. Thoreau's Journals served him as raw material for his formal pieces, as a place where he could develop his ideas, as an outlet for his interests in wild life and plants, in writing as an art, in classics of literature, Walt Whitman and other contemporaries, in politics, slavery, individual's relation to the State, etc. The Journals present a portrait of a remarkable man, and are an observant social history. Unabridged republication of 1906 edition, Bradford Torrey and Francis H. Allen, editors. Illustrations. Total of 1888pp. 8⅜ x 12¼.
Two volume set, clothbound $25.00

A SHAKESPEARIAN GRAMMAR, *E. A. Abbott*
Basic reference to Shakespeare and his contemporaries, explaining through thousands of quotations from Shakespeare, Jonson, Beaumont and Fletcher, North's *Plutarch* and other sources the grammatical usage differing from the modern. First published in 1870 and written by a scholar who spent much of his life isolating principles of Elizabethan language, the book is unlikely ever to be superseded. Indexes. xxiv + 511pp. 5⅜ x 8½.   Paperbound $2.75

FOLK-LORE OF SHAKESPEARE, *T. F. Thistelton Dyer*
Classic study, drawing from Shakespeare a large body of references to supernatural beliefs, terminology of falconry and hunting, games and sports, good luck charms, marriage customs, folk medicines, superstitions about plants, animals, birds, argot of the underworld, sexual slang of London, proverbs, drinking customs, weather lore, and much else. From full compilation comes a mirror of the 17th-century popular mind. Index. ix + 526pp. 5⅜ x 8½.
Paperbound $2.50

THE NEW VARIORUM SHAKESPEARE, *edited by H. H. Furness*
By far the richest editions of the plays ever produced in any country or language. Each volume contains complete text (usually First Folio) of the play, all variants in Quarto and other Folio texts, editorial changes by every major editor to Furness's own time (1900), footnotes to obscure references or language, extensive quotes from literature of Shakespearian criticism, essays on plot sources (often reprinting sources in full), and much more.

HAMLET, *edited by H. H. Furness*
Total of xxvi + 905pp. 5⅜ x 8½.   Two volume set, paperbound $4.75

TWELFTH NIGHT, *edited by H. H. Furness*
Index. xxii + 434pp. 5⅜ x 8½.   Paperbound $2.25

LA BOHEME BY GIACOMO PUCCINI,
translated and introduced by Ellen H. Bleiler
Complete handbook for the operagoer, with everything needed for full enjoyment except the musical score itself. Complete Italian libretto, with new, modern English line-by-line translation—the only libretto printing all repeats; biography of Puccini; the librettists; background to the opera, Murger's La Boheme, etc.; circumstances of composition and performances; plot summary; and pictorial section of 73 illustrations showing Puccini, famous singers and performances, etc. Large clear type for easy reading. 124pp. 5⅜ x 8½.
Paperbound $1.00

ANTONIO STRADIVARI: HIS LIFE AND WORK (1644-1737),
W. Henry Hill, Arthur F. Hill, and Alfred E. Hill
Still the only book that really delves into life and art of the incomparable Italian craftsman, maker of the finest musical instruments in the world today. The authors, expert violin-makers themselves, discuss Stradivari's ancestry, his construction and finishing techniques, distinguished characteristics of many of his instruments and their locations. Included, too, is story of introduction of his instruments into France, England, first revelation of their supreme merit, and information on his labels, number of instruments made, prices, mystery of ingredients of his varnish, tone of pre-1684 Stradivari violin and changes between 1684 and 1690. An extremely interesting, informative account for all music lovers, from craftsman to concert-goer. Republication of original (1902) edition. New introduction by Sydney Beck, Head of Rare Book and Manuscript Collections, Music Division, New York Public Library. Analytical index by Rembert Wurlitzer. Appendixes. 68 illustrations. 30 full-page plates. 4 in color. xxvi + 315pp. 5⅜ x 8½.
Paperbound $2.25

MUSICAL AUTOGRAPHS FROM MONTEVERDI TO HINDEMITH,
Emanuel Winternitz
For beauty, for intrinsic interest, for perspective on the composer's personality, for subtleties of phrasing, shading, emphasis indicated in the autograph but suppressed in the printed score, the mss. of musical composition are fascinating documents which repay close study in many different ways. This 2-volume work reprints facsimiles of mss. by virtually every major composer, and many minor figures—196 examples in all. A full text points out what can be learned from mss., analyzes each sample. Index. Bibliography. 18 figures. 196 plates. Total of 170pp. of text. 7⅞ x 10¾.
Vol. 1 Paperbound $2.00, Vol. 2 Paperbound $2.00,
The set $4.00

J. S. BACH,
Albert Schweitzer
One of the few great full-length studies of Bach's life and work, and the study upon which Schweitzer's renown as a musicologist rests. On first appearance (1911), revolutionized Bach performance. The only writer on Bach to be musicologist, performing musician, and student of history, theology and philosophy, Schweitzer contributes particularly full sections on history of German Protestant church music, theories on motivic pictorial representations in vocal music, and practical suggestions for performance. Translated by Ernest Newman. Indexes. 5 illustrations. 650 musical examples. Total of xix + 928pp. 5⅜ x 8½.
Vol. 1 Paperbound $2.00, Vol. 2 Paperbound $2.00,
The set $4.00

THE METHODS OF ETHICS, *Henry Sidgwick*
Propounding no organized system of its own, study subjects every major methodological approach to ethics to rigorous, objective analysis. Study discusses and relates ethical thought of Plato, Aristotle, Bentham, Clarke, Butler, Hobbes, Hume, Mill, Spencer, Kant, and dozens of others. Sidgwick retains conclusions from each system which follow from ethical premises, rejecting the faulty. Considered by many in the field to be among the most important treatises on ethical philosophy. Appendix. Index. xlvii + 528pp. 5⅜ x 8½.
Paperbound $2.50

TEUTONIC MYTHOLOGY, *Jakob Grimm*
A milestone in Western culture; the work which established on a modern basis the study of history of religions and comparative religions. 4-volume work assembles and interprets everything available on religious and folkloristic beliefs of Germanic people (including Scandinavians, Anglo-Saxons, etc.). Assembling material from such sources as Tacitus, surviving Old Norse and Icelandic texts, archeological remains, folktales, surviving superstitions, comparative traditions, linguistic analysis, etc. Grimm explores pagan deities, heroes, folklore of nature, religious practices, and every other area of pagan German belief. To this day, the unrivaled, definitive, exhaustive study. Translated by J. S. Stallybrass from 4th (1883) German edition. Indexes. Total of lxxvii + 1887pp. 5⅜ x 8½.   Four volume set, paperbound $10.00

THE I CHING, *translated by James Legge*
Called "The Book of Changes" in English, this is one of the Five Classics edited by Confucius, basic and central to Chinese thought. Explains perhaps the most complex system of divination known, founded on the theory that all things happening at any one time have characteristic features which can be isolated and related. Significant in Oriental studies, in history of religions and philosophy, and also to Jungian psychoanalysis and other areas of modern European thought. Index. Appendixes. 6 plates. xxi + 448pp. 5⅜ x 8½.
Paperbound $2.75

HISTORY OF ANCIENT PHILOSOPHY, *W. Windelband*
One of the clearest, most accurate comprehensive surveys of Greek and Roman philosophy. Discusses ancient philosophy in general, intellectual life in Greece in the 7th and 6th centuries B.C., Thales, Anaximander, Anaximenes, Heraclitus, the Eleatics, Empedocles, Anaxagoras, Leucippus, the Pythagoreans, the Sophists, Socrates, Democritus (20 pages), Plato (50 pages), Aristotle (70 pages), the Peripatetics, Stoics, Epicureans, Sceptics, Neo-platonists, Christian Apologists, etc. 2nd German edition translated by H. E. Cushman. xv + 393pp. 5⅜ x 8.
Paperbound $2.25

THE PALACE OF PLEASURE, *William Painter*
Elizabethan versions of Italian and French novels from *The Decameron,* Cinthio, Straparola, Queen Margaret of Navarre, and other continental sources — the very work that provided Shakespeare and dozens of his contemporaries with many of their plots and sub-plots and, therefore, justly considered one of the most influential books in all English literature. It is also a book that any reader will still enjoy. Total of cviii + 1,224pp.
Three volume set, Paperbound $6.75

THE WONDERFUL WIZARD OF OZ, *L. F. Baum*

All the original W. W. Denslow illustrations in full color—as much a part of "The Wizard" as Tenniel's drawings are of "Alice in Wonderland." "The Wizard" is still America's best-loved fairy tale, in which, as the author expresses it, "The wonderment and joy are retained and the heartaches and nightmares left out." Now today's young readers can enjoy every word and wonderful picture of the original book. New introduction by Martin Gardner. A Baum bibliography. 23 full-page color plates. viii + 268pp. 5⅜ x 8.

Paperbound $1.50

THE MARVELOUS LAND OF OZ, *L. F. Baum*

This is the equally enchanting sequel to the "Wizard," continuing the adventures of the Scarecrow and the Tin Woodman. The hero this time is a little boy named Tip, and all the delightful Oz magic is still present. This is the Oz book with the Animated Saw-Horse, the Woggle-Bug, and Jack Pumpkinhead. All the original John R. Neill illustrations, 10 in full color. 287pp. 5⅜ x 8.

Paperbound $1.50

ALICE'S ADVENTURES UNDER GROUND, *Lewis Carroll*

The original *Alice in Wonderland*, hand-lettered and illustrated by Carroll himself, and originally presented as a Christmas gift to a child-friend. Adults as well as children will enjoy this charming volume, reproduced faithfully in this Dover edition. While the story is essentially the same, there are slight changes, and Carroll's spritely drawings present an intriguing alternative to the famous Tenniel illustrations. One of the most popular books in Dover's catalogue. Introduction by Martin Gardner. 38 illustrations. 128pp. 5⅜ x 8½.

Paperbound $1.00

THE NURSERY "ALICE," *Lewis Carroll*

While most of us consider *Alice in Wonderland* a story for children of all ages, Carroll himself felt it was beyond younger children. He therefore provided this simplified version, illustrated with the famous Tenniel drawings enlarged and colored in delicate tints, for children aged "from Nought to Five." Dover's edition of this now rare classic is a faithful copy of the 1889 printing, including 20 illustrations by Tenniel, and front and back covers reproduced in full color. Introduction by Martin Gardner. xxiii + 67pp. 6⅛ x 9¼.

Paperbound $1.50

THE STORY OF KING ARTHUR AND HIS KNIGHTS, *Howard Pyle*

A fast-paced, exciting retelling of the best known Arthurian legends for young readers by one of America's best story tellers and illustrators. The sword Excalibur, wooing of Guinevere, Merlin and his downfall, adventures of Sir Pellias and Gawaine, and others. The pen and ink illustrations are vividly imagined and wonderfully drawn. 41 illustrations. xviii + 313pp. 6⅛ x 9¼.

Paperbound $1.50

Prices subject to change without notice.

Available at your book dealer or write for free catalogue to Dept. Adsci, Dover Publications, Inc., 180 Varick St., N.Y., N.Y. 10014. Dover publishes more than 150 books each year on science, elementary and advanced mathematics, biology, music, art, literary history, social sciences and other areas.